AMERICAN POLITICAL, ECONOMIC, AND SECURITY ISSUES

NATIONAL SECURITY LETTERS: BACKGROUND AND ISSUES. VOLUME 1

AMERICAN POLITICAL, ECONOMIC, AND SECURITY ISSUES

Additional books in this series can be found on Nova's website under the Series tab.

Additional E-books in this series can be found on Nova's website under the E-books tab.

AMERICAN POLITICAL, ECONOMIC, AND SECURITY ISSUES

NATIONAL SECURITY LETTERS: BACKGROUND AND ISSUES. VOLUME 1

CAROLYN D. HINES
EDITOR

Nova Science Publishers, Inc.
New York

For permission to use material from this book please contact us:
Telephone 631-231-7269; Fax 631-231-8175
Web Site: http://www.novapublishers.com

Additional color graphics may be available in the e-book version of this book.

LIBRARY OF CONGRESS CATALOGING-IN-PUBLICATION DATA
National security letters : background and issues / editors, Carolyn D.
Hines.
p. cm.
Includes bibliographical references and index.
ISBN 978-1-61668-941-4 (v. 1 : hardcover : alk. paper) -- ISBN
978-1-61668-942-1 (v. 2 : hardcover : alk. paper)
1. Terrorism--Prevention--Law and legislation--United States. 2. National
security--Law and legislation--United States. 3. Criminal
investigation--United States. 4. Searches and seizures--United States. I.
Hines, Carolyn D. II. Doyle, Charles.
KF9430.N38 2010
344.7305'325--dc22
2010026738

Published by Nova Science Publishers, Inc. ✢ New York

CONTENTS

PREFACE

National Security Letters (NSL) are roughly comparable to administrative subpoenas. Intelligence agencies issue them for intelligence gathering purposes to telephone companies; internet service providers, consumer credit reporting agencies, banks, and other financial institutions, directing the recipients to turn over certain customer records and similar information. This book and its corresponding volumes present an overview of the background and issues surrounding the use of National Security Letters, the Patriot Act and First Amendment implications.

Chapter 1- Five federal statutes authorize intelligence officials to request certain business record information in connection with national security investigations. The authority to issue these national security letters (NSLs) is comparable to the authority to issue administrative subpoenas. The USA PATRIOT Act expanded the authority under four of the NSL statutes and created the fifth. Thereafter, the authority has been reported to have been widely used. Prospects of its continued use dimmed, however, after two lower federal courts held the lack of judicial review and the absolute confidentiality requirements in one of the statutes rendered it constitutionally suspect.

A report by the Department of Justice's Inspector General (IG) found that in its pre-amendment use of expanded USA PATRIOT Act authority the FBI had "used NSLs in violation of applicable NSL statutes, Attorney General Guidelines, and internal FBI policies," but that no criminal laws had been broken. A year later, a second IG report confirmed the findings of the first, and noted the corrective measures taken in response.

The USA PATRIOT Improvement and Reauthorization Act (H.R. 3199), P.L. 109-177, and its companion P.L. 109-178, amended the five NSL sections to expressly provide for judicial review of both the NSLs and the confidentiality requirements that attend them. The sections have also been made explicitly judicially enforceable and sanctions recognized for failure to comply with an NSL request or to breach NSL confidentiality requirements with the intent to obstruct justice. The use of the authority has been made subject to greater congressional oversight. Following amendment, an appellate court dismissed one of the earlier cases as moot and remanded the second for reconsideration in light of the amendments. On remand, the lower court found the amended procedure contrary to the demands of the First Amendment. The Court of Appeals, however, ruled that the amended statutes could withstand constitutional scrutiny, if the government confined itself to a procedure which requires (1) notice to the recipient of its option to object to a secrecy requirement; (2) upon recipient objection, prompt judicial review at the government's petition and burden; and (3) meaningful judicial review without conclusive weight afforded a government certification of risk. Using this procedure, the district court upheld continuation of the *Doe* nondisclosure requirement following an ex parte, in camera hearing and granted the plaintiff's motion for an unclassified, redacted summary of the government declaration on which the court's decision was based.

Chapter 2- Five federal statutes authorize various intelligence agencies to demand, through National Security Letters (NSLs), certain customer information from communications providers, financial institutions, and consumer credit reporting agencies, under the Right to Financial Privacy Act, the Fair Credit Reporting Act, the National Security Act, and Electronic Communications Privacy Act. The USA PATRIOT Act expanded NSL authority. Later reports of the Department of Justice Inspector General indicated that (1) the FBI considered the expanded authority very useful; (2) after expansion the number of NSLs requests increased dramatically; (3) the number of requests relating to Americans increased substantially; and (4) FBI use of NSL authority had sometimes failed to comply with statutory, Attorney General, or FBI policies.

Originally, the NSL statutes authorized nondisclosure requirements prohibiting recipients from disclosing receipt or the content of the NSL to anyone, ever. They now permit judicial review of these secrecy provisions. As understood by the courts, recipients may request the issuing agency to seek and justify to the court the continued binding effect of any secrecy requirement.

Several USA PATRIOT Act provisions are scheduled to expire on December 31, 2009. The NSL statutory provisions are not among them. Nevertheless, several bills have been introduced which would amend and in some cases repeal NSL authority. The bills include (1) the National Security Letter Reform Act of 2009 (H.R. 1800), introduced by Representative Nadler; (2) the USA PATRIOT Amendments Act of 2009 (H.R. 3845), introduced by Representative Conyers; (3) the Judicious Use of Surveillance Tools in Counterterrorism Efforts Act of 2009 (JUSTICE Act) (S. 1686), introduced by Senator Feingold; and (4) the USA PATRIOT Act Sunset Extension Act of 2009 (S. 1692), introduced by Senator Leahy and reported to the floor by the Senate Judiciary Committee, S.Rept. 111-92.

Chapter 3- In the USA PATRIOT Improvement and Reauthorization Act of 2005 (Patriot Reauthorization Act), Congress directed the Department of Justice (Department) Office of the Inspector General (OIG) to review "the effectiveness and use, including any improper or illegal use, of national security letters issued by the Department of Justice." See Pub. L. No. 109-177, § 119. Four federal statutes contain five specific provisions authorizing the Federal Bureau of Investigation (FBI) to issue national security letters (NSLs) to obtain information from third parties, such as telephone companies, financial institutions, Internet service providers, and consumer credit agencies. In these letters, the FBI can direct third parties to provide customer account information and transactional records, such as telephone toll billing records.

Congress directed the OIG to review the use of NSLs for two time periods - calendar years (CY) 2003 through 2004 and CY 2005 through 2006. The first report is due to Congress on March 9, 2007; the second is due on December 31, 2007.[1] Although we were only required to review calendar years 2003 and 2004 in the first review, we elected to include data from calendar year 2005 as well.

In the Patriot Reauthorization Act, Congress directed the OIG's review to include:

(1) an examination of the use of national security letters by the Department of Justice during calendar years 2003 through 2006;
(2) a description of any noteworthy facts or circumstances relating to such use, including any improper or illegal use of such authority; and
(3) an examination of the effectiveness of national security letters as an investigative tool, including -
  (A) the importance of the information acquired by the Department of Justice to the intelligence activities of the Department of Justice or to any other department or agency of the Federal Government;
  (B) the manner in which such information is collected, retained, analyzed, and disseminated by the Department of Justice, including any direct access to such information (such as access to "raw data") provided to any other department, agency, or instrumentality of Federal, State, local, or tribal governments or any private sector entity;
  (C) whether, and how often, the Department of Justice utilized such information to produce an analytical intelligence product for distribution within the Department of Justice, to the intelligence community . . ., or to other Federal, State, local, or tribal government departments, agencies or instrumentalities;
  (D) whether, and how often, the Department of Justice provided such information to law enforcement authorities for use in criminal proceedings . . . .[2]

In: National Security Letters: Background and Issues. Volume 1 ISBN: 978-1-61668-941-4
Editor: Carolyn D. Hines

Chapter 1

NATIONAL SECURITY LETTERS IN FOREIGN INTELLIGENCE INVESTIGATIONS: LEGAL BACKGROUND AND RECENT AMENDMENTS*

Charles Doyle

SUMMARY

Five federal statutes authorize intelligence officials to request certain business record information in connection with national security investigations. The authority to issue these national security letters (NSLs) is comparable to the authority to issue administrative subpoenas. The USA PATRIOT Act expanded the authority under four of the NSL statutes and created the fifth. Thereafter, the authority has been reported to have been widely used. Prospects of its continued use dimmed, however, after two lower federal courts held the lack of judicial review and the absolute confidentiality requirements in one of the statutes rendered it constitutionally suspect.

A report by the Department of Justice's Inspector General (IG) found that in its pre-amendment use of expanded USA PATRIOT Act authority the FBI had "used NSLs in violation of applicable NSL statutes, Attorney General Guidelines, and internal FBI policies," but that no criminal laws had been broken. A year later, a second IG report confirmed the findings of the first, and noted the corrective measures taken in response.

The USA PATRIOT Improvement and Reauthorization Act (H.R. 3199), P.L. 109-177, and its companion P.L. 109-178, amended the five NSL sections to expressly provide for judicial review of both the NSLs and the confidentiality requirements that attend them. The sections have also been made explicitly judicially enforceable and sanctions recognized for failure to comply with an NSL request or to breach NSL confidentiality requirements with the intent to obstruct justice. The use of the authority has been made subject to greater congressional oversight. Following amendment, an appellate court dismissed one of the

* This is an edited, reformatted and augmented edition of a United States Congressional Research Service publication, Report RL33320, dated September 8, 2009.

earlier cases as moot and remanded the second for reconsideration in light of the amendments. On remand, the lower court found the amended procedure contrary to the demands of the First Amendment. The Court of Appeals, however, ruled that the amended statutes could withstand constitutional scrutiny, if the government confined itself to a procedure which requires (1) notice to the recipient of its option to object to a secrecy requirement; (2) upon recipient objection, prompt judicial review at the government's petition and burden; and (3) meaningful judicial review without conclusive weight afforded a government certification of risk. Using this procedure, the district court upheld continuation of the *Doe* nondisclosure requirement following an ex parte, in camera hearing and granted the plaintiff's motion for an unclassified, redacted summary of the government declaration on which the court's decision was based.

The text of the five provisions—section 11 14(a)(5) of the Right to Financial Privacy Act (12 U.S.C. 3414(a)(5)); sections 626 and 627 of the Fair Credit Reporting Act (15 U.S.C. 1681u, 168 1v); section 2709 of title 18 of the United States Code; and section 802 of the National Security Act (50 U.S.C. 436)—in their amended form have been appended.

INTRODUCTION

Five statutory provisions vest government agencies responsible for certain foreign intelligence investigations (principally the Federal Bureau of Investigation (FBI)) with authority to issue written commands comparable to administrative subpoenas.[1] A National Security Letter (NSL) seeks customer and consumer transaction information in national security investigations from communications providers, financial institutions and credit agencies. Section 505 of the USA PATRIOT Act expanded the circumstances under which an NSL could be used.[2] Subsequent press accounts suggested that their use had become wide-spread.[3] Two lower federal courts, however, found the uncertainties, practices and policies associated with the use of NSL authority contrary to the First Amendment right of freedom of speech, and thus brought into question the extent to which NSL authority could be used in the future.[4] The USA PATRIOT Improvement and Reauthorization Act,[5] and P.L. 109-178 (S. 2271) amended the NSL statutes and related law to address some of the concerns raised by critics and the courts.[6] As a consequence, the Second Circuit dismissed one of the lower court cases as moot and remanded the other for reconsideration in light of the amendments.[7] On reconsideration, the district court opinion continued to be troubled by the First Amendment implications of the nondisclosure features of 18 U.S.C. 2709, even as amended.[8] The appellate court was comparable concerned, but concluded that the government might invoke the authority of 18 U.S.C. 2709 and 18 U.S.C. 3511 in a limited but constitutionally acceptable manner.[9] On remand under the procedure envisioned by the Second Circuit panel, the district court found a continuing need to maintain the original secrecy order, but ordered the government to provide the plaintiffs with an unclassified, redacted summary of the declaration upon which the court's decision was based.[10]

BACKGROUND

The ancestor of the first NSL letter provision is a statutory exception to privacy protections afforded by the Right to Financial Privacy Act (RFPA).[11] Its history is not particularly instructive and consists primarily of a determination that the exception in its original form should not be too broadly construed.[12] But the exception was just that, an exception. It was neither an affirmative grant of authority to request information nor a command to financial institutions to provided information when asked. It removed the restrictions on the release of customer information imposed on financial institutions by the Right to Financial Privacy Act, but it left them free to decline to comply when asked to do so.

> [I]n certain significant instances, financial institutions [had] declined to grant the FBI access to financial records in response to requests under Section 1114(a). The FBI informed the Committee that the problem occurs particularly in States which have State constitutional privacy protection provisions or State banking privacy laws. In those States, financial institutions decline to grant the FBI access because State law prohibits them from granting such access and the RFPA, since it permits but does not mandate such access, does not override State law. In such a situation, the concerned financial institutions which might otherwise desire to grant the FBI access to a customer's record will not do so, because State law does not allow such cooperation, and cooperation might expose them to liability to the customer whose records the FBI sought access. H.Rept. 99-690, at 15-6 (1986).

Congress responded with passage of the first NSL statute as an amendment to the Right to Financial Privacy Act, affirmatively giving the FBI access to financial institution records in certain foreign intelligence cases.[13] At the same time in the Electronic Communications Privacy Act, it afforded the FBI comparable access to the telephone company and other communications service provider customer information. [14] Together the two NSL provisions afforded the FBI access to communications and financial business records under limited circumstances—customer and customer transaction information held by telephone carriers and banks pertaining to a foreign power or its agents relevant to a foreign counter-intelligence investigation. [15]

Both the communications provider section and the Right to Financial Privacy Act section contained nondisclosure provisions[16] and limitations on further dissemination except pursuant of guidelines promulgated by the Attorney General.[17] Neither had an express enforcement mechanism nor identified penalties for failure to comply with either the NSL or the nondisclosure instruction.

In the mid-1990s, Congress added two more NSL provisions—one permits NSL use in connection with the investigation of government employee leaks of classified information under the National Security Act;[18] and the other grants the FBI access to credit agency records pursuant to the Fair Credit Reporting Act, under much the same conditions as apply to the records of financial institutions.[19] The FBI asked for the Fair Credit Reporting Act amendment as a threshold mechanism to enable it to make more effective use of its bank record access authority:

> FBI's right of access under the Right of Financial Privacy Act cannot be effectively used, however, until the FBI discovers which financial institutions are being utilized by the subject

> of a counterintelligence investigation. Consumer reports maintained by credit bureaus are a ready source of such information, but, although such report[s] are readily available to the private sector, they are not available to FBI counterintelligence investigators....
>
> FBI has made a specific showing ... that the effort to identify financial institutions in order to make use of FBI authority under the Right to Financial Privacy Act can not only be time- consuming and resource-intensive, but can also require the use of investigative techniques— such as physical and electronic surveillance, review of mail covers, and canvassing of all banks in an area—that would appear to be more intrusive than the review of credit reports. H.Rept. 104-427, at 36 (1996).[20]

The National Security Act NSL provision authorized access to credit and financial institution records of federal employees with security clearances who were required to give their consent as a condition for clearance.[21] Passed in the wake of the Ames espionage case, it is limited to investigations of classified information leaks. As noted at the time, "The Committee believes section 801 will serve as a deterrent to espionage for financial gain without burdening investigative agencies with unproductive recordkeeping or subjecting employees to new reporting requirements.... The Committee recognizes that consumer credit records have been notoriously inaccurate, and expects that information obtained pursuant to this section alone will not be the basis of an action or decision adverse to the interest of the employee involved."[22]

Both the Fair Credit Reporting Act section and the National Security Act section contain dissemination restrictions;[23] as well as safe harbor (immunity),[24] and nondisclosure provisions.[25] Neither has an explicit penalty for improper disclosure of the request, but the Fair Credit Reporting Act section expressly authorizes judicial enforcement.[26]

The USA PATRIOT Act amended three of the four existing NSL statutes and added a fifth. In each of the three NSL statutes available exclusively to the FBI—the Electronic Communications Privacy Act section (18 U.S.C. 2709), the Right to Financial Privacy Act section (12 U.S.C. 3414(a)(5)), and the Fair Credit Reporting Act section (15 U.S.C. 1681u)—Section 505 of the USA PATRIOT Act:

- expanded FBI issuing authority beyond FBI headquarter officials to include the heads of the FBI field offices (i.e., Special Agents in Charge (SAC));
- eliminated the requirement that the record information sought pertain to a foreign power or the agent of a foreign power;
- required instead that the NSL request be relevant to an investigation to protect against international terrorism or foreign spying;
- added the caveat that no such investigation of an American can be predicated exclusively of First Amendment protected activities.[27]

The amendments allowed NSL authority to be employed more quickly (without the delays associated with prior approval from FBI headquarters) and more widely (without requiring that the information pertain to a foreign power or its agents).[28]

Subsection 358(g) of the USA PATRIOT Act amended the Fair Credit Reporting Act to add a fifth and final NSL section; the provision had one particularly noteworthy feature, it was available not merely to the FBI but to any government agency investigating or analyzing international terrorism:

> Notwithstanding section 1681b of this title or any other provision of this subchapter, a consumer reporting agency shall furnish a consumer report of a consumer and all other information in a consumer's file to a government agency authorized to conduct investigations of, or intelligence or counterintelligence activities or analysis related to, international terrorism when presented with a written certification by such government agency that such information is necessary for the agency's conduct or such investigation, activity or analysis.[29]

Although the subsection's legislative history treats it as a matter of first impression,[30] Congress's obvious intent was to provide other agencies with the national security letter authority comparable to that enjoyed by the FBI under the Fair Credit Reporting Act. The new section had a nondisclosure and a safe harbor subsection, 15 U.S.C. 168 1v(c), (e), but no express means of judicial enforcement or penalties for improper disclosure of a request under the section.

In the 108th Congress, the scope of the Right to Financial Privacy Act NSL was enlarged by defining the financial institutions subject to the authority to include not only banks and credit unions but also car dealers, jewelers, and real estate agents, among others.[31] The same Congress saw a number of proposals introduced to exempt libraries from the reach of the communications NSL,[32] to increase congressional oversight over the use of NSL authority,[33] and to add the USA PATRIOT Act section 505 NSL amendments to the list of those temporary sections scheduled to expire on December 31, 2005.[34] The 108th also witnessed the introduction of proposals that ultimately evolved into the NSL amendments in the USA PATRIOT Improvement and Reauthorization Act. H.R. 3179, introduced by Representative Sensenbrenner. They would have reinforced the five national security letter provisions with explicit authority for judicial enforcement[35] and with criminal penalties for improper disclosure of the issuance of such letters. The penalties were to be the same as those proposed under the general administrative subpoena bills offered in the 108th—imprisonment for not more than five years when committed with the intent to obstruct and for not more than one year otherwise, proposed 18 U.S.C. 1510(e). A Justice Department witness explained that, "Oftentimes, the premature disclosure of an ongoing terrorism investigation can lead to a host of negative repercussions, including the destruction of evidence, the flight of suspected terrorists, and the frustration of efforts to identify additional terrorist conspirators. For these reasons, the FBI has forgone using NSLs in some investigations for fear that the recipients of those NSLs would compromise an investigation by disclosing the fact that they had been sent an NSL."[36] The enforcement provision would have been backed by the court's contempt power, proposed 18 U.S.C. 2332h.[37] It had no explicit provisions, however, to permit the recipient to file a motion to quash or modify the NSL request.

Pre-amendment Judicial Action

Proponents of legislative proposals in the 108th Congress did not enjoy the benefit of two court decisions that colored the debate over NSL authority during the 109th Congress. *Doe v. Ashcroft*,[38] reached much the same conclusion on the First Amendment issue: narrowly defined, the government's and *Doe v. Gonzales*[39] suggested that the NSL statutes could not withstand constitutional scrutiny unless more explicit provisions were made for judicial review and permissible disclosure by recipients. In essence, *Doe v. Ashcroft* found that the language of 18 U.S.C. 2709 and the practices surrounding its use offended (1) the Fourth Amendment because "in all but the exceptional case it [had] the effect of authorizing coercive searches effectively immune from any judicial process," 334 F.Supp.2d at 506, and (2) the First Amendment because its sweeping, permanent secrecy order feature applied "in every case, to every person, in perpetuity, with no vehicle for the ban to ever be lifted from the recipient or other persons affected under any circumstances, either by the FBI itself, or pursuant to judicial process," *id.* at 476.

NSL Amendments in the 109th Congress

Both USA PATRIOT Act reauthorization statutes—P.L. 109-177(H.R. 3199) and P.L. 109-178 (S. 2271)[40]—amended each of the NSL statutes. They

- created a judicial enforcement mechanism and a judicial review procedure for both the requests and accompanying nondisclosure requirements;[41]
- established specific penalties for failure to comply or to observe the nondisclosure requirements;[42]
- made it clear that the nondisclosure requirements did not preclude a recipient from consulting an attorney;[43]
- provided a process to ease the nondisclosure requirement;[44]
- expanded congressional oversight;[45]
- called for an Inspector General's audit of use of the authority.[46]

POST-AMENDMENT NSL ATTRIBUTES

Addressees and Certifying Officials

The five NSL statutes share a number of common attributes, although each has its own individual features as well. They are most distinctive with respect to the nature of the businesses to whom they may be addressed. The Electronic Communication Privacy Act NSLs are addressed to communications providers.[47] Those issued under the authority of the Right to Financial Privacy Act may be directed to any financial institution, which as noted earlier, includes not only banks and credit unions, but credit card companies, car dealers, jewelers and a number of entities that are likely the scene of large cash transactions.[48] The Fair Credit Reporting Act NSLs may be addressed to consumer credit reporting agencies.[49] Recipients of the National Security Act NSLs may include either financial institutions or consumer credit reporting agencies as well as any commercial entity with information concerning an agency employee's travel.[50]

FBI officials are authorized to provide the initial certification required for issuance of an NSL under any of the five statutes. In three instances, the authority is exclusive; in the other two, it is enjoyed by other federal officials as well. In the case of the Electronic Communications Privacy Act NSL section, the Right to Financial Privacy Act section, and one of the Fair Credit Report Act NSL sections, issuance requires the certification of either the Director of the FBI, a senior FBI official (no lower than the Deputy Assistant Director), or the Special Agent in Charge of an FBI field office.[51]

Certifying officials under the other statutes are described more broadly. The National Security Act NSL section contemplates certification by officials from a wider range of agencies; the second Fair Credit Reporting Act NSL section allows certification by both a wider range of agencies and a wider range of officials. Senior officials no lower than Assistant Secretary or Assistant Director of an agency whose employee with access to classified material is under investigation may certify a National Security Act NSL request.[52] A designated supervisory official of any agency "authorized to conduct investigations of, or intelligence or counterintelligence activities and analysis related to, international terrorism" may certify a NSL request under the second, more recent Fair Credit Reporting Act section.[53]

Purpose, Standards, Information Covered

Although variously phrased, the purpose for each of the NSLs is to acquire information related to the requesting agency's national security concerns. The most common statement of purpose is "to protect against international terrorism or clandestine intelligence activities."[54] The more recent of the Fair Credit Reporting Act NSL sections simply indicates that the information must be sought for the requesting intelligence agency's investigation, activity or analysis.[55] The National Security Act NSL authority is available to conduct law enforcement investigations, counterintelligence inquiries, and security determinations.[56] As to standards, the Electronic Communications Privacy Act authorizes NSLs for relevant information.[57] The same standard may apply to the others which are a little more cryptic, authorizing NSLs when the information is "sought for"[58] or "is necessary"[59] for the statutory purpose.

The communications NSL provision and the earlier of the two credit agency NSL statutes are fairly specific in their descriptions of the information that may be requested through an NSL. An Electronic Communications Privacy Act NSL may request a customer's name, address, length of service and billing records.[60] The older of the two Fair Credit Report Act sections authorizes a NSL to acquire name, address or former address, place or former place of employment, and the name and address of any financial institution with which the consumer has or once had an account.[61] The Right to Financial Privacy Act NSL provision covers the financial records of a financial institution's customers;[62] the second and more recent Fair Credit Reporting Act NSL provision covers a consumer reporting agency's consumer reports and "all other" consumer information in its files.[63] The National Security Act provision is at once the most inclusive and the most restricted. It authorizes NSLs for financial information and records and consumer reports held by any financial agency, institution, holding company or consumer reporting agency, and for travel information held by any commercial entity.[64] On the other hand, it is the only provision that limits the information provided to that pertaining to the target of the agency's investigation and to information of a kind whose disclosure the target has previously approved.[65]

Confidentiality

Prior to their amendment in the 109th Congress, the NSL statutes generally featured an open ended confidentiality clause. The communications NSL provision for example declared, "No wire or electronic communication service provider, or officer, or employee, or agent thereof, shall disclose to any person that the Federal Bureau of Investigation has sought or obtained access to information or records under this section."[66] The statutes did not indicate whether a recipient might consult an attorney in order to ascertain his rights and obligations nor whether it might ever be lifted. It was this silence in the face of a seemingly absolute, permanent nondisclosure command that the early *Doe* courts found constitutionally unacceptable[67] and that perhaps led to the reconstruction of the NSL confidentiality requirements in their current form.

As NSL statutes now read, secrecy is not absolutely required. Instead NSL recipients are bound to secrecy only upon the certification of the requesting agency that disclosure of the request or response may result in a danger to national security; may interfere with diplomatic relations or with a criminal, counterterrorism, or counterintelligence investigation; or may endanger the physical safety of an individual. A recipient may disclose the request to those necessary to comply with the request and to an attorney the recipient consults for related legal advice or assistance. In doing so, the recipient must advise them of the secrecy requirements. Aside from its attorney and at the agency's election, the recipient must also identify those to whom it has disclosed the request. A recipient may petition the court to modify or extinguish any NSL secrecy requirement within a year of issuance.[68] Thereafter, it may petition to have the veil of secrecy lifted, although it may resubmit a rejected request only once a year.[69] In all instances, section 3511 declares conclusive and warranting continued secrecy the certification by certain officials that disclosure might create a danger to national security, interfere with diplomatic relations or ongoing investigations, or jeopardize personal safety.[70] A breach of a confidentiality requirement committed knowingly and with the intent to obstruct an investigation or related judicial proceedings is punishable by imprisonment for not more than five years and/or a fine of not more than $250,000 (not more than $500,000 for an organization).[71]

Judicial Review and Enforcement

In addition to authority to review and set aside NSL nondisclosure requirements, the federal courts also enjoy jurisdiction to review and enforce the underlying NSL requests. Recipients may petition and be granted an order modifying or setting aside an NSL, if the court finds that compliance would be unreasonable, oppressive, or otherwise unlawful.[72] Subpoenas issued under the Federal Rules of Criminal Procedure may be modified or quashed if compliance would be unreasonable or oppressive.[73] The Rule affords protection against undue burdens and protects privileged communications.[74] Compliance with a particular NSL might be unduly burdensome in some situations, but the circumstances under which NSLs are used suggest few federally recognized privileges. The Rule also imposes a relevancy requirement, but in the context of an investigation a motion to quash will be denied unless it can be shown that "there is no reasonable possibility that the category of materials the

Government seeks will produce information relevant" to the investigation.[75] The authority to modify or set aside a NSL that is unlawful affords the court an opportunity to determine whether the NSL in question complies with the statutory provisions under which it was issued. On the other hand, the court's authority may be invoked to enforce the NSL against a recalcitrant recipient and failure to comply thereafter is punishable as contempt of court.[76]

Dissemination

Attorney General guidelines govern the sharing of information acquired in response to NSLs under two statutes.[77] A third, the older of the two Fair Credit Report Act sections, limits dissemination to sharing within the FBI, with other agencies to the extent necessary to secure approval of a foreign counterintelligence investigation, or with military investigators when the information concerns a member of the Armed Forces.[78] The National Security Act authorizes dissemination of NSL information to the agency of the employee under investigation, to the Justice Department for law enforcement or counterintelligence purposes, or to another federal agency if the information is clearly relevant to its mission.[79] The more recent Fair Credit Reporting Act NSL section has no explicit provision on restricting dissemination.[80]

Liability, Fees and Oversight

Since judicial enforcement is a feature new to all but one of the NSL statutes,[81] they might be expected to include other incentives to overcome recipient resistance. Three do offer immunity from civil liability for recipients who comply in good faith,[82] and two offer fees or reimbursement to defer the costs of compliance.[83]

NSL statute	18 U.S.C. 2709	12 U.S.C. 3414	15 U.S.C. 1681u	15 U.S.C. 1681v	50 U.S.C. 436
Addressee	communications providers	financial institutions	consumer credit agencies	consumer credit agencies	financial institutions, consumer credit agencies, travel agencies
Certifying officials	senior FBI offi-ceals and SACs	senior FBI officials and SACs	senior FBI officials and SACs	supervisory official of an agency nvestigating, conducting intelligence activities relating to or nalyzing int'l terrorism	senior officials no lower than Ass't Secretary or Ass't Director of agency w/ employees w/ access to classi-fied material

Chart (Continued)

Information covered	Identified customer's name, address, length of service, and billing info	identified customer financial records	identified consumer's name, address, former address,place and former place of employment	all information relating to an identified consumer	all financial information relating to consenting, identified employee
Standard/ Purpose	relevant to an investigation to protect against int'l terrorism or clandestine intelligence activities	sought for foreign counter-intelligence purposes to protect against int'l terrorism or clandestine intelligence activities	sought for an investigation to protect against int'l terrorism or clandestine intelligence activities	necessary for the agency's investigation, activities, or analysis relating to int'l terrorism	necessary to conduct a law enforcement investigation, counter-intelligence inquiry or security determination
Dissemination	only per Att'y Gen. guidelines	only per Att'y Gen. guidelines	w/i FBI, to secure approval for intell. investigation, to military investigators when inform. relates to military member	no statutory provision	only to agency of employee under investingation, DoJ for law enforcement or intell. purposes, or fed. agency when clearly relevant to mission
Immunity/fees	no provisions	no provisions	fees; immunity for good faith compliance with a NSL	immunity for good faith compliance with a NSL	reimbursement; immunity for good faith compliance with a NSL

The confidentiality that necessarily surrounds NSL requests could give rise to concerns of governmental overreaching. Consequently, regular reports on the use of NSL authority must be made to the congressional intelligence and judiciary committees and in some instances to the banking committees.[84] Moreover, section 119 of the USA PATRIOT Improvement and Reauthorization Act instructs the Inspector General of the Department of Justice to audit and to report to the judiciary and intelligence committees as to the Department's use of the authority in the years following expansion of the authority in the USA PATRIOT Act. The section also directs the Attorney General and the Director of National Intelligence to report to Congress on the feasibility of establishing minimization requirements for the NSLs.

The chart summarizes the differences among the five NSL sections.

INSPECTOR GENERAL'S REPORTS

IG Report I

Section 119 of the USA PATRIOT Improvement and Reauthorization Act, P.L. 109-177, 120 Stat. 219 (2006), instructed the Department of Justice's Inspector General to review and report on the FBI's use of NSLs. In early March 2007, the Inspector General released the first of two required reports that covered calendar years 2003 through 2005. The second, covering the time period through the end of calendar year 2006, was released in March 2008.

The initial report notes that FBI use of NSLs has increased dramatically, expanding from 8,500 requests in 2000 to 47,000 in 2005, *IG Report I* at 120. Seventy-four percent were issued in conjunction with counterterrorism investigations, most of the rest in connection with counterintelligence investigations, and less than 1 percent as part of a foreign computer intrusion investigation, *Id.* During the three years under review, the percentage of NSLs used to investigate Americans ("U.S. persons") increased from 39% in 2003 to 53% in 2005.[85] A substantial majority of the requests involve records relating to telephone or e-mail communications, *IG Report I* at 120.

The report is somewhat critical of the FBI's initial performance:

> [W]e found that the FBI used NSLs in violation of applicable NSL statutes, Attorney General Guidelines, and internal FBI policies. In addition, we found that the FBI circumvented the requirements of the ECPA NSL statute when it issued at least 739 "exigent letters" to obtain telephone toll billing records and subscriber information from three telephone companies without first issuing NSLs. Moreover, in a few other instances, the FBI sought or obtained telephone toll billing records in the absence of a national security investigation, when it sought and obtained consumer full credit reports in a counterintelligence investigation, and when it sought and obtained financial records and telephone toll billing records without first issuing NSLs. *Id.* at 124.

More specifically, the Report found that:

- a "significant number of NSL-related possible violations are not being identified or reported" as required
- the only FBI data collection system produced "inaccurate" results
- a "significant number of NSL-related possible violations are not being identified or reported" as required
- the FBI issued over 700 exigent letters acquiring information in a manner that "circumvented the ECPA NSL statute and violated the Attorney General's Guidelines ... and internal FBI policy"
- the FBI's Counterterrorism Division initiated over 300 NSLs in a manner that precluded effective review prior to approval
- 60% of the individual files examined showed violations of FBI internal control policies
- the FBI did not retain signed copies of the NSLs it issues
- the FBI had not provided clear guidance on the application of the Attorney General's least-intrusive-feasible-investigative-technique standard in the case of NSLs

- the precise interpretation of toll billing information as it appears in the ECPA NSL statute is unclear
- SAC supervision of the attorneys responsible for review of the legal adequacy of proposed NSLs made some of the attorneys reluctant to question the adequacy of the underlying investigation previously approved by the SAC
- there was no indication that the FBI's misuse of NSL authority constituted criminal conduct
- personnel both at FBI headquarters and in the field consider NSL use indispensable
- information generated by NSLs is fed into a number of FBI systems. *IG Report I* at 121-24.

Exigent Letters

Prior to enactment of the ECPA, the Supreme Court held that customers had no Fourth Amendment protected privacy rights in the records the telephone company maintained relating to their telephone use.[86] Where a recognized expectation of privacy exists for Fourth Amendment purposes, the Amendment's usual demands such as those of probable cause, particularity, and a warrant may be eased in the face of exigent circumstances. For example, the Fourth Amendment requirement that officers must knock and announce their purpose before forcibly entering a building to execute a warrant can be eased in the presence of certain exigent circumstances such as the threat of the destruction of evidence or danger to the officers.[87] Satisfying Fourth Amendment requirements, however, does not necessary satisfy statutory demands.

The ECPA prohibits communications service providers from supplying information concerning customer records unless one of the statutory exceptions applies.[88] There are specific exceptions for disclosure upon receipt of a grand jury subpoena[89] or an NSL.[90] A service provider who knowingly or intentionally violates the prohibition is subject to civil liability,[91] but there are no criminal penalties for the breach.

The Inspector General found that contrary to assertions that "the FBI would obtain telephone records only after it served NSLs or grand jury subpoenas, the FBI obtained telephone bill records and subscriber information prior to serving NSLs or grand jury subpoenas" by use "exigent letters."[92] The FBI responded that it had barred the use of exigent letters, but emphasized that the term "exigent letter" does not include emergency disclosures under the exception now found in 18 U.S.C. 2702(c) (4). Thus, the FBI might request that a service provider invoke that exception to the record disclosure bar "if the provider reasonably believes that an emergency involving immediate danger of death or serious physical injury to any person justifies disclosure of the information," 18 U.S.C. 2702(c)(4).

IG Report II

The second IG Report reviewed the FBI's use of national security letter authority during calendar year 2006 and the corrective measures taken following the issuance of the IG's first report. The second Report concluded that:

- "the FBI's use of national security letters in 2006 continued the upward trend ... identified ... for the period covering 2003 through 2006"
- "the percentage of NSL requests generated from investigations of U.S. persons continued to increase significantly, from approximately 39% of all NSL requests issued in 2003 to approximately 57% of all NSL requests issued in 2006"
- the FBI and DoJ are committed to correcting the problems identified in *IG Report I* and "have made significant progress in addressing the need to improve compliance in the FBI's use of NSLs"
- "it is too early to definitively state whether the new systems and controls developed by the FBI and the Department will eliminate fully the problems with NSLs that we identified," *IG Report II* at 8-9.

Post-Amendment Judicial Action

Following the 2006 USA PATRIOT Act amendments, the District Court for the Southern District of New York revisited the issue anew and concluded that the revised NSL procedures violated both First Amendment and separation of powers principles.[93] It enjoined Justice Department officials from issuing NSLs under section 2709 or from enforcing compliance with existing orders.[94] However, it stayed the order pending appeal.[95] The Court of Appeals was similarly disposed, but concluded that the government could invoke the secrecy and judicial review authority of the 18 U.S.C. 2709 and 18 U.S.C. 3511 in a limited, but constitutionally permissible manner.[96]

The issues before the Court of Appeals were (1) whether the nondisclosure features of section 2709(c) should be subject to First Amendment strict scrutiny and (2) whether judicial review subject to the conclusive weight of an executive branch certification under section 3511 posed constitutional concerns.

The pre-amendment *Doe* cases had concluded that section 27 09(c), which then broadly prohibited disclosure of receipt of an NSL, "work[ed] as both a prior restraint on speech and a content-based restriction, and hence, [was] subject to strict scrutiny."[97] "Under strict scrutiny review," the Supreme Court has explained, "the Government must demonstrate that the nondisclosure requirement is narrowly tailored to promote a compelling Government interest."[98] Moreover, there can be "no less restrictive alternatives that would be at least as effective in achieving the legitimate purpose that the statute was enacted to serve."[99] When a suspect prior restraint comes in the form of a licensing scheme, under which expression is banned for want government permission as in *Freedman v. Maryland*, the scheme must include prompt judicial review at the petition and burden of the regulator.[100]

Yet, the courts have been unwilling to classify as constitutionally suspect all instances of apparent prior restraint. The government in its presentation to the Second Circuit point to a number of instances where withstanding an apparent prior restraint regulators were held to a less demanding standard—citing cases involving pre-trial discovery gag orders, grand jury secrecy, the confidentiality surrounding inquiry into judicial misconduct, and the secrecy agreements signed by national security employees.[101]

In fact when the Supreme Court assessed the First Amendment validity of a pre-trial discovery gag order, it concluded that the relevant questions were two: first, "whether the practice in question furthers an important or substantial governmental interest unrelated to the suppression of expression;" and second, "whether the limitation of First Amendment freedoms is no greater than is necessary or essential to the protection of the particular governmental interest involved."[102]

The members of the Second Circuit panel could not agree on whether section 2709(c), as amended, constituted a prior restraint subject to strict scrutiny analysis, or should be judged by a somewhat less demanding standard. The lack of consensus proved of little consequence, because the government conceded that strict scrutiny analysis was appropriate,[103] and because the panel agreed the result would be the same under the factor common to both standards—is the restriction on expression narrowly tailored as possible to protect the governmental interest.[104]

The government's interest in national security is indisputably compelling. [105] Unwilling to read section 2709(c) procedure as a licensing scheme, the Second Circuit panel nevertheless concluded that "in the absence of Government-initiated judicial review, subsection 3511(b) is not narrowly tailored to conform to First Amendment protected standards."[106] Moreover, the judicial review must be real. It must "place on the Government the burden to show a good reason to believe that disclosure may result in an enumerated harm, *i.e.* a harm related to an authorized investigation to protect against international terrorism or clandestine intelligence activities."[107] Such judicial review may occur ex parte and in camera, but it may not be bound by the executive's conclusive certification of harm feature of section 3511. In the eyes of the court, there is no meaningful judicial review "of the decision of the Executive Branch to prohibit speech if the position of the Executive Branch that speech would be harmful is 'conclusive' on the reviewing court, absent only a demonstration of bad faith."[108] "To accept deference to that extraordinary degree would be to reduce strict scrutiny to no scrutiny, save only in the rarest of situations where bad faith could be shown," it concluded.[109]

Yet the court envisioned a procedure under which NSL secrecy provision might survive:

> We deem it beyond the authority of a court to "interpret" or "revise" the NSL statutes to create the constitutionally required obligation of the Government to initiate judicial review of a nondisclosure requirement. However, the Government might be able to assume such an obligation without additional legislation....
>
> If the Government uses the suggested reciprocal notice procedure as a means of initiating judicial review, there appears to be no impediment to the Government's including notice of a recipient's opportunity to contest the nondisclosure requirement in an NSL. If such notice is given, time limits on the nondisclosure requirement pending judicial review, as reflected in *Freedman*, would have to be applied to make the review procedure constitutional. We would deem it to be within our judicial authority to conform subsection 2709(c) to First Amendment requirements, by limiting the duration of the nondisclosure requirement, absent a ruling favorable to the Government upon judicial review, to the 1 0-day period in which the NSL recipient decides whether to contest the nondisclosure requirement, the 30-day period in which the Government considers whether to seek judicial review, and a further period of 60 days in which a court must adjudicate the merits, unless special circumstances warrant additional time. If the NSL recipient declines timely to precipitate Government-initiated judicial review, the nondisclosure requirement would continue, subject to the recipient's existing opportunities for annual challenges to the nondisclosure requirement provided by subsection 3511(b). If such an annual challenge is made, the standards and burden of proof

that we have specified for an initial challenge would apply, although the Government would not be obliged to initiate judicial review.[110]

Given the possibility of constitutional application, the court saw no reason to invalidate sections 2709(c) and 3511(b) in toto. The exclusive presumptions of section 3511 cannot survive, the court declared, but the First Amendment finds no offense in the remainder of the two sections except "to the extent that they fail to provide for Government-initiated judicial review. The Government can respond to this partial invalidation ruling by using the suggested reciprocal notice procedure."[111]

On remand under the procedure suggested by the Court of Appeals, the government submitted the declaration of the senior FBI official concerning the continued need for secrecy concerning the NSL. Following an ex parte, in camera hearing, the district court concluded the government had met its burden, but granted the plaintiff's motion for a unclassified, redacted summary of the FBI declaration.[112]

APPENDICES

(Language added by P.L. 109-177(H.R. 3199): in italics)
(Language added by P.L. 109-178 (S. 2271): in bold)
(Language repealed by either: struck out)

12 U.S.C. 3414

(a) (1) Nothing in this chapter (except sections 3415, 3417, 3418, and 3421 of this title) shall apply to the production and disclosure of financial records pursuant to requests from:
   (A) a Government authority authorized to conduct foreign counter- or foreign positive- intelligence activities for purposes of conducting such activities;
   (B) the Secret Service for the purpose of conducting its protective functions (18 U.S.C. 3056; 3 U.S.C. 202, Public Law 90-331, as amended); or
   (C) a Government authority authorized to conduct investigations of, or intelligence or counterintelligence analyses related to, international terrorism for the purpose of conducting such investigations or analyses.
(2) In the instances specified in paragraph (1), the Government authority shall submit to the financial institution the certificate required in section 3403(b) of this title signed by a supervisory official of a rank designated by the head of the Government authority.
   (A) If the Government authority described in paragraph (1) or the Secret Service, as the case may be, certifies that otherwise there may result a danger to the national security of the United States, interference with a criminal, counterterrorism, or counterintelligence investigation, interference with diplomatic relations, or danger to the life or physical safety of any person, no financial institution, or officer, employee, or agent of such institution, shall

disclose to any person (other than those to whom such disclosure is necessary to comply with the request or an attorney to obtain legal advice or legal assistance with respect to the request) that the Government authority or the Secret Service has sought or obtained access to a customer's financial records.

(B) The request shall notify the person or entity to whom the request is directed of the nondisclosure requirement under subparagraph (A).

(C) Any recipient disclosing to those persons necessary to comply with the request or to an attorney to obtain legal advice or legal assistance with respect to the request shall inform such persons of any applicable nondisclosure requirement. Any person who receives a disclosure under this subsection shall be subject to the same prohibitions on disclosure under subparagraph (A).

(D) At the request of the authorized Government agency or the Secret Service, any person making or intending to make a disclosure under this section shall identify to the requesting official of the authorized Government agency or the Secret Service the person to whom such disclosure will be made or to whom such disclosure was made prior to the request, except that nothing in this section shall require a person to inform the requesting official of the authorized Government authority or the Secret Service of the identity of an attorney to whom disclosure was made or will be made to obtain legal advice or legal assistance with respect to the request for financial records under this subsection.

(4) The Government authority specified in paragraph (1) shall compile an annual tabulation of the occasions in which this section was used.

(5)

(A) Financial institutions, and officers, employees, and agents thereof, shall comply with a request for a customer's or entity's financial records made pursuant to this subsection by the Federal Bureau of Investigation when the Director of the Federal Bureau of Investigation (or the Director's designee in a position not lower than Deputy Assistant Director at Bureau headquarters or a Special Agent in Charge in a Bureau field office designated by the Director) certifies in writing to the financial institution that such records are sought for foreign counter intelligence purposes to protect against international terrorism or clandestine intelligence activities, provided that such an investigation of a United States person is not conducted solely upon the basis of activities protected by the first amendment to the Constitution of the United States.

(B) The Federal Bureau of Investigation may disseminate information obtained pursuant to this paragraph only as provided in guidelines approved by the Attorney General for foreign intelligence collection and foreign counter-intelligence investigations conducted by the Federal Bureau of Investigation, and, with respect to dissemination to an agency of the United States, only if such information is clearly relevant to the authorized responsibilities of such agency.

(C) On the dates provided in section 415b of Title 50, the Attorney General shall fully inform the congressional intelligence committees (as defined in section 401a of Title 50) concerning all requests made pursuant to this paragraph.

(D) No prohibition of certain disclosure. –

(i) If the Director of the Federal Bureau of Investigation, or his designee in a position not lower than Deputy Assistant Director at Bureau headquarters or a

Special Agent in Charge in a Bureau field office designated by the Director, certifies that otherwise there may result a danger to the national security of the United States, interference with a criminal, counterterrorism, or counterintelligence investigation, interference with diplomatic relations, or danger to the life or physical safety of any person, no financial institution, or officer, employee, or agent of such institution, shall disclose to any person (other than those to whom such disclosure is necessary to comply with the request or an attorney to obtain legal advice or legal assistance with respect to the request) that the Federal Bureau of Investigation has sought or obtained access to a customer's or entity's financial records under subparagraph (A).

(ii) The request shall notify the person or entity to whom the request is directed of the nondisclosure requirement under clause (i).

(iii) Any recipient disclosing to those persons necessary to comply with the request or to an attorney to obtain legal advice or legal assistance with respect to the request shall inform such persons of any applicable nondisclosure requirement. Any person who receives a disclosure under this subsection shall be subject to the same prohibitions on disclosure under clause (i).

(iv) At the request of the Director of the Federal Bureau of Investigation or the designee of the Director, any person making or intending to make a disclosure under this section shall identify to the Director or such designee the person to whom such disclosure will be made or to whom such disclosure was made prior to the request, except that nothing in this section shall require a person to inform the Director or such designee of the identity of an attorney to whom disclosure was made or will be made to obtain legal advice or legal assistance with respect to the request for financial records under subparagraph (A).

(b)

(1) Nothing in this chapter shall prohibit a Government authority from obtaining financial records from a financial institution if the Government authority determines that delay in obtaining access to such records would create imminent danger of –

(A) physical injury to any person;

(B) serious property damage; or

(C) flight to avoid prosecution.

(2) In the instances specified in paragraph (1), the Government shall submit to the financial institution the certificate required in section 3403(b) of this title signed by a supervisory official of a rank designated by the head of the Government authority.

(3) Within five days of obtaining access to financial records under this subsection, the Government authority shall file with the appropriate court a signed, sworn statement of a supervisory official of a rank designated by the head of the Government authority setting forth the grounds for the emergency access. The Government authority shall thereafter comply with the notice provisions of section 3409(c) of this title.

(4) The Government authority specified in paragraph (1) shall compile an annual tabulation of the occasions in which this section was used.

[there is no subsection (c)]

(d) For purposes of this section, and sections 1115 and 1117 [12 U.S.C. 3415, 3417 relating to cost reimbursement and civil penalties respectively] insofar as they relate to the operation of this section, the term "financial institution" has the same meaning as in subsections (a)(2) and (c)(1) of section 5312 of title 31, United States Code, except that, for purposes of this section, such term shall include only such a financial institution any part of which is located inside any State or territory of the United States, the District of Columbia, Puerto Rico, Guam, American Samoa, the Commonwealth of the Northern Mariana Islands, or the United States Virgin Islands. [Subsection (d) was added by subsection 3 74(a) of the Intelligence Authorization Act for Fiscal Year 2004, P.L. 108-177, 117 Stat. 2628 (2003).]

18 U.S.C. 2709

(a) Duty to provide. – A wire or electronic communication service provider shall comply with a request for subscriber information and toll billing records information, or electronic communication transactional records in its custody or possession made by the Director of the Federal Bureau of Investigation under subsection (b) of this section.

(b) Required certification. – The Director of the Federal Bureau of Investigation, or his designee in a position not lower than Deputy Assistant Director at Bureau headquarters or a Special Agent in Charge in a Bureau field office designated by the Director, may –

  (1) request the name, address, length of service, and local and long distance toll billing records of a person or entity if the Director (or his designee) certifies in writing to the wire or electronic communication service provider to which the request is made that the name, address, length of service, and toll billing records sought are relevant to an authorized investigation to protect against international terrorism or clandestine intelligence activities, provided that such an investigation of a United States person is not conducted solely on the basis of activities protected by the first amendment to the Constitution of the United States; and

  (2) request the name, address, and length of service of a person or entity if the Director (or his designee) certifies in writing to the wire or electronic communication service provider to which the request is made that the information sought is relevant to an authorized investigation to protect against international terrorism or clandestine intelligence activities, provided that such an investigation of a United States person is not conducted solely upon the basis of activities protected by the first amendment to the Constitution of the United States.

(c) Prohibition of certain disclosure.

  (1) If the Director of the Federal Bureau of Investigation, or his designee in a position not lower than Deputy Assistant Director at Bureau headquarters or a Special Agent in Charge in a Bureau field office designated by the Director, certifies that otherwise there may result a danger to the national security of the United States, interference with a criminal, counterterrorism, or counterintelligence investigation, interference with diplomatic relations, or

danger to the life or physical safety of any person, no wire or electronic communications service provider, or officer, employee, or agent thereof, shall disclose to any person (other than those to whom such disclosure is necessary to comply with the request or an attorney to obtain legal advice or legal assistance with respect to the request) that the Federal Bureau of Investigation has sought or obtained access to information or records under this section.

(2) *The request shall notify the person or entity to whom the request is directed of the nondisclosure requirement under paragraph (1).*

(3) *Any recipient disclosing to those persons necessary to comply with the request or to an attorney to obtain legal advice or legal assistance with respect to the request shall inform such person of any applicable nondisclosure requirement. Any person who receives a disclosure under this subsection shall be subject to the same prohibitions on disclosure under paragraph (1).*

(4) *At the request of the Director of the Federal Bureau of Investigation or the designee of the Director, any person making or intending to make a disclosure under this section shall identify to the Director or such designee the person to whom such disclosure will be made or to whom such disclosure was made prior to the request except that nothing in this section shall require a person to inform the Director or such designee of the identity of an attorney to whom disclosure was made or will be made to obtain legal advice or legal assistance with respect to the request under subsection (a).*

(d) Dissemination by bureau. – The Federal Bureau of Investigation may disseminate information and records obtained under this section only as provided in guidelines approved by the Attorney General for foreign intelligence collection and foreign counterintelligence investigations conducted by the Federal Bureau of Investigation, and, with respect to dissemination to an agency of the United States, only if such information is clearly relevant to the authorized responsibilities of such agency.

(e) Requirement that certain congressional bodies be informed. – On a semiannual basis the Director of the Federal Bureau of Investigation shall fully inform the Permanent Select Committee on Intelligence of the House of Representatives and the Select Committee on Intelligence of the Senate, and the Committee on the Judiciary of the House of Representatives and the Committee on the Judiciary of the Senate, concerning all requests made under subsection (b) of this section.

(f) Libraries- A library (as that term is defined in section 213(1) of the Library Services and Technology Act (20 U.S.C. 9122(1)), the services of which include access to the Internet, books, journals, magazines, newspapers, or other similar forms of communication in print or digitally by patrons for their use, review, examination, or circulation, is not a wire or electronic communication service provider for purposes of this section, unless the library is providing the services defined in section 2510(15) (`electronic communication service') of this title.

15 U.S.C. 1681u.

(a) Identity of financial institutions

Notwithstanding section 168 1b of this title or any other provision of this subchapter, a consumer reporting agency shall furnish to the Federal Bureau of Investigation the names and addresses of all financial institutions (as that term is defined in section 3401 of Title 12) at which a consumer maintains or has maintained an account, to the extent that information is in the files of the agency, when presented with a written request for that information, signed by the Director of the Federal Bureau of Investigation, or the Director's designee in a position not lower than Deputy Assistant Director at Bureau headquarters or a Special Agent in Charge of a Bureau field office designated by the Director, which certifies compliance with this section. The Director or the Director's designee may make such a certification only if the Director or the Director's designee has determined in writing, that such information is sought for the conduct of an authorized investigation to protect against international terrorism or clandestine intelligence activities, provided that such an investigation of a United States person is not conducted solely upon the basis of activities protected by the first amendment to the Constitution of the United States.

(b) Identifying information

Notwithstanding the provisions of section 1681b of this title or any other provision of this subchapter, a consumer reporting agency shall furnish identifying information respecting a consumer, limited to name, address, former addresses, places of employment, or former places of employment, to the Federal Bureau of Investigation when presented with a written request, signed by the Director or the Director's designee in a position not lower than Deputy Assistant Director at Bureau headquarters or a Special Agent in Charge of a Bureau field office designated by the Director, which certifies compliance with this subsection. The Director or the Director's designee may make such a certification only if the Director or the Director's designee has determined in writing that such information is sought for the conduct of an authorized investigation to protect against international terrorism or clandestine intelligence activities, provided that such an investigation of a United States person is not conducted solely upon the basis of activities protected by the first amendment to the Constitution of the United States.

(c) Court order for disclosure of consumer reports

Notwithstanding section 1681b of this title or any other provision of this subchapter, if requested in writing by the Director of the Federal Bureau of Investigation, or a designee of the Director in a position not lower than Deputy Assistant Director at Bureau headquarters or a Special Agent in Charge in a Bureau field office designated by the Director, a court may issue an order ex parte directing a consumer reporting agency to furnish a consumer report to the Federal Bureau of Investigation, upon a showing in camera that the consumer report is sought for the conduct of an authorized investigation to protect against international terrorism or clandestine intelligence activities, provided that such an investigation of a United States person is not conducted solely upon the basis of activities protected by the first amendment to the Constitution of the United States.

The terms of an order issued under this subsection shall not disclose that the order is issued for purposes of a counterintelligence investigation.

(d) Confidentiality

(1) If the Director of the Federal Bureau of Investigation, or his designee in a position not lower than Deputy Assistant Director at Bureau headquarters or a Special Agent in Charge in a Bureau field office designated by the Director, certifies that otherwise there may result a danger to the national security of the United States, interference with a criminal, counterterrorism, or counterintelligence investigation, interference with diplomatic relations, or danger to the life or physical safety of any person, no consumer reporting agency or officer, employee, or agent of a consumer reporting agency shall disclose to any person (other than those to whom such disclosure is necessary to comply with the request or an attorney to obtain legal advice or legal assistance with respect to the request) that the Federal Bureau of Investigation has sought or obtained the identity of financial institutions or a consumer report respecting any consumer under subsection (a), (b), or (c), and no consumer reporting agency or officer, employee, or agent of a consumer reporting agency shall include in any consumer report any information that would indicate that the Federal Bureau of Investigation has sought or obtained such information on a consumer report.

(2) The request shall notify the person or entity to whom the request is directed of the nondisclosure requirement under paragraph (1).

(3) Any recipient disclosing to those persons necessary to comply with the request or to an attorney to obtain legal advice or legal assistance with respect to the request shall inform such persons of any applicable nondisclosure requirement. Any person who receives a disclosure under this subsection shall be subject to the same prohibitions on disclosure under paragraph (1).

(4) At the request of the Director of the Federal Bureau of Investigation or the designee of the Director, any person making or intending to make a disclosure under this section shall identify to the Director or such designee the person to whom such disclosure will be made or to whom such disclosure was made prior to the request; except that nothing in this section shall require a person to inform the Director or such designee of the identity of an attorney to whom disclosure was made or will be made to obtain legal advice or legal assistance with respect to the request for the identity of financial institutions or a consumer report respecting any consumer under this section.

(e) Payment of fees

The Federal Bureau of Investigation shall, subject to the availability of appropriations, pay to the consumer reporting agency assembling or providing report or information in accordance with procedures established under this section a fee for reimbursement for such costs as are reasonably necessary and which have been directly incurred in searching, reproducing, or transporting books, papers, records, or other data required or requested to be produced under this section.

(f) Limit on dissemination

The Federal Bureau of Investigation may not disseminate information obtained pursuant to this section outside of the Federal Bureau of Investigation, except to other Federal agencies as may be necessary for the approval or conduct of a foreign counterintelligence investigation, or, where the information concerns a person subject to the Uniform Code of Military Justice, to appropriate investigative authorities within the military department concerned as may be necessary for the conduct of a joint foreign counterintelligence investigation.

(g) Rules of construction

Nothing in this section shall be construed to prohibit information from being furnished by the Federal Bureau of Investigation pursuant to a subpoena or court order, in connection with a judicial or administrative proceeding to enforce the provisions of this subchapter. Nothing in this section shall be construed to authorize or permit the withholding of information from the Congress.

(h) Reports to Congress

(1) On a semiannual basis, the Attorney General shall fully inform the Permanent Select Committee on Intelligence and the Committee on Banking, Finance and Urban Affairs of the House of Representatives, and the Select Committee on Intelligence and the Committee on Banking, Housing, and Urban Affairs of the Senate concerning all requests made pursuant to subsections (a), (b), and (c) of this section.

(2) In the case of the semiannual reports required to be submitted under paragraph (1) to the Permanent Select Committee on Intelligence of the House of Representatives and the Select Committee on Intelligence of the Senate, the submittal dates for such reports shall be as provided in section 41 5b of Title 50.

(i) Damages

Any agency or department of the United States obtaining or disclosing any consumer reports, records, or information contained therein in violation of this section is liable to the consumer to whom such consumer reports, records, or information relate in an amount equal to the sum of –

(1) $100, without regard to the volume of consumer reports, records, or information involved;

(2) any actual damages sustained by the consumer as a result of the disclosure;

(3) if the violation is found to have been willful or intentional, such punitive damages as a court may allow; and

(4) in the case of any successful action to enforce liability under this subsection, the costs of the action, together with reasonable attorney fees, as determined by the court.

(j) Disciplinary actions for violations

If a court determines that any agency or department of the United States has violated any provision of this section and the court finds that the circumstances surrounding the violation raise questions of whether or not an officer or employee of the agency or department acted willfully or intentionally with respect to the violation, the agency or department shall promptly initiate a proceeding to determine whether or not disciplinary action is warranted against the officer or employee who was responsible for the violation.

(k) Good-faith exception

Notwithstanding any other provision of this subchapter, any consumer reporting agency or agent or employee thereof making disclosure of consumer reports or identifying information pursuant to this subsection in good-faith reliance upon a certification of the Federal Bureau of Investigation pursuant to provisions of this section shall not be liable to any person for such disclosure under this subchapter, the constitution of any State, or any law or regulation of any State or any political subdivision of any State.

(l) Limitation of remedies

Notwithstanding any other provision of this subchapter, the remedies and sanctions set forth in this section shall be the only judicial remedies and sanctions for violation of this section.

(m) Injunctive relief

In addition to any other remedy contained in this section, injunctive relief shall be available to require compliance with the procedures of this section. In the event of any successful action under this subsection, costs together with reasonable attorney fees, as determined by the court, may be recovered.

15 U.S.C. 1681v.

(a) Disclosure

Notwithstanding section 1681b of this title or any other provision of this subchapter, a consumer reporting agency shall furnish a consumer report of a consumer and all other information in a consumer's file to a government agency authorized to conduct investigations of, or intelligence or counterintelligence activities or analysis related to, international terrorism when presented with a written certification by such government agency that such information is necessary for the agency's conduct or such investigation, activity or analysis.

(b) Form of certification

The certification described in subsection (a) shall be signed by a supervisory official designated by the head of a Federal agency or an officer of a Federal agency whose appointment to office is required to be made by the President, by and with the advice and consent of the Senate.

(c) Confidentiality

(1) If the head of a government agency authorized to conduct investigations of intelligence or counterintelligence activities or analysis related to international terrorism, or his designee, certifies that otherwise there may result a danger to the national security of the United States, interference with a criminal, counterterrorism, or counterintelligence investigation, interference with diplomatic relations, or danger to the life or physical safety of any person, no consumer reporting agency or officer, employee, or agent of such consumer reporting agency, shall disclose to any person (other than those to whom such disclosure is necessary to comply with the request or an attorney to obtain legal advice or legal assistance with respect to the request), or specify in any consumer report, that a government agency has sought or obtained access to information under subsection (a).

(2) The request shall notify the person or entity to whom the request is directed of the nondisclosure requirement under paragraph (1).

(3) *Any recipient disclosing to those persons necessary to comply with the request or to any attorney to obtain legal advice or legal assistance with respect to the request shall inform such persons of any applicable nondisclosure requirement. Any person who receives a disclosure under this subsection shall be subject to the same prohibitions on disclosure under paragraph (1).*

(4) *At the request of the authorized Government agency, any person making or intending to make a disclosure under this section shall identify to the requesting official of the authorized Government agency the person to whom such disclosure will be made or to whom such disclosure was made prior to the request, except that nothing in this section shall require a person to inform the requesting official of the identity of an attorney to whom disclosure was made or will be made to obtain legal advice or legal assistance with respect to the request for information under subsection (a).*

(d) Rule of construction
Nothing in section 168 1u of this title shall be construed to limit the authority of the Director of the Federal Bureau of Investigation under this section.

(d) Safe harbor
Notwithstanding any other provision of this subchapter, any consumer reporting agency or agent or employee thereof making disclosure of consumer reports or other information pursuant to this section in good-faith reliance upon a certification of a governmental agency pursuant to the provisions of this section shall not be liable to any person for such disclosure under this subchapter, the constitution of any State, or any law or regulation of any State or any political subdivision of any State.

(f) Reports to Congress- (1) On a semi-annual basis, the Attorney General shall fully inform the Committee on the Judiciary, the Committee on Financial Services, and the Permanent Select Committee on Intelligence of the House of Representatives and the Committee on the Judiciary, the Committee on Banking, Housing, and Urban Affairs, and the Select Committee on Intelligence of the Senate concerning all requests made pursuant to subsection (a).

(2) *In the case of the semiannual reports required to be submitted under paragraph (1) to the Permanent Select Committee on Intelligence of the House of Representatives and the Select Committee on Intelligence of the Senate, the submittal dates for such reports shall be as provided in section 507 of the National Security Act of 1947 (50 U.S. C. 415b).*

50 U.S.C. 436.

(a) Generally

(1) Any authorized investigative agency may request from any financial agency, financial institution, or holding company, or from any consumer reporting agency, such financial records, other financial information, and consumer reports as may be necessary in order to conduct any authorized law enforcement investigation, counterintelligence inquiry, or security determination. Any authorized investigative agency may also request records maintained by any

commercial entity within the United States pertaining to travel by an employee in the executive branch of Government outside the United States.

(2) Requests may be made under this section where –

(A) the records sought pertain to a person who is or was an employee in the executive branch of Government required by the President in an Executive order or regulation, as a condition of access to classified information, to provide consent, during a background investigation and for such time as access to the information is maintained, and for a period of not more than three years thereafter, permitting access to financial records, other financial information, consumer reports, and travel records; and

(B) (i) there are reasonable grounds to believe, based on credible information, that the person is, or may be, disclosing classified information in an unauthorized manner to a foreign power or agent of a foreign power;

(ii) information the employing agency deems credible indicates the person has incurred excessive indebtedness or has acquired a level of affluence which cannot be explained by other information known to the agency; or

(iii) circumstances indicate the person had the capability and opportunity to disclose classified information which is known to have been lost or compromised to a foreign power or an agent of a foreign power.

(3) Each such request –

(A) shall be accompanied by a written certification signed by the department or agency head or deputy department or agency head concerned, or by a senior official designated for this purpose by the department or agency head concerned (whose rank shall be no lower than Assistant Secretary or Assistant Director), and shall certify that –

(i) the person concerned is or was an employee within the meaning of paragraph (2)(A);

(ii) the request is being made pursuant to an authorized inquiry or investigation and is authorized under this section; and

(iii) the records or information to be reviewed are records or information which the employee has previously agreed to make available to the authorized investigative agency for review;

(B) shall contain a copy of the agreement referred to in subparagraph (A)(iii);

(C) shall identify specifically or by category the records or information to be reviewed; and

(D) shall inform the recipient of the request of the prohibition described in subsection (b) of this section.

(b) Disclosure of requests

(1) If an authorized investigative agency described in subsection (a) certifies that otherwise there may result a danger to the national security of the United States, interference with a criminal, counterterrorism, or counterintelligence investigation, interference with diplomatic relations, or danger to the life or physical safety of any person, no governmental or private entity, or officer, employee, or agent of such entity, may disclose to any person (other than those to whom such disclosure is necessary to comply with the request or an attorney to obtain legal advice or legal assistance with respect to the request) that such

entity has received or satisfied a request made by an authorized investigative agency under this section.

(2) *The request shall notify the person or entity to whom the request is directed of the nondisclosure requirement under paragraph (1).*

(3) *Any recipient disclosing to those persons necessary to comply with the request or to an attorney to obtain legal advice or legal assistance with respect to the request shall inform such persons of any applicable nondisclosure requirement. Any person who receives a disclosure under this subsection shall be subject to the same prohibitions on disclosure under paragraph (1).*

(4) *At the request of the authorized investigative agency, any person making or intending to make a disclosure under this section shall identify to the requesting official of the authorized investigative agency the person to whom such disclosure will be made or to whom such disclosure was made prior to the request, except that nothing in this section shall require a person to inform the requesting official of the identity of an attorney to whom disclosure was made or will be made to obtain legal advice or legal assistance with respect to the request under subsection (a).*

(c) Records or information; inspection or copying

(1) Notwithstanding any other provision of law (other than section 6103 of Title 26), an entity receiving a request for records or information under subsection (a) of this section shall, if the request satisfies the requirements of this section, make available such records or information within 30 days for inspection or copying, as may be appropriate, by the agency requesting such records or information.

(2) Any entity (including any officer, employee, or agent thereof) that discloses records or information for inspection or copying pursuant to this section in good faith reliance upon the certifications made by an agency pursuant to this section shall not be liable for any such disclosure to any person under this subchapter, the constitution of any State, or any law or regulation of any State or any political subdivision of any State.

(d) Reimbursement of costs

Any agency requesting records or information under this section may, subject to the availability of appropriations, reimburse a private entity for any cost reasonably incurred by such entity in responding to such request, including the cost of identifying, reproducing, or transporting records or other data.

(e) Dissemination of records or information received

An agency receiving records or information pursuant to a request under this section may disseminate the records or information obtained pursuant to such request outside the agency only –

(1) to the agency employing the employee who is the subject of the records or information;

(2) to the Department of Justice for law enforcement or counterintelligence purposes; or

(3) with respect to dissemination to an agency of the United States, if such information is clearly relevant to the authorized responsibilities of such agency.

(f) Construction of section

Nothing in this section may be construed to affect the authority of an investigative agency to obtain information pursuant to the Right to Financial Privacy Act (12 U.S.C. 3401 et seq.) or the Fair Credit Reporting Act (15 U.S.C. 1681 et seq.).

18 U.S.C. 1510

(e) Whoever, having been notified of the applicable disclosure prohibitions or confidentiality requirements of section 2709(c)(1) of this title, section 626(d)(1) or 627(c)(1) of the Fair Credit Reporting Act (15 U.S.C. 1681u(d)(1) or 1681v(c)(1)), section 1114(a)(3)(A) or 1114(a)(5)(D)(i) of the Right to Financial Privacy Act (12 U.S.C. 3414(a)(3)(A) or 3414(a)(5)(D)(i)), or section 802(b)(1) of the National Security Act of 1947 (50 U.S.C. 436(b)(1)), knowingly and with the intent to obstruct an investigation or judicial proceeding violates such prohibitions or requirements applicable by law to such person shall be imprisoned for not more than five years, fined under this title, or both.

P.L. 109-177, Sec. 118

Reports on National Security Letters.

(a) Existing Reports – Any report made to a committee of Congress regarding national security letters under section 2709(c)(1) of title 18, United States Code, sections 626(d) or 627(c) of the Fair Credit Reporting Act (15 U.S.C. 1681u(d) or 1681v(c)), section 1114(a)(3) or 1114(a)(5)(D) of the Right to Financial Privacy Act (12 U.S.C. 3414(a)(3) or 3414(a)(5)(D)), or section 802(b) of the National Security Act of 1947 (50 U.S.C. 436(b)) shall also be made to the Committees on the Judiciary of the House of Representatives and the Senate.

(c) Report on Requests for National Security Letters-

(1) IN GENERAL- In April of each year, the Attorney General shall submit to Congress an aggregate report setting forth with respect to the preceding year the total number of requests made by the Department of Justice for information concerning different United States persons under –

(A) section 2709 of title 18, United States Code (to access certain communication service provider records), excluding the number of requests for subscriber information;

(B) section 1114 of the Right to Financial Privacy Act (12 U.S.C. 3414) (to obtain financial institution customer records);

(C) section 802 of the National Security Act of 1947 (50 U.S.C. 436) (to obtain financial information, records, and consumer reports);

(D) section 626 of the Fair Credit Reporting Act (15 U.S.C. 1681u) (to obtain certain financial information and consumer reports); and

(E) section 627 of the Fair Credit Reporting Act (15 U.S.C. 1681v) (to obtain credit agency consumer records for counterterrorism investigations).

(2) UNCLASSIFIED FORM- The report under this section shall be submitted in unclassified form.

(d) National Security Letter Defined- In this section, the term 'national security letter' means a request for information under one of the following provisions of law:

(1) Section 2709(a) of title 18, United States Code (to access certain communication service provider records).
(2) Section 1114(a)(5)(A) of the Right to Financial Privacy Act (12 U.S.C. 3414(a)(5)(A)) (to obtain financial institution customer records).
(3) Section 802 of the National Security Act of 1947 (50 U.S.C. 436) (to obtain financial information, records, and consumer reports).
(4) Section 626 of the Fair Credit Reporting Act (15 U.S.C. 1681u) (to obtain certain financial information and consumer reports).
(5) Section 627 of the Fair Credit Reporting Act (15 U.S.C. 1681v) (to obtain credit agency consumer records for counterterrorism investigations).

P.L. 109-177, Sec. 119

Audit of Use of National Security Letters.

(a) Audit – The Inspector General of the Department of Justice shall perform an audit of the effectiveness and use, including any improper or illegal use, of national security letters issued by the Department of Justice.

(b) Requirements- The audit required under subsection (a) shall include –

(1) an examination of the use of national security letters by the Department of Justice during calendar years 2003 through 2006;

(2) a description of any noteworthy facts or circumstances relating to such use, including any improper or illegal use of such authority; and

(3) an examination of the effectiveness of national security letters as an investigative tool, including –

(A) the importance of the information acquired by the Department of Justice to the intelligence activities of the Department of Justice or to any other department or agency of the Federal Government;

(B) the manner in which such information is collected, retained, analyzed, and disseminated by the Department of Justice, including any direct access to such information (such as access to 'raw data') provided to any other department, agency, or instrumentality of Federal, State, local, or tribal governments or any private sector entity;

(C) whether, and how often, the Department of Justice utilized such information to produce an analytical intelligence product for distribution within the Department of Justice, to the intelligence community (as such term is defined in section 3(4) of the National Security Act of 1947 (50 U.S. C. 401a(4))), or to other Federal, State, local, or tribal government departments, agencies, or instrumentalities;

(D) *whether, and how often, the Department of Justice provided such information to law enforcement authorities for use in criminal proceedings;*

(E) *with respect to national security letters issued following the date of the enactment of this Act, an examination of the number of occasions in which the Department of Justice, or an officer or employee of the Department of Justice, issued a national security letter without the certification necessary to require the recipient of such letter to comply with the nondisclosure and confidentiality requirements potentially applicable under law; and*

(F) *the types of electronic communications and transactional information obtained through requests for information under section 2709 of title 18, United States Code, including the types of dialing, routing, addressing, or signaling information obtained, and the procedures the Department of Justice uses if content information is obtained through the use of such authority.*

(c) *Submission Dates-*

(1) *PRIOR YEARS- Not later than one year after the date of the enactment of this Act, or upon completion of the audit under this section for calendar years 2003 and 2004, whichever is earlier, the Inspector General of the Department of Justice shall submit to the Committee on the Judiciary and the Permanent Select Committee on Intelligence of the House of Representatives and the Committee on the Judiciary and the Select Committee on Intelligence of the Senate a report containing the results of the audit conducted under this subsection for calendar years 2003 and 2004.*

(2) *CALENDAR YEARS 2005 AND 2006- Not later than December 31, 2007, or upon completion of the audit under this subsection for calendar years 2005 and 2006, whichever is earlier, the Inspector General of the Department of Justice shall submit to the Committee on the Judiciary and the Permanent Select Committee on Intelligence of the House of Representatives and the Committee on the Judiciary and the Select Committee on Intelligence of the Senate a report containing the results of the audit conducted under this subsection for calendar years 2005 and 2006.*

(d) *Prior Notice to Attorney General and Director of National Intelligence; Comments-*

(1) *NOTICE- Not less than 30 days before the submission of a report under subsections (c)(1) or (c)(2), the Inspector General of the Department of Justice shall provide such report to the Attorney General and the Director of National Intelligence.*

(2) *COMMENTS- The Attorney General or the Director of National Intelligence may provide comments to be included in the reports submitted under subsections (c)(1) or (c)(2) as the Attorney General or the Director of National Intelligence may consider necessary.*

(e) *Unclassified Form- The reports submitted under subsections (c)(1) or (c)(2) and any comments included under subsection (d)(2) shall be in unclassified form, but may include a classified annex.*

(f) *Minimization Procedures Feasibility- Not later than February 1, 2007, or upon completion of review of the report submitted under subsection (c)(1), whichever is earlier, the Attorney General and the Director of National Intelligence shall jointly submit to the Committee on the Judiciary and the Permanent Select Committee on Intelligence of the House of Representatives and the Committee on the Judiciary and the Select Committee on Intelligence of the Senate a report on the feasibility of applying minimization procedures in the context of national security letters to ensure the protection of the constitutional rights of United States persons.*

(g) *National Security Letter Defined- In this section, the term 'national security letter' means a request for information under one of the following provisions of law:*
   (1) *Section 2709 (a) of title 18, United States Code (to access certain communication service provider records).*
   (2) *Section 1114(a) (5) (A) of the Right to Financial Privacy Act (12 U.S. C. 3414(a) (5) (A)) (to obtain financial institution customer records).*
   (3) *Section 802 of the National Security Act of 194 7 (50 U.S. C. 436) (to obtain financial information, records, and consumer reports).*
   (4) *Section 626 of the Fair Credit Reporting Act (15 U.S. C. 1681u) (to obtain certain financial information and consumer reports).*
   (5) *Section 627 of the Fair Credit Reporting Act (15 U.S. C. 1681v) (to obtain credit agency consumer records for counterterrorism investigations).*

18 U.S.C. 3511

(a) *The recipient of a request for records, a report, or other information under section 2709(b) of this title, section 626(a) or (b) or 627(a) of the Fair Credit Reporting Act, section 1114(a) (5) (A) of the Right to Financial Privacy Act, or section 802(a) of the National Security Act of 1947 may, in the United States district court for the district in which that person or entity does business or resides, petition for an order modifying or setting aside the request. The court may modify or set aside the request if compliance would be unreasonable, oppressive, or otherwise unlawful.*

(b) *(1) The recipient of a request for records, a report, or other information under section 2709(b) of this title, section 626(a) or (b) or 62 7(a) of the Fair Credit Reporting Act, section 1114(a) (5) (A) of the Right to Financial Privacy Act, or section 802(a) of the National Security Act of 1947, may petition any court described in subsection (a) for an order modifying or setting aside a nondisclosure requirement imposed in connection with such a request.*

   (2) If the petition is filed within one year of the request for records, a report, or other information under section 2709(b) of this title, section 626(a) or (b) or 62 7(a) of the Fair Credit Reporting Act, section 1114(a) (5) (A) of the Right to Financial Privacy Act, or section 802(a) of the National Security Act of 1947, the court may modify or set aside such a nondisclosure requirement if it finds that there is no reason to believe that disclosure may endanger the national security of the United States, interfere with a criminal, counterterrorism, or counterintelligence investigation, interfere with diplomatic relations, or endanger the life or physical safety of any person. If, at the time of the petition, the Attorney General, Deputy Attorney General, an Assistant Attorney General, or the Director of the Federal Bureau of Investigation, or in the case of a request by a department, agency, or instrumentality

of the Federal Government other than the Department of Justice, the head or deputy head of such department, agency, or instrumentality, certifies that disclosure may endanger the national security of the United States or interfere with diplomatic relations, such certification shall be treated as conclusive unless the court finds that the certification was made in bad faith.

(3) If the petition is filed one year or more after the request for records, a report, or other information under section 2709(b) of this title, section 626(a) or (b) or 627(a) of the Fair Credit Reporting Act, section 1114 (a) (5) (A) of the Right to Financial Privacy Act, or section 802(a) of the National Security Act of 1947, the Attorney General, Deputy Attorney General, an Assistant Attorney General, or the Director of the Federal Bureau of Investigation, or his designee in a position not lower than Deputy Assistant Director at Bureau headquarters or a Special Agent in Charge in a Bureau field office designated by the Director, or in the case of a request by a department, agency, or instrumentality of the Federal Government other than the Federal Bureau of Investigation, the head or deputy head of such department, agency, or instrumentality, within ninety days of the filing of the petition, shall either terminate the nondisclosure requirement or recertify that disclosure may result in a danger to the national security of the United States, interference with a criminal, counterterrorism, or counterintelligence investigation, interference with diplomatic relations, or danger to the life or physical safety of any person. In the event of re-certification, the court may modify or set aside such a nondisclosure requirement if it finds that there is no reason to believe that disclosure may endanger the national security of the United States, interfere with a criminal, counterterrorism, or counterintelligence investigation, interfere with diplomatic relations, or endanger the life or physical safety of any person. If the recertification that disclosure may endanger the national security of the United States or interfere with diplomatic relations is made by the Attorney General, Deputy Attorney General, an Assistant Attorney General, or the Director of the Federal Bureau of Investigation, such certification shall be treated as conclusive unless the court finds that the recertification was made in bad faith. If the court denies a petition for an order modifying or setting aside a nondisclosure requirement under this paragraph, the recipient shall be precluded for a period of one year from filing another petition to modify or set aside such nondisclosure requirement.

(c) *In the case of a failure to comply with a request for records, a report, or other information made to any person or entity under section 2709(b) of this title, section 626(a) or (b) or 62 7(a) of the Fair Credit Reporting Act, section 1114(a) (5)(A) of the Right to Financial Privacy Act, or section 802(a) of the National Security Act of 1947, the Attorney General may invoke the aid of any district court of the United States within the jurisdiction in which the investigation is carried on or the person or entity resides, carries on business, or may be found, to compel compliance with the request. The court may issue an order requiring the person or entity to comply with the request. Any failure to obey the order of the court may be punished by the court as contempt thereof. Any process under this section may be served in any judicial district in which the person or entity may be found.*

(d) *In all proceedings under this section, subject to any right to an open hearing in a contempt proceeding, the court must close any hearing to the extent necessary to prevent an unauthorized disclosure of a request for records, a report, or other information made to any person or entity under section 2709(b) of this title, section 626(a) or (b) or 62 7(a) of the Fair Credit Reporting Act, section 1114(a) (5) (A) of the Right to Financial Privacy Act, or section 802(a) of the National Security Act of 1947. Petitions, filings, records, orders, and subpoenas must also be kept under seal to the extent and as long as necessary to prevent the unauthorized disclosure of a request for records, a report, or other information made to any person or entity under section 2709(b) of this title, section 626(a) or (b) or 627(a) of the Fair Credit Reporting Act, section 1114(a) (5) (A) of the Right to Financial Privacy Act, or section 802(a) of the National Security Act of 194 7.*

(e) *In all proceedings under this section, the court shall, upon request of the government, review ex parte and in camera any government submission or portions thereof, which may include classified information.*

End Notes

[1] 18 U.S.C. 2709; 12 U.S.C. 3414; 15 U.S.C. 1681v; 15 U.S.C. 1681u; 50 U.S.C. 436; the text of each is appended. Federal administrative subpoena authority is discussed in U.S. Department of Justice, Office of Legal Policy, *Report to Congress on the Use of Administrative Subpoena Authorities by Executive Branch Agencies and Entities* [2002], available on March 6, 2006 at http://www.usdoj.gov/olp/intro.pdf; see also CRS Report RL33321, *Administrative Subpoenas in Criminal Investigations: A Brief Legal Analysis*, abridged as CRS Report RS22407, *Administrative Subpoenas in Criminal Investigations: A Sketch*, both by Charles Doyle.

[2] P.L. 1-7-56, 115 Stat. 365 (2001).

[3] From calendar year 2003 through 2005, the FBI issued approximately 44,000 NSLs containing 143,074 requests. In one investigation, it issued 9 NSLs requesting information relating to 11,000 telephone numbers. U.S. Department of Justice, Office of the Inspector General, *A Review of the Federal Bureau of Investigation's Use of National Security Letters (IG Report I)* at xviii-xix (March 2007), available on Sept. 3, 2009 at http://www.usdoj.gov/oig/special/s0703b/ final.pdf. It issued another 49, 425 requests in 2006 for a total 192,499 requests over the four year period from 2003 through 2006, U.S. Department of Justice, Office of the Inspector General, *A Review of the Federal Bureau of Investigation's Use of National Security Letters (IG Report II)* at 9 (March 2008), available on Sept. 3, 2009 at http://www.usdoj.gov/oig/special/s0803b/final.pdf.

[4] *Doe v. Ashcroft*, 334 F. Supp.2d 471, 526-27 (S.D.N.Y. 2004)("the Court concludes that the compulsory, secret, and unreviewable production of information required by the FBI's application of 18 U.S.C. 2709 violates the Fourth Amendment and that the non-disclosure provision of 18 U.S.C. 2709(c) violates the First Amendment"); *Doe v. Gonzales*, 386 F. Supp.2d 66, 78-82 (D.Conn. 2005)(the court did not reach the Fourth Amendment issue). Justice Ginsburg declined to lift the stay of Connecticut court's injunction pending appeal in the Second Circuit, 126 S.Ct. 1 (2005).

[5] P.L. 109-177 (H.R. 3199), 120 Stat. 192 (2006).

[6] The appended statutes note the amendments and additions.

[7] *Doe v. Gonzalez*, 449 F.3d 415 (2d Cir. 2006).

[8] *Doe v. Gonzalez*, 500 F. Supp.2d 379 (S.D.N.Y. 2007).

[9] *John Doe, Inc. v. Mukasey*, 549 F.3d 861 (2d Cir. 2008).

[10] *Doe v. Holder*, ____ F.Supp.2d ____ (2009 WL 2432320) (S.D.N.Y. Aug. 5, 2009).

[11] Section 1114, P.L. 95-630, 92 Stat. 3706 (1978); now codified at 12 U.S.C. 3414(a)(1) (A), (B): "Nothing in this chapter (except sections 3415, 3417, 3418, and 3421 of this title) shall apply to the production and disclosure of financial records pursuant to requests from – (A) a Government authority authorized to conduct foreign counter- or foreign positive- intelligence activities for purposes of conducting such activities; [or] (B) the Secret Service for the purpose of conducting its protective functions (18 U.S.C. 3056; 3 U.S.C. 202, P.L.90-331, as amended)."

[12] "Section 1114 provides for special procedures in the case of foreign intelligence ... though the committee believes that some privacy protections may well be necessary for financial records sought during a foreign intelligence investigation, there are special problems in this area which make consideration of such protections in other congressional forums more appropriate. Nevertheless, the committee intends that this exemption be used only for legitimate foreign intelligence investigations: investigations proceeding only under the rubric of "national

security" do not qualify. Rather this exception is available only to those U.S. Government officials specifically authorized to investigate the intelligence operations of foreign governments," H.Rept. 95-1383, at 55 (1978).

[13] P.L. 99-569, §404, 100 Stat. 3197 (1986); 12 U.S.C. 3414(a)(5)(A)(1988 ed.).

[14] 18 U.S.C. 2709 (1988 ed.); *see also*, S.Rept. 99-541, at 43 (1986)("This provision is substantially the same as language recently reported by the Intelligence Committee as section 503 of the Intelligence Authorization Act for Fiscal Year 1987, [P.L. 99-569]").

[15] 18 U.S.C. 2709 (1988 ed.); 12 U.S.C. 3414(a)(5)(A)(1988 ed.).

[16] 18 U.S.C. 2709(c)("No wire or electronic communication service provider, or officer, employee, or agent thereof, shall disclose to any person that the Federal Bureau of Investigation has sought or obtained access to information or records under this section"); *see also*, 12 U.S.C. 3414(a)(5)(D). Note that unlike section 3486, the prohibition is neither temporary nor judicially supervised.

[17] 18 U.S.C. 2709(d)(1988 ed.); 12 U.S.C. 3414(a)(5)(B)(1988 ed.).

[18] 50 U.S.C. 436.

[19] 15 U.S.C. 1681u.

[20] The Senate Intelligence Committee had made similar observations in a prior Congress when considering legislation that ultimately became the National Security Amendment, H.Rept. 103-256, at 17-22 (1994).

[21] 50 U.S.C. 456 (1994 ed.).

[22] H.Rep.No.103-541 at 53-4 (1994).

[23] 15 U.S.C. 1681u(f), 50 U.S.C. 436(e).

[24] 15 U.S.C. 1681u(k), 50 U.S.C. 436(c).

[25] 15 U.S.C. 1681u(d); 50 U.S.C. 436(b).

[26] 15 U.S.C. 1681u(c).

[27] P.L. 107-56, §505, 115 Stat. 365-66 (2001).

[28] "The information acquired through NSLs is extremely valuable to national security investigations.... Unfortunately, however, NSLs were of limited utility prior to the PATRIOT Act. While records held by third parties may generally be subpoenaed by a grand jury in a criminal investigation so long as those records are relevant, the standard for obtaining such records through an NSL was much higher before October of 2001.

"The FBI had to have specific and articulable facts that the information requested pertained to a foreign power or an agent of a foreign power. This requirement often prohibited the FBI from using NSLs to develop evidence at the early stage of an investigation, which is precisely when they are the most useful.

"The prior standard, Mr. Chairman, put the cart before the horse. Agents trying to determine whether or not there were specific and articulable facts that a certain individual was a terrorist or spy were precluded from using an NSL in this inquiry because, in order to use an NSL, they first had to be in possession of such facts.

"Suppose, for example, investigators were tracking a known al-Qaeda operative and saw him having lunch with three individuals. A responsible agent would want to conduct a preliminary investigation of those individuals and find out, among other things, with whom they had recently been in communication.

"Before the passage of the PATRIOT Act, however, the FBI could not have issued an NSL to obtain such information. While investigators could have demonstrated that this information was relevant to an ongoing terrorism investigation, they could not have demonstrated sufficient specific, and articulable facts that the individuals in question were agents of a foreign power," *Material Witness Provisions of the Criminal Code, and the Implementation of the USA PATRIOT Act: Section 505 That Addresses National Security Letters, and Section 804 That Addresses Jurisdiction Over Crimes Committed at U.S. Facilities Abroad: Hearing Before the Subcomm. on Crime, Terrorism, and Homeland Security of the House Comm. on the Judiciary*, 109th Cong., 1st Sess. at 9-10 (2005) (testimony of Matthew Berry, Office of Legal Policy, U.S. Department of Justice).

[29] P.L. 107-56, §358(g), 115 Stat. 327 (2001).

[30] E.g., H.Rept. 107-250, at 60-1 ("This section facilitates government access to information contained in suspected terrorists' credit reports when the government inquiry relates to an investigation, of or intelligence activity or analysis relating to, domestic or international terrorism. Even though private entities such as lender and insurers can access an individual's credit history, the government is strictly limited in its ability under current law to obtain the information. This section would permit those investigating suspected terrorists prompt access to credit histories that may reveal key information about the terrorist's plan or source of refunding – without notifying the target").

[31] P.L. 108-177, §374, 117 Stat. 2628 (2004), 12 U.S.C. 3414(d), adopts the definition of financial institution found in 31 U.S.C. 5312(a)(2), (c)(1), *i.e.*: "(A) an insured bank (as defined in 12 U.S.C. 1813(h)); (B) a commercial bank or trust company; (C) a private banker; (D) an agency or branch of a foreign bank in the United States; (E) any credit union; (F) a thrift institution; (G) a broker or dealer registered with the Securities and Exchange Commission; (H) a broker or dealer in securities or commodities; (I) an investment banker or investment company; (J) a currency exchange; (K) an issuer, redeemer, or cashier of travelers' checks, checks, money orders, or similar instruments; (L) an operator of a credit card system; (M) an insurance company; (N) a dealer in precious metals, stones, or jewels; (O) a pawnbroker; (P) a loan or finance company; (Q) a travel agency; (R) a licensed sender of money or any other person who engages as a business in the transmission of funds,

including any person who engages as a business in an informal money transfer system or any network of people who engage as a business in facilitating the transfer of money domestically or internationally outside of the conventional financial institutions system; (S) a telegraph company; (T) a business engaged in vehicle sales, including automobile, airplane, and boat sales; (U) persons involved in real estate closings and settlements; (V) the United States Postal Service; (W) an agency of the United States Government or of a State or local government carrying out a duty or power of a business described in this paragraph; (X) a casino, gambling casino, or gaming establishment with an annual gaming revenue of more than $1,000,000 which – (i) is licensed as a casino, gambling casino, or gaming establishment under the laws of any State or any political subdivision of any State; or (ii) is an Indian gaming operation conducted under or pursuant to the Indian Gaming Regulatory Act other than an operation which is limited to class I gaming (as defined in section 4(6) of such Act); (Y) any business or agency which engages in any activity which the Secretary of the Treasury determines, by regulation, to be an activity which is similar to, related to, or a substitute for any activity in which any business described in this paragraph is authorized to engage; (Z) any other business designated by the Secretary whose cash transactions have a high degree of usefulness in criminal, tax, or regulatory matters; [or (AA)] any futures commission merchant, commodity trading advisor, or commodity pool operator registered, or required to register, under the Commodity Exchange Act."

[32] H.R. 3352, §5 (Rep. Otter); S. 1158, §3 (Sen. Boxer); S. 1507, §2 (Sen. Feingold); S. 1552, §4(b) (Sen. Murkowski); and S. 1709, §5 (Sen. Craig).

[33] S. 436, §3 (Sen. Leahy).

[34] H.R. 3171, §4 (Rep. Kucinich); H.R. 3352, §7 (Rep. Otter); S. 1695, §2 (Sen. Leahy); and S. 1709, §6 (Sen. Craig).

[35] In *Doe v. Ashcroft*, 334 F.Supp.2d 471, 496-501 (S.D.N.Y. 2004), the Government argued unsuccessfully that the NSL statutes should be understood to include an implicit judicial enforcement component.

[36] *Anti-Terrorism Intelligence Tools Improvement Act of 2003: Hearing Before the Subcomm. on Crime, Terrorism, and Homeland Security (House Hearing)*, 108th Cong., 2nd Sess., 7-8 (2004)(prepared statement of United States Assistant Attorney General Daniel J. Bryant).

[37] Proposed 18 U.S.C. 2332h ("In the case of a refusal to comply with a request for records, a report, or other information made to any person under section 2709(b) of this title, section 625 (a) or (b) or 626 of the Fair Credit Reporting Act [15 U.S.C. 1681u, 1681v], section 11 14(a)(5)A) of the right to Financial Privacy Act [12 U.S.C. 3414, or section 802(a) of the National Security Act of 1947 [50 U.S.C. 436(a)], the Attorney General may invoke the aid of any court of the United States within the jurisdiction of which the investigation is carried on or the person resides, carries on business, or may be found, to compel compliance with the request. The court may issue an order requiring the person to comply with the request. Any failure to obey the order of the court may be punished by the court as contempt thereof. Any process under this section may be served in any judicial district in which the person may be found").

[38] 334 F.Supp.2d 471 (S.D.N.Y. 2004), vac'd and remanded, 449 F.3d 415 (2d Cir. 2006), after remand, 500 F.Supp.2d 379 (S.D.N.Y. 2007), aff'd in part, rev'd in part and remanded, 549 F.3d 861 (2d Cir. 2008), after remand, ____ F.Supp.2d ____ (2009 WL 2432320)(S.D.N.Y. Aug. 5, 2009).

[39] 386 F.Supp.2d 66 (D.Conn. 2005), dism'd as moot, 449 F.3d 415 (2d Cir. 2006).

[40] 120 Stat. 192 (2006) and 120 Stat. 278 (2006), respectively.

[41] 28 U.S.C. 3511.

[42] 28 U.S.C. 3511(c), 18 U.S.C. 1510(e).

[43] 12 U.S.C. 3414((a)(3)(A); 15 U.S.C. 1681v(c)(1), 1681u(d)(1); 18 U.S.C. 2709(c)(1); 50 U.S.C. 436(B)(1).

[44] 28 U.S.C. 3511(b).

[45] P.L. 109-177, §118.

[46] P.L. 109-177, §119.

[47] 18 U.S.C. 2709.

[48] 12 U.S.C. 3414(a), (d).

[49] 15 U.S.C. 1681u(a), 1681v(a).

[50] 50 U.S.C. 43 6(a).

[51] 18 U.S.C. 2709 (b); 12 U.S.C. 3414(a)(5)(A); 15 U.S.C. 1681u(b).

[52] 50 U.S.C. 436 (a)(3).

[53] 15 U.S.C. 1681v(a).

[54] 18 U.S.C. 2709(b); 12 U.S.C. 3414(a)(5)(A); 15 U.S.C. 1681u(b).

[55] 15 U.S.C. 1681v(a).

[56] 50 U.S.C. 436(a)(1).

[57] 18 U.S.C. 2709(b).

[58] 15 U.S.C. 1681u(a); 12 U.S.C. 3414(a)(5)(A).

[59] 15 U.S.C. 1681v; 50 U.S.C. 436(a).

[60] 18 U.S.C. 2709(b).

[61] 15 U.S.C. 1681u(a),(b).

[62] 12 U.S.C. 3414(a)(5)(A).

[63] 15 U.S.C. 1681v(a)
[64] 50 U.S.C. 436(a)(1).
[65] 50 U.S.C. 436(a)(2),(3).
[66] 18 U.S.C. 2709(c) (2000 ed.); see also, 12 U.S.C. 3414(a)(5)(D) (2000 ed.); 15 U.S.C. 1681u(d) (2000 ed.); 15 U.S.C. 1681v(c) (2002 Supp.); 50 U.S.C. 436(b) (2000 ed.).
[67] *Doe v. Ashcroft*, 334 F.Supp.2d 471, 522 (S.D.N.Y. 2004). and *Doe v. Gonzales*, 386 F.Supp.2d 66, 78-81 (D.Conn. 2005).
[68] 28 U.S.C. 351 1(b)(2). As construed by the Second Circuit, the government is obliged to advise a recipient that the recipient has a period of time within which to decide if he would like the government to seek judicial review of its determination of the need for secrecy, *John Doe, Inc.v. Mukasey*, 549 F.3d 861, 883 (2d Cir. 2008).
[69] 28 U.S.C. 3511(b)(3).
[70] 28 U.S.C. 351 1(b)(2), (3). The Second Circuit has declared this component of the procedure unconstitutional, *John Doe, Inc.v. Mukasey*, 549 F.3d at 883.
[71] 18 U.S.C. 1510(e), 3571, 3559.
[72] 28 U.S.C. 3511.
[73] F.R.Crim.P. 17(c)(2).
[74] 2 WRIGHT, FEDERAL PRACTICE AND PROCEDURE §275 (Crim. 3d ed. 2000).
[75] *United States v. R. Enterprises, Inc.*, 498 U.S. 292, 301 (1991).
[76] 28 U.S.C. 3511(c).
[77] 12 U.S.C. 3414(a)(5)(B)("The Federal Bureau of Investigation may disseminate information obtained pursuant to this paragraph only as provided in guidelines approved by the Attorney General for foreign intelligence collection and foreign counterintelligence investigations conducted by the Federal Bureau of Investigation, and, with respect to dissemination to an agency of the United States, only if such information is clearly relevant to the authorized responsibilities of such agency"); see also, 18 U.S.C. 2709(d).
[78] 15 U.S.C. 1681u(f).
[79] 50 U.S.C. 43 6(e).
[80] 15 U.S.C. 1681v.
[81] In addition to the newly added judicial enforcement mechanism in 28 U.S.C. 3511, the earlier Fair Credit Report Act NSL sections had a limited judicial enforcement subsection, as it had for some time, 15 U.S.C. 1681u(c).
[82] 15 U.S.C. 1681u(k), 1681v(e); 50 U.S.C. 436(c)(2).
[83] 15 U.S.C. 1681u(e); 50 U.S.C. 4356(d).
[84] P.L. 109-177, §1 18(a)(adding the judiciary committees as recipients of all NSL required reports); 12 U.S.C. 3414(a)(5)(C)(intelligence committees); 18 U.S.C. 2709 (intelligence and judiciary committees); 15 U.S.C. 168 1u(h)(intelligence and banking committees), 168 1v(judiciary, intelligence, and banking committees).
[85] *Id.* A "U.S. person" is generally understood to mean "a citizen of the United States, an alien lawfully admitted for permanent residence (as defined in section 1 101(a)(2) of title 8), an unincorporated association a substantial number of members of which are citizens of the United States or aliens lawfully admitted for permanent residence, or a corporation which is incorporated in the United States, but does not include a corporation or an association which is a foreign power, as defined in subsection(a)(1), (2), or (3) of this section," 50 U.S.C. 1801.
[86] *Smith v. Maryland*, 442 U.S. 735, 745 (1979)
[87] *Richards v. Wisconsin*, 520 U.S. 385, 391 (1997); *Wilson v. Arkansas*, 514 U.S. 927, 936 (1995).
[88] 18 U.S.C. 2702(c).
[89] 18 U.S.C. 2703(c)(2).
[90] 18 U.S.C. 2709(a).
[91] 18 U.S.C. 2707(a).
[92] *IG Report I* at 90.
[93] *Doe v. Gonzalez*, 500 F.Supp.2d 379 (S.D.N.Y. 2007), aff'd in part, rev'd in part, and remanded, sub nom., *John Doe, Inc. v. Mukasey*, 549 F.861 (2d Cir. 2008).
[94] *Doe v. Gonzalez* at 425-26.
[95] *Id.* at 426.
[96] *John Doe, Inc. v. Mukasey*, 549 F.3d at 883-84.
[97] *Doe v. Ashcroft*, 334 F.Supp.2d 471, 511 (S.D.N.Y. 2004); *Doe v. Gonzales*, 386 F.Supp.2d 66, 75 (D.Conn. 2005)("Section 2709(c) is subject to strict scrutiny not only because it is a prior restraint, but also because it is a content-based restriction").
[98] *Playboy Entertainment* 529 U.S. 803, 813 (2000).
[99] *Reno v. ACLU*, 521 U.S. 844, 874 (1997).
[100] *FW/PHS, Inc. v. Dallas*, 493 U.S. 215, (1990)("In *Freedman*, we determined that the following three procedural safeguards were necessary to ensure expeditious decisionmaking by the motion picture censorship board: (1) any restraint prior to judicial review can be imposed only for a specified brief period during which the status

quo msut be maintained; (2) expeditious judicial review of that decision must be available; and (3) the censor must bear the burden of proof once in court"), citing *Freedman v. Maryland*, 380 U.S. 51, 58-60 (1965).

[101] *John Doe, Inc. v. Mukasey*, 549 F.3d 861, 876-77 (2d Cir. 2008) noting the government contentions based on *Seattle Times Co. v. Rhinehard,* 467 U.S. 20 (1984)(pre-trial discover); *Douglas Oil Co. v. Petrol Stops Northwest*, 441 U.S. 211 (1979)(grand jury); *Kamasinski v. Judicial Review Council*, 44 F.3d 106 (2d Cir. 1994)(judicial misconduct); *United States v. Snepp*, 897 F.2d 138 (4th Cir. 1990)(CIA employees); *United States v. Marchetti*, 466 F.2d 1309 (4th Cir. 1972)(same).

[102] *Seattle Times Co. v. Rhinehard,* 467 U.S. at 32.

[103] *John Doe, Inc. v. Mukasey*, 549 F.3d at 878.

[104] *Id.*

[105] *John Doe, Inc. v. Mukasey*, 549 F.3d at 878, citing *Haig v. Agee*, 453 U.S. 280, 307 (1981).

[106] *John Doe, Inc. v. Mukasey*, 549 F.3d at 880-8 1.

[107] *Id.* at 881.

[108] *Id.* at 882.

[109] *Id.*

[110] *Id.* at 883-84.

[111] *Id.* at 884.

[112] *Doe v. Holder*, F.Supp.2d, (2009 WL 2432320)(S.D.N.Y. Aug. 5, 2009).

In: National Security Letters: Background and Issues. Volume 1 ISBN: 978-1-61668-941-4
Editor: Carolyn D. Hines

Chapter 2

NATIONAL SECURITY LETTERS: PROPOSED AMENDMENTS IN THE 111TH CONGRESS*

Charles Doyle

SUMMARY

Five federal statutes authorize various intelligence agencies to demand, through National Security Letters (NSLs), certain customer information from communications providers, financial institutions, and consumer credit reporting agencies, under the Right to Financial Privacy Act, the Fair Credit Reporting Act, the National Security Act, and Electronic Communications Privacy Act. The USA PATRIOT Act expanded NSL authority. Later reports of the Department of Justice Inspector General indicated that (1) the FBI considered the expanded authority very useful; (2) after expansion the number of NSLs requests increased dramatically; (3) the number of requests relating to Americans increased substantially; and (4) FBI use of NSL authority had sometimes failed to comply with statutory, Attorney General, or FBI policies.

Originally, the NSL statutes authorized nondisclosure requirements prohibiting recipients from disclosing receipt or the content of the NSL to anyone, ever. They now permit judicial review of these secrecy provisions. As understood by the courts, recipients may request the issuing agency to seek and justify to the court the continued binding effect of any secrecy requirement.

Several USA PATRIOT Act provisions are scheduled to expire on December 31, 2009. The NSL statutory provisions are not among them. Nevertheless, several bills have been introduced which would amend and in some cases repeal NSL authority. The bills include (1) the National Security Letter Reform Act of 2009 (H.R. 1800), introduced by Representative Nadler; (2) the USA PATRIOT Amendments Act of 2009 (H.R. 3845), introduced by Representative Conyers; (3) the Judicious Use of Surveillance Tools in Counterterrorism Efforts Act of 2009 (JUSTICE Act) (S. 1686), introduced by Senator Feingold; and (4) the

* This is an edited, reformatted and augmented edition of a United States Congressional Research Service publication, Report R40887, dated October 28, 2009.

USA PATRIOT Act Sunset Extension Act of 2009 (S. 1692), introduced by Senator Leahy and reported to the floor by the Senate Judiciary Committee, S.Rept. 111-92.

In addition to sunset and repeal, the bills raise issues involving amendment of nondisclosure requirements; the promulgation of standards to minimize capturing, using, and holding (long term) NSL generated information, continued periodic IG audits and reports, and limitations on statutory provisions thought by some to permit circumvention of NSL statutory requirements.

This report includes a chart comparing the provisions of the bills and current law. It also reprints the text of the five NSL statutes as they now appear and as they appeared prior to amendment by the USA PATRIOT Act (to which form they would return under some of the bills).

INTRODUCTION

National security letters (NSL) are roughly comparable to administrative subpoenas. Intelligence agencies issue them for intelligence gathering purposes to telephone companies, Internet service providers, consumer credit reporting agencies, banks, and other financial institutions, directing the recipients to turn over certain customer records and similar information. Four bills, introduced in the 111th Congress, propose substantial changes in the law governing NSL authority: H.R. 1800, the National Security Letters Reform Act of 2009 (Rep. Nadler); H.R. 3845, the USA PATRIOT Amendments Act of 2009 (Rep. Conyers); S. 1686, the Judicious Use of Surveillance Tools in Counterterrorism Efforts Act (JUSTICE Act) of 2009 (Sen. Feingold); and S. 1692, the USA PATRIOT Act Sunset Extension Act of 2009 (Sen. Leahy). The Senate Judiciary Committee sent an amended version of S. 1692 to floor on October 13, 2009, 155 *Cong. Rec.* S 10361 (daily ed. Oct. 13, 2009), with a report on October 28, 2009, 155 *Cong. Rec.*S10850 (daily ed. Oct. 28, 2009).[1]

The Feingold bill would repeal immediately one of the existing NSL statutes, section 627 of the Fair Credit Reporting Act (15 U.S.C. 168 1v), created in the USA PATRIOT Act.[2] The Leahy bill would repeal section 627 effective December 31, 2013 and on that date would return the other NSL statutes to their pre-USA PATRIOT Act form.[3] The Conyers bill would return all five NSL statutes to pre-USA PATRIOT Act form effective December 31, 2013, thereby effectively repealing section 627.[4] The Nadler bill would return all but the National Security Act statute (50 U.S.C. 436) to their pre-USA PATRIOT Act form after five years;[5] which has the effect of repealing section 627, the NSL created by the USA PATRIOT Act. While the Nadler bill deals exclusive with NSL matters, the Leahy bill addresses other national security issues, as do the Feingold and Conyers bills, which also speak to related law enforcement issues.[6]

BACKGROUND

Prior to the USA PATRIOT Act, the NSL statutes were four. One, 18 U.S.C. 2709, obligated communications providers to supply certain customer information upon the written request of the Director of the Federal Bureau of Investigation (FBI) or a senior FBI headquarters official.[7] When customer identity, length of service, and toll records were sought, the letters had to certify (1) that the information was relevant to a foreign counterintelligence investigation and (2) that specific and articulable facts gave reason to believe the information pertained to a foreign power or its agents.[8] When only customer identity and length of service records (but not toll records) were sought, the letters had to certify (1) again that the information was relevant to a foreign counterintelligence investigation, but (2) that specific and articulable facts gave reason to believe that the customer information pertained to use of the provider's facilities to communicate with foreign powers, their agents or those engaged in international terrorism or criminal clandestine intelligence activities.[9]

In like manner a second statute, section 1114(a)(5) of the Right to Financial Privacy Act, obligated financial institutions to provide the FBI with customers' financial records upon written certification of the FBI Director or his designee (1) that the records were sought for foreign counterintelligence purposes and (2) that specific and articulable facts gave reason to believe that the records were those of a foreign power or its agents.[10]

And so it was with a third, section 626 of the Fair Credit Report Act, which obligated consumer credit reporting agencies to provide customer identification, and the names and addresses of financial institutions at which a designated consumer maintained accounts.[11] Here too, the obligation was triggered by written certification of the FBI Director or his designee (1) that the information was necessary for a foreign counterintelligence investigation, and (2) that specific and articulable facts gave reason to believe that the consumer was either a foreign power, a foreign official, or the agent of a foreign power and was engaged in international terrorism or criminal clandestine intelligence activities. [12]

The fourth, section 802 of the National Security Act, was a bit different.[13] It reached a wider range of potential recipients at the demand of large group of federal officials, but for a more limited purpose. It rested the obligation to provide consumer reports, together with financial information and records, upon consumer reporting agencies, financial agencies, and financial institutions, or holding companies.[14] The requirement was triggered by the certification of senior officials of law enforcement and intelligence agencies, but confined to information pertaining to federal employees with access to classified information and being sought for clearance purposes and inquiries into past or potential security leaks.[15]

USA PATRIOT Act

Section 505 of the USA PATRIOT Act altered the FBI's NSL authority under section 2709, the Right to Financial Privacy Act, and the Fair Credit Reporting Act in several ways:

- It expanded issuing authority to include the heads of FBI field offices (special agents in charge (SACs));
- It eliminated the requirement of specific and articulable facts demonstrating a nexus to a foreign power or its agents;
- It required instead that the information was sought for or relevant to various national security investigations; and

- It directed that no NSL related investigation of a "U.S. person" (American citizen or foreign resident alien) be predicated exclusively on First Amendment protected activities.[16]
- The National Security Act NSL section remained unchanged, but section 358(g) of the USA PATRIOT Act added a new Fair Credit Reporting Act NSL section 627, 15 U.S.C. 168 1v. The new section obligated consumer reporting agencies to provide consumer information and reports to a federal agency "authorized to conduct investigations of, or intelligence or counterintelligence activities or analysis related to, international terrorism."[17] Senior federal agency officials were empowered to issue the NSL with a certification that the information was "necessary for the agency's conduct or such investigation, activity, or analysis."[18]

2006 Amendments

Several of the USA PATRIOT Act's intelligence gathering provisions were temporary and originally set to expire after five years.[19] The NSL statutes were not among them, but Congress amended the statutes in the USA PATRIOT Improvement and Reauthorization Act of 2005 and the USA PATRIOT Act Additional Reauthorizing Amendments Act of 2006 nonetheless.[20] The NSL statute amendments were driven both by sensitivity to an Administration desire for more explicit enforcement authority[21] and by judicial developments which had raised questions as to the statutes' constitutional vitality as then written.[22] The statutes then came with open-ended nondisclosure provisions which barred recipients from disclosing the fact or content of the NSL – ever or to anyone. Yet, they featured neither a penalty provision should the confidential requirement be breached nor in most cases an enforcement mechanism should a NSL obligation be ignored (the original Fair Credit Report Act statute alone had an explicit judicial enforcement component).

The amendments:

- created a judicial enforcement mechanism and a judicial review procedure for both the requests and accompanying nondisclosure requirements;[23]
- established specific penalties for failure to comply with the nondisclosure requirements;[24]
- made it clear that the nondisclosure requirements did not preclude a recipient from consulting an attorney;[25]
- provided a process to ease the nondisclosure requirement;[26]
- expanded Congressional oversight;[27] and
- called for Inspector General's audits of use of NSL authority.[28]

IG Reports

The First IG Report

The Department of Justice Inspector General audit reports, one released in March of 2007 and the second in March of 2008, were less than totally favorable.[29] The first report noted that

FBI use of NSLs had increased dramatically, expanding from 8,500 requests in 2000 to 47,000 in 2005, *IG Report I* at 120. During the 3 years under review, the percentage of NSLs used to investigate Americans ("U.S. persons") increased from 39% in 2003 to 53% in 2005.[30] A substantial majority of the requests involved records relating to telephone or e-mail communications, Id.

The report and the subsequent report a year later provided a glimpse at how the individual NSL statutes were used and why they were considered available. In case of the 18 U.S.C. 2709, the Electronic Communications Privacy Act (ECPA) NSL statute, the reports explained that:

> Through national security letters, an FBI field office obtained telephone toll billing records and subscriber information about an investigative subject in a counterterrorism case. The information obtained identified the various telephone numbers with which the subject had frequent contact. Analysis of the telephone records enabled the FBI to identify a group of individuals residing in the same vicinity as the subject. The FBI initiated investigations on these individuals to determine if there was a terrorist cell operating in the city.[31]
>
> Headquarters and field personnel told us that the principal objective of the most frequently used type of NSL – ECPA NSLs seeking telephone toll billing records, electronic communication transactional records, or subscriber information (telephone and e-mail) – is to develop evidence to support applications for FISA orders.[32]

The Right to Financial Privacy Act (RFPA) NSL statute, 12 U.S.C. 3414(a)(5), also affords authorities access a wide range of information (bank transaction records v. telephone transaction records) as demonstrated by the instances where it proved useful:

> The FBI conducted a multi-jurisdictional counterterrorism investigation of convenience store owners in the United States who allegedly sent funds to known Hawaladars (persons who use the Hawala money transfer system in lieu of or parallel to traditional banks) in the Middle East. The funds were transferred to suspected Al Qaeda affiliates. The possible violations committed by the subjects of these cases included money laundering, sale of untaxed cigarettes, check cashing fraud, illegal sale of pseudoephedrine (the precursor ingredient used to manufacture methamphetamine), unemployment insurance fraud, welfare fraud, immigration fraud, income tax violations, and sale of counterfeit merchandise.[33]
>
> The FBI issued national security letters for the convenience store owners' bank account records. The records showed that two persons received millions of dollars from the subjects and that another subject had forwarded large sums of money to one of these individuals. The bank analysis identified sources and recipients of the money transfers and assisted in the collection of information on targets of the investigation overseas.[34]

The Fair Credit Reporting Act NSL statutes, 15 U.S.C. 168 1u (FCRAu) and 168 1v (FCRAv) can be even more illuminating, "The supervisor of a counterterrorism squad told us that the FCRA NSLs enable the FBI to see 'how their investigative subjects conduct their day-to-day activities, how they get their money, and whether they are engaged in white collar crime that could be relevant to their investigations.'"[35]

Overall, the report notes that the FBI used the information gleaned from NSLs for a variety of purposes, "to determine if further investigation is warranted; to generate leads for other field offices, Joint Terrorism Task Forces, or other federal agencies; and to corroborate information developed from other investigative techniques."[36] Moreover, information supplied in response to NSLs provides the grist of FBI analytical intelligence reports and various FBI databases.[37]

The report was somewhat critical, however, of the FBI's initial performance:

> [W]e found that the FBI used NSLs in violation of applicable NSL statutes, Attorney General Guidelines, and internal FBI policies. In addition, we found that the FBI circumvented the requirements of the ECPA NSL statute when it issued at least 739 "exigent letters" to obtain telephone toll billing records and subscriber information from three telephone companies without first issuing NSLs. Moreover, in a few other instances, the FBI sought or obtained telephone toll billing records in the absence of a national security investigation, when it sought and obtained consumer full credit reports in a counterintelligence investigation, and when it sought and obtained financial records and telephone toll billing records without first issuing NSLs. *Id.* at 124.

More specifically, the Report found that:

- a "significant number of NSL-related possible violations were not being identified or reported" as required;
- the only FBI data collection system produced "inaccurate" results;
- the FBI issued over 700 exigent letters acquiring information in a manner that "circumvented the ECPA NSL statute and violated the Attorney General's Guidelines . . . and internal FBI policy;"
- the FBI's Counterterrorism Division initiated over 300 NSLs in a manner that precluded effective review prior to approval;
- 60% of the individual files examined showed violations of FBI internal control policies;
- the FBI did not retain signed copies of the NSLs it issued;
- the FBI had not provided clear guidance on the application of the Attorney General's least-intrusive-feasible-investigative-technique standard in the case of NSLs;
- the precise interpretation of toll billing information as it appears in the ECPA NSL statute is unclear;
- SAC supervision of the attorneys responsible for review of the legal adequacy of proposed NSLs made some of the attorneys reluctant to question the adequacy of the underlying investigation previously approved by the SAC;
- there was no indication that the FBI's misuse of NSL authority constituted criminal conduct;
- personnel both at FBI headquarters and in the field considered NSL use indispensable; and
- information generated by NSLs was fed into a number of FBI systems. *IG Report I* at 121-24.

Exigent Letters

Prior to enactment of the Electronic Communications Privacy Act (ECPA), the Supreme Court held that customers had no Fourth Amendment protected privacy rights in the records the telephone company maintained relating to their telephone use.[38]

Table 1. Profile of the Current NSL Statutes

NSL statute	18 U.S.C. 2709	12 U.S.C. 3414	15 U.S.C. 1681u	15 U.S.C. 1681v	50 U.S.C. 436
Addressee	Communications providers	financial institutions	consumer credit agencies	consumer credit agencies	Financial instit-utions, consu-mer credit age-ncies, travel agencies
Certifying officials	senior FBI officials and SACs	senior FBI officials and SACs	senior FBI officials and SACs	supervisory official of an agency investigating, conducting intelligence activeities relating to or analyzing int'l terrorism	senior officials no lower than Ass't Secretary or Ass't Director of agency w/ employees w/access to classified material
Information covered	Identified custo-mer's name, address, length of service, and billing info	identified customer financial records	identified consumer's name, address, former address, pla-e and former place of employment	all inform-ation relating to an identified consumer	all financial information relating to consenting, identified employee
Standard/ Purpose	relevant to an investigation to protect against int'l terrorism or clandestine intelligence activities	sought for foreign counter-intelligence purposes to protect ag-ainst int'l terrorism or clande-stine intell-igence activities	sought for an investigation to protect against int'l terrorism or landestine intelligence activities	necessary for the agency's investigation, activities, or analysis relating to int'l terrorism	necessary to conduct a law enforcement investigation, counter-intelligence inquiry or security determination
Dissemin-ation	only per Att'y Gen. guidelines	only per Att'y Gen. guidelines	w/i FBI, to secure app-roval for intell. invest-igation, to military	no statutory provision	only to agency of employee under investig-ation, DoJ for law enforcem-ent or intell.
			investigators when inform. relates to military member		purposes, or fed. agency when clearly relevant to mission
Immunity/ fees	no provisions	no provisions	fees; immunity for good faith compliance with a NSL	immunity for good faith compliance with a NSL	reimbursement; immunity for good faith compliance with a NSL

Where a recognized expectation of privacy exists for Fourth Amendment purposes, the Amendment's usual demands such as those of probable cause, particularity, and a warrant may be eased in the face of exigent circumstances.

For example, the Fourth Amendment requirement that officers must knock and announce their purpose before forcibly entering a building to execute a warrant can be eased in the presence of certain exigent circumstances such as the threat of the destruction of evidence or danger to the officers.[39] Satisfying Fourth Amendment requirements, however, does not necessarily satisfy statutory prohibitions.

The ECPA prohibits communications service providers from supplying information concerning customer records unless one of the statutory exceptions applies.[40] There are specific exceptions for disclosure upon receipt of a grand jury subpoena[41] or an NSL.[42] A service provider who knowingly or intentionally violates the prohibition is subject to civil liability,[43] but there are no criminal penalties for the breach.

The Inspector General found that contrary to assertions that "the FBI would obtain telephone records only after it served NSLs or grand jury subpoenas, the FBI obtained telephone bill records and subscriber information prior to serving NSLs or grand jury subpoenas" by using "exigent letters."[44] The FBI responded that it had barred the use of exigent letters, but emphasized that the term "exigent letter" does not include emergency disclosures under the exception now found in 18 U.S.C. 2702(c)(4). Thus, the FBI might request that a service provider invoke that exception to the record disclosure bar "if the provider reasonably believes that an emergency involving immediate danger of death or serious physical injury to any person justifies disclosure of the information," 18 U.S.C. 2702(c)(4).

The Second IG Report

The second IG Report reviewed the FBI's use of national security letter authority during calendar year 2006 and the corrective measures taken following the issuance of the IG's first report. The second Report concluded that:

- "the FBI's use of national security letters in 2006 continued the upward trend . . . identified . . . for the period covering 2003 through 2006;
- "the percentage of NSL requests generated from investigations of U.S. persons
- continued to increase significantly, from approximately 39% of all NSL requests issued in 2003 to approximately 57% of all NSL requests issued in 2006;"
- the FBI and DoJ are committed to correcting the problems identified in *IG Report I* and "have made significant progress in addressing the need to improve compliance in the FBI's use of NSLs;" [and]
- "it [was] too early to definitively state whether the new systems and controls developed by the FBI and the Department will eliminate fully the problems with NSLs that we identified," *IG Report II* at 8-9.

Secrecy, Judicial Review & the Second Circuit

The current secrecy and judicial review provisions applicable to NSLs must be read in light of the Second Circuit's *John Doe, Inc. v. Mukasey* decision, 549 F.3d 861 (2d Cir. 2008). Under the NSL statutes, secrecy is not absolutely required. Instead NSL recipients are bound to secrecy only upon the certification of the requesting agency that disclosure of the request or response may result in a danger to national security; may interfere with diplomatic relations or with a criminal, counterterrorism, or counterintelligence investigation; or may endanger the physical safety of an individual.[45] A recipient may disclose the request to those necessary to comply with the request and to an attorney the recipient consults for related legal advice or assistance.[46] In doing so, the recipient must advise them of the secrecy requirements.[47] Aside from its attorney the recipient must also identify, at the requesting agency's election, those to whom it has disclosed the request.[48]

Judicial Review of NSLs

Under the statute, 18 U.S.C. 3511, *a recipient may petition the court to modify or extinguish any NSL secrecy requirement* within a year of issuance.[49] Thereafter, it may petition to have the veil of secrecy lifted, although it may resubmit a rejected request only once a year.[50] Section 3511 provides that the court may modify or set aside the restriction if it finds "no reason to believe that disclosure may" endanger national security or personal safety or interfere with diplomatic relations or a criminal, countterrorism, or counterintelligence investigation.[51] The section, however, *binds the court to the assertion of a senior executive branch official that such an adverse consequence is possible.*[52]

In addition to authority to review and set aside NSL nondisclosure requirements, the federal courts also enjoy jurisdiction to review and enforce the underlying NSL requests. Under section 3511, recipients may petition and be granted an order modifying or setting aside an NSL, if the court finds that compliance would be unreasonable, oppressive, or otherwise unlawful.[53] The "unreasonable or oppressive" standard is used for grand jury and other subpoenas issued under the Federal Rules of Criminal Procedure.[54] The Rules afford protection against undue burdens and protect privileged communications.[55] Compliance with a particular NSL might be unduly burdensome in some situations, but the circumstances under which NSLs are used suggest few federally recognized privileges. The Rules also impose a relevancy requirement, but in the context of a grand jury investigation a motion to quash will be denied unless it can be shown that "there is no reasonable possibility that the category of materials the Government seeks will produce information relevant" to the investigation.[56] The authority to modify or set aside a NSL that is "unlawful" affords the court an opportunity to determine whether the NSL in question complies with the statutory provisions under which it was issued. Section 3511 also vests the court with authority to enforce the NSL against a recalcitrant recipient. Failure to comply with the court's order thereafter is punishable as contempt of court.[57] A breach of a confidentiality requirement committed knowingly and with the intent to obstruct an investigation or related judicial proceedings is punishable by imprisonment for not more than five years and/or a fine of not more than $250,000 (not more than $500,000 for an organization).[58]

The Second Circuit has concluded that the procedure can survive First Amendment scrutiny only if it involves the following:

- notice to NSL recipients that they may contest any secrecy order;
- expeditious government petition for judicial review of a secrecy order upon recipient request;
- government burden to establish the validity of its narrowly tailored secrecy order;
- no conclusive weigh may be afforded governmental assertions; and
- recipients may apply or reapply annually for judicial review where the government's burden remains the same.[59]

On remand, the district upheld continuation of the nondisclosure order under the procedure suggested by the Second Circuit.[60]

Proposed Amendments

Sunset and Repeal

Three provisions governing foreign intelligence investigations sunset on December 31, 2009. The NSL provisions are not among them. Nevertheless, each of the bills propose sunset in one form or another. The Feingold bill would repeal immediately one of the existing NSL statutes, section 627 of the Fair Credit Reporting Act (15 U.S.C. 168 1v).[61] The Leahy bill would repeal section 627 effective December 31, 2013 and on that date would return the others to their pre-USA PATRIOT Act form.[62] The Conyers bill would return all five NSL statutes to pre-USA PATRIOT Act form effective December 31, 2013, thereby effectively repealing section 627.[63] The Nadler bill would return all but the National Security Act statute (50 U.S.C. 436) to their pre-USA PATRIOT Act form after five years.[64]

The USA PATRIOT Act expanded existing authority under 18 U.S.C. 2709, the Right to Financial Privacy Act, and the Fair Credit Reporting Act.[65] It also created new NSL authority in the form of section 627 of the Fair Credit Reporting Act (15 U.S.C. 168 1v).[66] It did not expand the reach of the National Security Act NSL statute. A return to the state of the law prior to enactment of the USA PATRIOT Act would have the effect of eliminating the amendments it made in the preexisting NSL statutes as well as any subsequent amendments, and of repealing section 627.

In general terms for the three pre-existing NSL statutes, the USA PATRIOT Act:

- expanded issuing authority to include the heads of FBI field offices (special agents in charge (SACs));
- eliminated the requirement of specific and articulable facts demonstrating a nexus to a foreign power or its agents;
- required instead that the information was sought for or relevant to various national security investigations; and
- directed that no NSL related investigation of a "U.S. person" (American citizen or foreign resident alien) be predicated exclusively on First Amendment protected activities.[67]

This means that:

- NSLs are more readily available to FBI field agents at a lower level of supervisory control;.
- NSLs can be used to obtain information pertaining to individuals two, three, or more steps removed from the foreign power or agent of a foreign power that is the focus of the investigation; and
- NSL-related investigations may not be predicated solely on the basis of activities protected by the First Amendment.

A return to the state of the law prior to the effective date of the USA PATRIOT Act would mean NSLs would have to be approved by the FBI Director or a senior FBI headquarters official, and it would have to be based on specific and articulable facts giving reason to believe that the information sought pertains to a foreign power or agent of a foreign power.[68] A witness at an earlier Congressional hearing indicated that the "specific and articulable" facts standard grew out of the standards employed in counterintelligence investigations and did not always translate well in a counterterrorism context:

> My point is that the "specific and articulable facts" standard was particularly suited to the counterintelligence operations of the era in which it was created. A FBI counterintelligence investigation involved examining a linear connection between a foreign intelligence officer (about whom much was known) and his contacts (potential spies). The information known about the intelligence officer was specific in nature, and could be readily used to meet the NSL legal standards . . . . Unlike the traditional linear counterintelligence case, in which the foreign agent tried to recruit the domestic spy using infrequent and highly secure forms of communication, many counterterrorism cases involved complex networks generating a much larger volume of communication and financial transactions. In counter-terrorism cases, the starting point was often not a clearly identifiable agent of a foreign power (as in counterintelligence); indeed, the relevant "foreign power" was itself an imperfectly understood terrorist organization that might defy precise definition. As a consequence, counter-terrorism investigators often had a far more difficult time meeting the "specific and articulable facts" standard.[69]

The language precluding NSL-related investigations grounded exclusively on the exercise of First Amendment rights would also disappear. It is at best unclear, however, that the First Amendment unaided does not embody a comparable prohibition.

At the first sunset of USA PATRIOT Act provisions, Congress amended each of the NSL statutes in the USA PATRIOT Improvement and Reauthorization Act and the USA PATRIOT Act Additional Reauthorization Amendments Act.[70] The amendments state the grounds upon which the NSLs may be made subject to a secrecy requirement (gag order);[71] advise recipients that the order does not preclude disclosure to the recipient's attorney or to those necessary for execution of the request; and notify recipients of their right to judicial review of the order.[72] They too would disappear were the law carried back to its pre-USA PATRIOT Act state.

The impact might be less significant that would at first appear. By and large, 18 U.S.C. 3511 governs judicial review of NSL nondisclosure requirements. When implemented as required by the Second Circuit's decision in *John Doe, Inc. v. Mukasey,* 549 U.S. 861 (2d Cir.

2008), and at the election of the recipient, the government has the burden of persuading the court of the validity of the gag order under the same standards as found in the expired portions of the NSL statutes. Although each of the legislative proposals would amend section 3511, explicitly or implicitly, they each reinforce rather than erode the recipient protections of section 3511 as discussed *infra*.

Section 627, the NSL statute created in the USA PATRIOT Act, is arguably the most sweeping of the NSL statutes. It offers the most extensive array of information (all information pertaining to a consumer held by a consumer credit reporting agency) to the widest range of requesters (any federal agency "authorized to conduct investigations of, or intelligence or counterintelligence activities or analysis relating to, international terrorism").[73] Its repeal might be seen to facilitate oversight, since it would centralize authority to issue NSLs in the FBI (other than in the case of employee security investigations under the National Security Act). Moreover, the Justice Department IG reported that both the FBI and consumer reporting agencies have experienced difficulty distinguishing between authority under 168 1u and 168 1v.[74]

In contrast, the National Security Act NSL statute, left unamended by the USA PATRIOT Act is arguably the least intrusive. It reaches only information pertaining to federal employees who have consented to their disclosure.[75]

Nondisclosure

Each of the NSL statutes has a nondisclosure provision.[76] They state that the issuing agency may prohibit recipients from disclosing the request – to anyone other than their attorney and those necessary to comply with the request, ever.[77] In order to activate the authority, agency officials must certify that disclosure may endanger national security, endanger individual safety, or may interfere with diplomatic relations or with a criminal, counterintelligence, or counterterrorism investigation.[78]

A federal district court may modify or set aside a NSL secrecy requirement on the petition of a recipient, if it concludes that there is no reason to believe that disclosure might result in any such danger or interference.[79] If the petition for review is filed more than a year after issuance of the NSL, the agency must either terminate the gag order or recertify the need for its continuation.[80] There is no explicit provision for disclosure to the party to whom the information pertains.

The Second Circuit in *John Doe, Inc. v. Mukasey* held that these provisions only survive First Amendment scrutiny if the agency petitions for judicial review and convinces the court that the agency proposed order is narrowly crafted to meet to the statutorily identified adverse consequences of disclosure.[81]

The Nadler, Conyers, Feingold and Leahy bills would each modify the statutory provisions governing the issuance and judicial review of NSL nondisclosure orders. The Conyers, Feingold and Leahy bills would codify a procedure comparable in many respects to that which the Second Circuit identified as constitutionally acceptable. Under all three bills, the agency issuing the NSL would make the initial determination of whether to include a nondisclosure provision in the NSL and that determination would be subject to judicial review.[82] The Nadler bill uses a different approach to meet the Second Circuit requirement that the government seek and justify judicial approval for a nondisclosure order. Under the Nadler bill, recipients would be under a disclosure ban for 30 days during which the agency might apply to the court to issue a nondisclosure order.[83]

The Leahy and Conyers bills would leave unchanged the concerns a requesting official might rely upon in order to impose a nondisclosure order: reason to believe disclosure may endanger national security or individual safety or interfere with diplomatic relations or a criminal, counterterrorism, or counterintelligence investigation (but in the Conyers bill the court would have to find that disclosure would – rather than might – result in one or more of the adverse consequences).[84] The Nadler and Feingold bills would adopt a higher threshold and would establish a narrower range of adverse consequences necessary to justify nondisclosure: reason to believe disclosure "will" (rather than "may") result in a danger to personal safety; flight from prosecution; destruction or tampering with evidence; witness intimidation; a serious danger to national security by tipping off the foreign agent who is the target of the investigation, or his associates, or the foreign power that is the agent's principal; or (only in the case of the Feingold bill) interfere with diplomatic relations.[85]

The Nadler and Feingold bills would adopt a higher threshold as well and would establish a narrower range of adverse consequences necessary to justify nondisclosure: reason to believe disclosure "will" (rather than "may") result in a danger to personal safety; flight from prosecution; destruction or tampering with evidence; witness intimidation; a serious danger to national security by tipping off the foreign agent who is the target of the investigation, or his associates, or the foreign power that is the agent's principal; or (only in the case of the Feingold bill) interfere with diplomatic relations.[86]

In all four bills, the government would bear the burden of petitioning for and securing U.S. district court approval of a nondisclosure provision. In the Nadler bill, the recipient would be subject to a preliminary 30 day nondisclosure requirement during which the issuing agency might seek a court nondisclosure order.[87] In the Feingold bill, should the agency determine that nondisclosure is appropriate it would inform the recipient that he had 21 days to ask for judicial review.[88] Those who elect not to request judicial review would be bound by the nondisclosure requirement for not more than a year.[89] In the case of those who request judicial review, the agency would have 21 days to petition the court for review.[90] In the Leahy and Conyers bills, the agency would notify the recipient of the right to judicial review and petition for review within 30 days of a recipient's request for judicial review.[91]

All four bills would require that the agency's application for judicial approval or review include a statement of facts giving reason to believe that disclosure would (or might in the case of the Leahy and Conyers bills) result in one of the statutory list of adverse consequences – (A) in the Leahy and Conyers bills, endanger national security or individual safety or interfere with diplomatic relations or with a criminal, counterterrorism, or counterintelligence investigation; or (B) in the Nadler and Feingold bills, endanger personal safety; flight from prosecution; destruction or tampering with evidence; witness intimidation; a serious danger to national security by tipping off the foreign agent who is the target of the investigation, or his associates, or the foreign power that is the agent's principal; or (only in the case of the Feingold bill) interfere with diplomatic relations.[92]

The Feingold bill would compel applicants to explain how the adverse consequences relate to the investigation in which NSL is sought and how the secrecy order is narrowly crafted to counter the possibility of those adverse consequences.[93] In addition, the Feingold bill would require that agency applicants recommend when the secrecy order should expire.[94]

Should the court feel the agency has met its burden, it would be authorized to approve the requested secrecy order. The Feingold bill limits the order to no more than a year; the Nadler and Conyers bills to no more than 180 days.[95] Renewals would be available under the same conditions and with the maximum duration as in the original.[96] Unlike the other bills, the Leahy bill has no such explicit provision for maximum duration of a gag order, and unlike existing law, it has no explicit provision to allow a recipient to petition for judicial review after the passage of time. On the other hand, it places no express time limit on the recipient's right to judicial review nor upon the court's jurisdiction over the question; it states only that the recipient has a right to judicial review of the order, that the recipient must notify the agency of any desire for judicial review, and that the agency must be petition the court for review within 30 days of receiving a recipient's request.[97]

Judicial Review of NSL Itself

Existing law permits the recipient of a NSL to petition the U.S. district court to modify it or set aside under the same grounds as a grand jury subpoena might be quashed or modified or if it is otherwise unlawful.[98] The Conyers, Feingold and Leahy bills would not change existing law here, although they would provide that a NSL include a statement informing the recipient of his right to seek judicial review and of the procedures for doing so.[99] The Nadler bill contains a provision which appears to be designed to replace existing law, although the bill would neither repeal nor expressly amend the current provision. The Nadler proposal would allow a recipient to petition the U.S. district court to modify or set aside the NSL for failure to comply with the statutory requirements associated with the issuance of NSL or based "upon any constitutional or other legal right or privilege" of the recipient.[100]

Issuance and Content

The NSL statutes now authorize the NSLs upon certification that the information is sought for, or is relevant to, various national security investigations.[101] The Nadler and Conyers bills would require certification of specific and articulable facts supporting a belief that the information pertains to a foreign power or one of its agents.[102] The Feingold bill would require certification of specific and articulable facts supporting a belief that the information pertains to (i) a suspected agent of a foreign power or the subject of a national security investigation, (ii) an individual in contact with or directly linked to such an individual, or (iii) the activities of such an individual when the activities are the subject of a national security investigation and the NSL is the least intrusive means to identifying persons involved.[103] The Leahy bill has no comparable provision, but it would insist upon a written statement of facts supporting the conclusion that the information sought is relevant to the investigation for which it is sought.[104]

Both the Nadler bill and the Feingold bill would prohibit NSL demands that would be considered unreasonable or privileged, if sought under a grand jury subpoena duces tecum.[105] The Conyers and Leahy bills have no comparable provisions.

Minimization Requirements

In a general sense "minimization" refers to limitations on what information is acquired; how it is acquired; how it is maintained; who has access to it within the capturing agency and under what circumstances; to whom and under what circumstances it is disclosed beyond the capturing agency; how long it is preserved; and when and under what circumstances it is expunged. Minimization standards are drawn with an eye to the purposes for which information is acquired; the authority under which it is acquired; the legitimate interests which may be affected by its acquisition, use, or disclosure; and the governmental interests served by its acquisition, maintenance, use, and disclosure.

Minimization standards ordinarily reinforce statutory and regulatory limitations that attend the use of possibly invasive means of acquiring information. For example, the Foreign Intelligence Surveillance Act (FISA) provides fairly rigorous statutory procedures that must be honored before electronic surveillance or physical searches may be authorized in a national security context, 50 U.S.C. 1801-1829. It also supplies statutory conditions under which information acquired using those techniques may be used, e.g., 50 U.S.C. 1806, and both judicial and legislative oversights procedures, e.g., 50 U.S.C. 1 805, 1808. As an additional safeguard, it also calls for the creation and implementation of minimization procedures to protect private information relating to Americans consistent with the U.S. foreign intelligence interests, *e.g.*, 50 U.S.C. 1801(h), 1 802(a)(2).[106]

Section 119(f) of the USA PATRIOT Improvement and Reauthorization Act directed the Attorney General and the Director of National Intelligence to report to the Congressional intelligence and judiciary committees on the feasibility of NSL minimization procedures "to ensure the protection of the constitutional rights of Untied States persons."[107] The Inspector General's reports noted the need for minimization standards or their regulatory equivalent:

> In our first NSL report, the OIG noted the proviso in the Attorney General's NSI Guidelines that national security investigations should use the "least intrusive collection techniques feasible" to carry out the investigations. The OIG reported that we found no clear guidance on how Special Agents should reconcile the Attorney General guidelines' limitations with the expansive authority provided in the NSL statutes. Our concerns over the lack of formal guidance were magnified because of the volume of NSLs generated by the FBI each year and because the information collected is retained for long periods in databases available to many authorized law enforcement personnel.[108]

The Justice Department convened a working group to study and make recommendations concerning possible NSL minimization standards in response to its statutory obligation and the Inspector General's initial report.[109] The working group's proposals have yet to be finalized and the Inspector General recently testified that "final guidance is needed and overdue."[110]

Each of the bills has minimization components. Some take the form of statutory limitations and others instructions for Justice Department guidelines. The Leahy and Feingold bills would direct the Attorney General to promulgate minimization procedures within 180 days with features comparable to the FISA definition in 50 U.S.C. 180 1(h): procedures that are calculated, consistent with U.S. needs for foreign intelligence information, to minimize the capture and retention of private information (information not publicly available) relating to a U.S. person (and to ban its retention); procedures that preclude the disclosure of private information relating to a U.S. person (that is not foreign intelligence information) that identifies the person, unless necessary to appreciate its significance; and procedures that permit evidence of a crime to be retained and disclosed.[111] The Feingold bill would also insist that the procedures call for the return or destruction of information acquired outside the scope of the NSL or in a manner that fails to comply with the NSL statute.[112]

The Nadler and Conyers bills would give the Attorney General 90 days to promulgate minimization procedures that are calculated to minimize the capture and retention of private information (information not publicly available) relating to a U.S. person (and to ban its dissemination).[113] The additional requirements would focus on procedures for the return or destruction of information that does not reflect the activity of an agent of a foreign power; that is superfluous; or that exceeds the bounds of the original NSL request.[114]

In provisions modeled after those in FISA, the Nadler and Feingold bills would also add explicit provisions describing some of the circumstances under which NSL generated information might be disclosed. They would:

- prohibit disclosure except for lawful purposes and in compliance with minimization procedures;
- require a statement of origin and of Attorney General approval when used in criminal proceedings;
- when the information is to be used in federal proceedings, direct that the person to whom the information relates and the tribunal be informed beforehand of the information's source;
- when the information is to be used in state proceedings, direct that the person to whom the information relates, the tribunal, and the Attorney General be informed beforehand of the information's source and intended use;
- when the information is to be used in either state or federal proceedings, afford the person to whom the information relates an opportunity to move for suppression based on the NSL statute, the Constitution, or other laws of the United States;
- authorize the U.S. district court to order suppression should it find that due process so requires or that the NSL was not issued in compliance with the NSL statute, the Constitution, or other laws of the United States; and
- make binding the U.S. district court's suppression decisions except for federal appellate purposes.[115]

The Conyers bill would require the Attorney General's prior approval before NSL information could be used in a criminal proceeding.[116]

The Feingold bill also includes a "least intrusive means" section.[117] The current Attorney General's guidelines governing FBI intelligence investigations in this country state that the FBI investigations should use the "least intrusive method feasible" in light of the circumstances.[118] The Feingold bill would establish a statutory least intrusive means NSL standard and would require recourse to other sources before the issuance of a NSL directed to a bookstore or library.[119]

Table 2. Chart of Proposed NSL Amendments: H.R. 3845, H.R. 1800, S. 1686, and S. 1692

Current Law	H.R. 3845 (Conyers)	H.R. 1800 (Nadler)	S. 1686 (Feingold)	S. 1692 (Leahy)
Sunset				
NSL statutes have no expiration date	Effective Dec. 3, 2013, NSL statutes revert to pre-USA PATRIOT Act versions and 15 USC 1681v is thereby repealed (§2C2)	After 5 years, NSL statutes (except 50 USC 436) revert to pre-USA PATRIOT Act versions and 15 USC 1681v is thereby repealed (§5(a))	Repeals 15 USC 1681v (§101(c)(2))	Effective Dec. 31, 2013, NSL statutes revert to pre-USA PATRIOT Act versions and 15 USC 1681v is repealed (§2(c))
Gag orders:				
Recipient may seek judicial review, 18 USC 3511 (2d Cir. valid only if agency secures court approval when recipient requests (549 F.3d 861)	Upon recipient request, agency has 30 days to seek a court order of < 180 days; renewals of < 180 days (§207)	Agency issued (up to 30 days) pending US district court order of <180 days; renewals of <180 days (§3(d))	Agency issued (recipient may request jud. rev. w/i 21 days); upon request, agency has 21 days to seek court order (orders limited to 1 year; renewals for 1 year possible) (§102)	Agency issued (recipient may request jud. rev.); upon request, agency has 30 days to seek a court order (no statu-tory max. duration); bill appears to contemplate continuous right to request review (§§5, 6(b))
Grounds				
Agency cert. & ct. approval if any reason to believe disclosure might: endanger US national security/individual safety; or interfere w/ diplomatic relations or w/ a criminal, counterintell, or counterterr. investigation (18 USC 3511)	Agency certification & court approval granted if there is any reason to believe disclosure might(agency)/will (ct): endanger US national security or individual safety; or inte-rfere with diplomatic relations or with a criminal, counteri-ntelligence, or counterte-rrorism investigation (§207)	Agency application stating specific and articulable facts for believe disclosure will result in : danger to individual safety; flight to avoid prosecution, destruction or tampering with evidence, or danger to national security (by tipping off the target of the investigation, his associates or foreign principal) (§3(d)(5),(d)(6))	Same as H.R. 1800 except adds interference with dip-lomatic relations to the list of adverse consequences that may justify a gag order (§101 –prop. 18 USC 2709(c), 12 USC 3414(b), 15 USC 1681u(b))	Agency statement of facts and court determination that discl-osure will result in: danger to US national security or individual safety; or interfere with diplomatic relations or with a criminal, counterintelligence, or counterterrorism investigation (§6(b))

Table 2. (Continued)

Current Law	H.R. 3845 (Conyers)	H.R. 1800 (Nadler)	S. 1686 (Feingold)	S. 1692 (Leahy)
NSL: Grounds				
Relevancy to various national security investigations (e.g., 18 USC 2709(b))	Specific/articulable facts showing info pertains to a foreign power/agent in separate letter for the files (§204)	Specific and articulable facts exist showing info pertains to a foreign power/agent (§3(a))	Specific and articulable facts showing info pertains to (i) suspected foreign power agent/individual subject of a national security investigation; (ii) individual in contact with/directly linked to (i); or (iii) activities of a suspected for. power agent (if activities are under national security investigation and NSL is least intrusive means) (§101)	Relevancy to various national security investigations and agency retains writtenstatement specific factual basis for conclusion (§7)
Minimization				
DoJ is finalizing minimization standards	Directs DoJ to issue standards	Same as H.R. 3845 (§6)	Directs DoJ to issue standards w/i 180	Same as S. 1686 (§12)
	w/i 90 days covering (1) minimum capture/keep (no passing on) nonpublic info in re US persons (consistent w/ US for. intell. needs); (2) burn ASAP info in re US person not a for. Power agent, info in excess of NSL, & superfluous info (§208)		days covering (1) minimum capture/keep (no passing on) nonpublic info in re US persons (consistent w/ US for. intell. needs); (2) passing on non public info in re US person (if not for. intell. info) that id.s person (unless needed for context); permit keep/pass on evidence of crime (§101)	

Table 2. (Continued)

Current Law	H.R. 3845 (Conyers)	H.R. 1800 (Nadler)	S. 1686 (Feingold)	S. 1692 (Leahy)
	Requires AG notification before use of NSL info in criminal proceedings (§206)	Adapts FISA-like use-in-official-proceeding features (§3(f))	Same as H.R. 1800 (§101)	
Audits & Reports				
Audits				
DoJ IG audited and reported on FBI NSL use for 2003, 2004, 2005 & 2006 (120 Stat. 219)	Requires DoJ IG audits and reports on FBI NSL use for 2007-2009 and annual audits/repts for, 2010, 2011, 2012 & 2013 (§105(b))			Requires DoJ IG audit and reports covering the years 2007, 2008 and 2009, and annual reports for 2010 and 2011 (§10(b))
Reports				
Requires annual DoJ report to Con-gress in unclassi-fied form on total number of NSL requests in re US persons (120 Stat. 218)		Requires semiannual DoJ report in unclassified form on: the total number of NSL requests under each NSL statute, for procedures and any changes to them; sum-mary of any judicial chall-enges; the extent to which NSLs aided investigations and prosecutions (§6(c)	Except with regard to sub-scriber information under 18 USC 2709, requires the annual report to include the nubmer NSL requests con-cerning US persons, non-US persons, persons who were the subject of nati-onal security investiga-tions, and those who were not (§104	Same as S. 1686
Emergency Practices				
Communications providers may dis-close the content and records of customer commu-nications in threat of death or serious physical injury cases (18 USC 2702((b)(8), (c)(4))		Limit such voluntary disclosures to threats of imm-inent or immediate death or serious injury cases (§7	Same as H.R. 1800(§105(a)) Permits financial institutions to disclose customer financial information to government authorities in cases of a threat of immediate death or serious physical injury (§1105(b))	

Emergency Practices

The IG's first report indicated that in a number of instances the FBI had used "exigent letters" and "certificate letters" rather than NSL statutory authority to "circumvent" NSL requirements.[120] Although they had not relied upon it, the FBI asserted that in some of those instances they might have invoked the voluntary disclosure provisions of 18 U.S.C. 2702.[121]

Section 2702 authorizes communications providers to supply "a governmental entity" with customer communications content and records, "if the provider, in good faith, believes that an emergency involving danger of death or serious physical injury to any person requires disclosure without delay of communications [or information] relating to the emergency."[122]

The Nadler and Feingold bills would amend section 2702 to limit the exception to where the risk of death or serious injury is imminent or immediate.[123] The Feingold bill would also add a provision to the Right to Financial Privacy Act to allow a comparable disclosure of customer records by financial institutions under similar circumstances.[124] The change seems intended to make clear that there are no implicit emergency grounds for disclosure of such records.

Reports and Audits

Some of the NSL statutes provide for periodic reports to various Congressional committees.[125] In addition, the USA PATRIOT Improvement and Reauthorization Act instructed the Attorney General to prepare, in unclassified form, an annual report to Congress on the number of NSLs issued in the previous year.[126] The same legislation directed the Inspector General of the Department of Justice to audit and report on the use of NSL authority for calendar years 2002 through 2006.[127]

The Nadler, Feingold and Leahy bills would each expand the annual statistical report to include a breakdown of the number of NSLs issued concerning U.S. persons, those who are not U.S. persons, the targets of national security investigation, and those who are not the target of a national security investigation.[128] The Leahy and Conyers bills would call for Inspector General audits and reports covering the years 2007 through 2009 and annual audits and reports for calendar years 2010 and 2011 (as well as 2012 and 2013 under the Conyers bill).[129]

Text of NSL Statutes on October 25, 2001 and Now (emphasis added)

12 U.S.C. 3414(a)(5) (on October 25, 2001)

(a) . . . .

(5) (A) Financial institutions, and officers, employees, and agents thereof, shall comply with a request for a customer's or entity's financial records made pursuant to this subsection by the Federal Bureau of Investigation when the Director of the Federal Bureau of Investigation (or the Director's designee) certifies in writing to the

financial institution that such records are sought for foreign counter intelligence purposes *and that there are specific and articulable facts giving reason to believe that the customer or entity whose records are sought is a foreign power or the agents of a foreign power as defined in section 1801 of title 50.*

(B) The Federal Bureau of Investigation may disseminate information obtained pursuant to this paragraph only as provided in guidelines approved by the Attorney General for foreign intelligence collection and foreign counterintelligence investigations conducted by the Federal Bureau of Investigation, and, with respect to dissemination to an agency of the United States, only if such information is clearly relevant to the authorized responsibilities of such agency.

(C) On a semiannual basis the Attorney General shall fully inform the Permanent Select Committee on Intelligence of the House of Representatives and the Select Committee on Intelligence of the Senate concerning all requests made pursuant to this paragraph.

(D) No financial institution, or officer, employee, or agent of such institution, shall disclose to any person that the Federal Bureau of Investigation has sought or obtained access to a customer's or entity's financial records under this paragraph.

12 U.S.C. 3414(a)(5) (now)

(a) . . .

(5) (A) Financial institutions, and officers, employees, and agents thereof, shall comply with a request for a customer's or entity's financial records made pursuant to this subsection by the Federal Bureau of Investigation when the Director of the Federal Bureau of Investigation (or the Director's designee *in a position not lower than Deputy Assistant Director at Bureau headquarters or a Special Agent in Charge in a Bureau field office designated by the Director*) certifies in writing to the financial institution that such records are sought for foreign counter intelligence purposes *to protect against international terrorism or clandestine intelligence activities, provided that such an investigation of a United States person is not conducted solely upon the basis of activities protected by the first amendment to the Constitution of the United States.*

(B) The Federal Bureau of Investigation may disseminate information obtained pursuant to this paragraph only as provided in guidelines approved by the Attorney General for foreign intelligence collection and foreign counterintelligence investigations conducted by the Federal Bureau of Investigation, and, with respect to dissemination to an agency of the United States, only if such information is clearly relevant to the authorized responsibilities of such agency.

(C) On the dates provided in section 41 5b of Title 50, the Attorney General shall fully inform the congressional intelligence committees (as defined in section 401 a of Title 50) concerning all requests made pursuant to this paragraph.

(D) Prohibition of certain disclosure. –

(i) *If the Director of the Federal Bureau of Investigation, or his designee in a position not lower than Deputy Assistant Director at Bureau headquarters or a Special Agent in Charge in a Bureau field office designated by the Director, certifies that otherwise there may result a danger to the national security of the United States, interference with a criminal, counterterrorism, or counterintelligence investigation, interference with diplomatic relations, or danger to the life or physical safety of any person, no financial institution, or officer, employee, or agent of such institution, shall disclose to any person (other than those to whom such disclosure is necessary to comply with the request or an attorney to obtain legal advice or legal assistance with respect to the request)* that the Federal Bureau of Investigation has sought or obtained access to a customer's or entity's financial records under subparagraph (A).

(ii) *The request shall notify the person or entity to whom the request is directed of the nondisclosure requirement under clause (i).*

(iii) *Any recipient disclosing to those persons necessary to comply with the request or to an attorney to obtain legal advice or legal assistance with respect to the request shall inform such persons of any applicable nondisclosure requirement. Any person who receives a disclosure under this subsection shall be subject to the same prohibitions on disclosure under clause (i).*

(iv) *At the request of the Director of the Federal Bureau of Investigation or the designee of the Director, any person making or intending to make a disclosure under this section shall identify to the Director or such designee the person to whom such disclosure will be made or to whom such disclosure was made prior to the request, except that nothing in this section shall require a person to inform the Director or such designee of the identity of an attorney to whom disclosure was made or will be made to obtain legal advice or legal assistance with respect to the request for financial records under subparagraph (A).*

15 U.S.C. 1681u(a), (b)(on October 25, 2001)

(a) Identity of financial institutions

Notwithstanding section 168 1b of this title or any other provision of this subchapter, a consumer reporting agency shall furnish to the Federal Bureau of Investigation the names and addresses of all financial institutions (as that term is defined in section 3401 of Title 12) at which a consumer maintains or has maintained an account, to the extent that information is in the files of the agency, when presented with a written request for that information, signed by the Director of the Federal Bureau of Investigation, or the Director's designee, which certifies compliance with this section. The Director or the Director's designee may make such a certification only if the Director or the Director's designee has determined in writing that –

(1) *such information is necessary for the conduct of an authorized foreign counterintelligence investigation; and*

(2) *there are specific and articulable facts giving reason to believe that the consumer –*

(A) *is a foreign power (as defined in section 1801 of title 50) or a person who is not a United States person (as defined in such section 1801 of title 50) and is an official of a foreign power; or*

(B) *is an agent of a foreign power and is engaging or has engaged in an act of international terrorism (as that term is defined in section 1801(c) of title 50) or clandestine intelligence activities that involve or may involve a violation of criminal statutes of the United States.*

(b) Identifying information

Notwithstanding the provisions of section 168 1b of this title or any other provision of this subchapter, a consumer reporting agency shall furnish identifying information respecting a consumer, limited to name, address, former addresses, places of employment, or former places of employment, to the Federal Bureau of Investigation when presented with a written request, signed by the Director or the Director's designee, which certifies compliance with this subsection. The Director or the Director's designee may make such a certification only if the Director or the Director's designee has determined in writing that –

(1) such information is necessary to the conduct of an authorized counterintelligence investigation; and

(2) there is information giving reason to believe that the consumer has been, or is about to be, in contact with a foreign power or an agent of a foreign power (as defined in section 1801 of title 50).

15 U.S.C. 1681u(a), (b)(now)

(a) Identity of financial institutions

Notwithstanding section 168 1b of this title or any other provision of this subchapter, a consumer reporting agency shall furnish to the Federal Bureau of Investigation the names and addresses of all financial institutions (as that term is defined in section 3401 of Title 12) at which a consumer maintains or has maintained an account, to the extent that information is in the files of the agency, when presented with a written request for that information, signed by the Director of the Federal Bureau of Investigation, or the Director's designee *in a position not lower than Deputy Assistant Director at Bureau headquarters or a Special Agent in Charge of a Bureau field office designated by the Director*, which certifies compliance with this section. The Director or the Director's designee may make such a certification only if the Director or the Director's designee has determined in writing, that *such information is sought for the conduct of an authorized investigation to protect against international terrorism or clandestine intelligence activities, provided that such an investigation of a United States person is not conducted solely upon the basis of activities protected by the first amendment to the Constitution of the United States.*

(b) Identifying information

Notwithstanding the provisions of section 168 1b of this title or any other provision of this subchapter, a consumer reporting agency shall furnish identifying information respecting a consumer, limited to name, address, former addresses, places of employment, or former places of employment, to the Federal Bureau of Investigation when presented with a written request, signed by the Director or the Director's designee *in a position not lower than Deputy Assistant Director at Bureau headquarters or a Special Agent in Charge of a Bureau field office designated by the Director*, which certifies compliance with this subsection. The Director or the Director's designee may make such a certification only if the Director or the Director's designee has determined in writing that *such information is sought for the conduct of an authorized investigation to protect against international terrorism or clandestine intelligence activities, provided that such an investigation of a United States person is not conducted solely upon the basis of activities protected by the first amendment to the Constitution of the United States.*

18 U.S.C. 2709 (as of October 25, 2001)

(a) Duty to provide. – A wire or electronic communication service provider shall comply with a request for subscriber information and toll billing records information, or electronic communication transactional records in its custody or possession made by the Director of the Federal Bureau of Investigation under subsection (b) of this section.

(b) Required certification. – The Director of the Federal Bureau of Investigation, or his designee in a position not lower than Deputy Assistant Director, may –

(1) request the name, address, length of service, and local and long distance toll billing records of a person or entity if the Director (or his designee in a position not lower than Deputy Assistant Director) certifies in writing to the wire or electronic communication service provider to which the request is made that –

(A) the name, address, length of service, and toll billing records sought are relevant to an authorized investigation to foreign counterintelligence investigation; and

(B) *there are specific and facts giving reason to believe that the person or entity to whom the information sought pertains is a foreign power or an agent of a foreign power as defined in section 101 of the Foreign intelligence Surveillance Act of 1978 (50 U.S. C. 1801)*; and

(2) request the name, address, and length of service of a person or entity if the Director (or his designee in a position not lower than Deputy Assistant Director) certifies in writing to the wire or electronic communication service provider to which the request is made that –

(A) the information sought is relevant to an authorized foreign counterintelligence investigation; and

(B) *There are specific and articulable facts giving reason to believe that communication facilities registered in the name of the person or entity have been used, through the services of such provider, in communications with –*

(i) an individual who is engaging or has engaged in international terrorism as defined in section 101(c) of the Foreign Intelligence Surveillance Act or clandestine intelligence activities that involve or may involve a violation of the criminal statutes of the United States; or

(ii) a foreign power or agent of a foreign power under circumstances giving reason to believe that the communication concerned international

terrorism as defined in section 101(c) of the Foreign Intelligence Surveillance Act or clandestine intelligence activities that involve or may involve a violation of the criminal statutes of the United States.

(c) Prohibition of certain disclosure. – No wire or electronic communication service provider, or officer, employee, or agent thereof, shall disclose to any person that the Federal Bureau of Investigation has sought or obtained access to information or records under this section.

(d) Dissemination by bureau. – The Federal Bureau of Investigation may disseminate information and records obtained under this section only as provided in guidelines approved by the Attorney General for foreign intelligence collection and foreign counterintelligence investigations conducted by the Federal Bureau of Investigation, and, with respect to dissemination to an agency of the United States, only if such information is clearly relevant to the authorized responsibilities of such agency.

(e) Requirement that certain congressional bodies be informed. – On a semiannual basis the Director of the Federal Bureau of Investigation shall fully inform the Permanent Select Committee on Intelligence of the House of Representatives and the Select Committee on Intelligence of the Senate, and the Committee on the Judiciary of the House of Representatives and the Committee on the Judiciary of the Senate, concerning all requests made under subsection (b) of this section.

18 U.S.C. 2709 (now)

(a) Duty to provide. – A wire or electronic communication service provider shall comply with a request for subscriber information and toll billing records information, or electronic communication transactional records in its custody or possession made by the Director of the Federal Bureau of Investigation under subsection (b) of this section.

(b) Required certification. – The Director of the Federal Bureau of Investigation, or his designee in a position not lower than Deputy Assistant Director *at Bureau headquarters or a Special Agent in Charge in a Bureau field office designated by the Director*, may –

(1) request the name, address, length of service, and local and long distance toll billing records of a person or entity if the Director (or his designee) certifies in writing to the wire or electronic communication service provider to which the request is made that the name, address, length of service, and toll billing records *sought are relevant to an authorized investigation to protect against international terrorism or clandestine intelligence activities, provided that such an investigation of a United States person is not conducted solely on the basis of activities protected by the first amendment to the Constitution of the United States.*; and

(2) request the name, address, and length of service of a person or entity if the Director (or his designee) certifies in writing to the wire or electronic communication service provider to which the request is made that the information *sought is relevant to an authorized investigation to protect against*

international terrorism or clandestine intelligence activities, provided that such an investigation of a United States person is not conducted solely upon the basis of activities protected by the first amendment to the Constitution of the United States.

(c) Prohibition of certain disclosure. –

(1) *If the Director of the Federal Bureau of Investigation, or his designee in a position not lower than Deputy Assistant Director at Bureau headquarters or a Special Agent in Charge in a Bureau field office designated by the Director, certifies that otherwise there may result a danger to the national security of the United States, interference with a criminal, counterterrorism, or counterintelligence investigation, interference with diplomatic relations, or danger to the life or physical safety of any person, no wire or electronic communications service provider, or officer, employee, or agent thereof, shall disclose to any person (other than those to whom such disclosure is necessary to comply with the request or an attorney to obtain legal advice or legal assistance with respect to the request) that the Federal Bureau of Investigation has sought or obtained access to information or records under this section.*

(2) *The request shall notify the person or entity to whom the request is directed of the nondisclosure requirement under paragraph (1).*

(3) *Any recipient disclosing to those persons necessary to comply with the request or to an attorney to obtain legal advice or legal assistance with respect to the request shall inform such person of any applicable nondisclosure requirement. Any person who receives a disclosure under this subsection shall be subject to the same prohibitions on disclosure under paragraph (1).*

(4) *At the request of the Director of the Federal Bureau of Investigation or the designee of the Director, any person making or intending to make a disclosure under this section shall identify to the Director or such designee the person to whom such disclosure will be made or to whom such disclosure was made prior to the request, except that nothing in this section shall require a person to inform the Director or such designee of the identity of an attorney to whom disclosure was made or will be made to obtain legal advice or legal assistance with respect to the request under subsection (a).*

(d) Dissemination by bureau. – The Federal Bureau of Investigation may disseminate information and records obtained under this section only as provided in guidelines approved by the Attorney General for foreign intelligence collection and foreign counterintelligence investigations conducted by the Federal Bureau of Investigation, and, with respect to dissemination to an agency of the United States, only if such information is clearly relevant to the authorized responsibilities of such agency.

(e) Requirement that certain congressional bodies be informed. – On a semiannual basis the Director of the Federal Bureau of Investigation shall fully inform the Permanent Select Committee on Intelligence of the House of Representatives and the Select Committee on Intelligence of the Senate, and the Committee on the Judiciary of the House of Representatives and the Committee on the Judiciary of the Senate, concerning all requests made under subsection (b) of this section.

(f) *Libraries. – A library (as that term is defined in section 213(1) of the Library Services and Technology Act (20 U.S. C. 9122 (1)), the services of which include access to the Internet, books, journals, magazines, newspapers, or other similar forms of communication in print or digitally by patrons for their use, review, examination, or circulation, is not a wire or electronic communication service provider for purposes of this section, unless the library is providing the services defined in section 2510(15) ("electronic communication service") of this title.*

15 U.S.C. 1681v (as of October 25, 2001)

NONE. This section was created by the USA PATRIOT Act, effective October 26, 2001.

15 U.S.C. 1681v (now)

(a) Disclosure
Notwithstanding section 1681b of this title or any other provision of this subchapter, a consumer reporting agency shall furnish a consumer report of a consumer and all other information in a consumer's file to a government agency authorized to conduct investigations of, or intelligence or counterintelligence activities or analysis related to, international terrorism when presented with a written certification by such government agency that such information is necessary for the agency's conduct or such investigation, activity or analysis.

(b) Form of certification
The certification described in subsection (a) of this section shall be signed by a supervisory official designated by the head of a Federal agency or an officer of a Federal agency whose appointment to office is required to be made by the President, by and with the advice and consent of the Senate.

(c) Confidentiality

(1) If the head of a government agency authorized to conduct investigations of intelligence or counterintelligence activities or analysis related to international terrorism, or his designee, certifies that otherwise there may result a danger to the national security of the United States, interference with a criminal, counterterrorism, or counterintelligence investigation, interference with diplomatic relations, or danger to the life or physical safety of any person, no consumer reporting agency or officer, employee, or agent of such consumer reporting agency, shall disclose to any person (other than those to whom such disclosure is necessary to comply with the request or an attorney to obtain legal advice or legal assistance with respect to the request), or specify in any consumer report, that a government agency has sought or obtained access to information under subsection (a) of this section.

(2) The request shall notify the person or entity to whom the request is directed of the nondisclosure requirement under paragraph (1).

(3) Any recipient disclosing to those persons necessary to comply with the request or to any attorney to obtain legal advice or legal assistance with respect to the request shall inform such persons of any applicable nondisclosure requirement.

Any person who receives a disclosure under this subsection shall be subject to the same prohibitions on disclosure under paragraph (1).

(4) At the request of the authorized government agency, any person making or intending to make a disclosure under this section shall identify to the requesting official of the authorized government agency the person to whom such disclosure will be made or to whom such disclosure was made prior to the request, except that nothing in this section shall require a person to inform the requesting official of the identity of an attorney to whom disclosure was made or will be made to obtain legal advice or legal assistance with respect to the request for information under subsection (a) of this section.

(d) Rule of construction

Nothing in section 1681u of this title shall be construed to limit the authority of the Director of the Federal Bureau of Investigation under this section.

(e) Safe harbor

Notwithstanding any other provision of this subchapter, any consumer reporting agency or agent or employee thereof making disclosure of consumer reports or other information pursuant to this section in good-faith reliance upon a certification of a government agency pursuant to the provisions of this section shall not be liable to any person for such disclosure under this subchapter, the constitution of any State, or any law or regulation of any State or any political subdivision of any State.

(f) Reports to Congress

(1) On a semi-annual basis, the Attorney General shall fully inform the Committee on the Judiciary, the Committee on Financial Services, and the Permanent Select Committee on Intelligence of the House of Representatives and the Committee on the Judiciary, the Committee on Banking, Housing, and Urban Affairs, and the Select Committee on Intelligence of the Senate concerning all requests made pursuant to subsection (a) of this section.

(2) In the case of the semiannual reports required to be submitted under paragraph (1) to the Permanent Select Committee on Intelligence of the House of Representatives and the Select Committee on Intelligence of the Senate, the submittal dates for such reports shall be as provided in section 41 5b of Title 50.

50 U.S.C. 436 (as of October 25, 2001)

(a) Generally

(1) Any authorized investigative agency may request from any financial agency, financial institution, or holding company, or from any consumer reporting agency, such financial records, other financial information, and consumer reports as may be necessary in order to conduct any authorized law enforcement investigation, counterintelligence inquiry, or security determination. Any authorized investigative agency may also request records maintained by any commercial entity within the United States pertaining to travel by an employee in the executive branch of Government outside the United States.

(2) Requests may be made under this section where –

(A) the records sought pertain to a person who is or was an employee in the executive branch of Government required by the President in an Executive order or regulation, as a condition of access to classified information, to provide consent, during a background investigation and for such time as access to the information is maintained, and for a period of not more than three years thereafter, permitting access to financial records, other financial information, consumer reports, and travel records; and

(B)

(i) there are reasonable grounds to believe, based on credible information, that the person is, or may be, disclosing classified information in an unauthorized manner to a foreign power or agent of a foreign power;

(ii) information the employing agency deems credible indicates the person has incurred excessive indebtedness or has acquired a level of affluence which cannot be explained by other information known to the agency; or

(iii) circumstances indicate the person had the capability and opportunity to disclose classified information which is known to have been lost or compromised to a foreign power or an agent of a foreign power.

(3) Each such request –

(A) shall be accompanied by a written certification signed by the department or agency head or deputy department or agency head concerned, or by a senior official designated for this purpose by the department or agency head concerned (whose rank shall be no lower than Assistant Secretary or Assistant Director), and shall certify that –

(i) the person concerned is or was an employee within the meaning of paragraph (2)(A);

(ii) the request is being made pursuant to an authorized inquiry or investigation and is authorized under this section; and

(iii) the records or information to be reviewed are records or information which the employee has previously agreed to make available to the authorized investigative agency for review;

(B) shall contain a copy of the agreement referred to in subparagraph (A)(iii);

(C) shall identify specifically or by category the records or information to be reviewed; and

(D) shall inform the recipient of the request of the prohibition described in subsection (b) of this section.

(b) *Disclosure of requests*

Notwithstanding any other provision of law, no governmental or private entity, or officer, employee, or agent of such entity, may disclose to any person that such entity has received or satisfied a request made by an authorized investigative agency under this section.

50 U.S.C. 436 (now)

(a) Generally

(1) Any authorized investigative agency may request from any financial agency, financial institution, or holding company, or from any consumer reporting agency, such financial records, other financial information, and consumer reports as may be necessary in order to conduct any authorized law enforcement investigation, counterintelligence inquiry, or security determination. Any authorized investigative agency may also request records maintained by any commercial entity within the United States pertaining to travel by an employee in the executive branch of Government outside the United States.

(2) Requests may be made under this section where –

(A) the records sought pertain to a person who is or was an employee in the executive branch of Government required by the President in an Executive order or regulation, as a condition of access to classified information, to provide consent, during a background investigation and for such time as access to the information is maintained, and for a period of not more than three years thereafter, permitting access to financial records, other financial information, consumer reports, and travel records; and

(B)

(i) there are reasonable grounds to believe, based on credible information, that the person is, or may be, disclosing classified information in an unauthorized manner to a foreign power or agent of a foreign power;

(ii) information the employing agency deems credible indicates the person has incurred excessive indebtedness or has acquired a level of affluence which cannot be explained by other information known to the agency; or

(iii) circumstances indicate the person had the capability and opportunity to disclose classified information which is known to have been lost or compromised to a foreign power or an agent of a foreign power.

(3) Each such request –

(A) shall be accompanied by a written certification signed by the department or agency head or deputy department or agency head concerned, or by a senior official designated for this purpose by the department or agency head concerned (whose rank shall be no lower than Assistant Secretary or Assistant Director), and shall certify that –

(i) the person concerned is or was an employee within the meaning of paragraph (2)(A);

(ii) the request is being made pursuant to an authorized inquiry or investigation and is authorized under this section; and

(iii) the records or information to be reviewed are records or information which the employee has previously agreed to make available to the authorized investigative agency for review;

(B) shall contain a copy of the agreement referred to in subparagraph (A)(iii);

(C) shall identify specifically or by category the records or information to be reviewed; and

(D) shall inform the recipient of the request of the prohibition described in subsection (b) of this section.

(b) *Prohibition of certain disclosure*

(1) *If an authorized investigative agency described in subsection (a) of this section certifies that otherwise there may result a danger to the national security of the United States, interference with a criminal, counterterrorism, or counterintelligence investigation, interference with diplomatic relations, or danger to the life or physical safety of any person, no governmental or private entity, or officer, employee, or agent of such entity, may disclose to any person (other than those to whom such disclosure is necessary to comply with the request or an attorney to obtain legal advice or legal assistance with respect to the request)* that such entity has received or satisfied a request made by an authorized investigative agency under this section.

(2) *The request shall notify the person or entity to whom the request is directed of the nondisclosure requirement under paragraph (1).*

(3) *Any recipient disclosing to those persons necessary to comply with the request or to an attorney to obtain legal advice or legal assistance with respect to the request shall inform such persons of any applicable nondisclosure requirement. Any person who receives a disclosure under this subsection shall be subject to the same prohibitions on disclosure under paragraph (1).*

(4) *At the request of the authorized investigative agency, any person making or intending to make a disclosure under this section shall identify to the requesting official of the authorized investigative agency the person to whom such disclosure will be made or to whom such disclosure was made prior to the request, except that nothing in this section shall require a person to inform the requesting official of the identity of an attorney to whom disclosure was made or will be made to obtain legal advice or legal assistance with respect to the request under subsection (a) of this section.*

End Notes

[1] For purposes of this report, S. 1692 and the Leahy bill refer to the bill as reported out unless otherwise noted; citations to H.R. 1800, the Nadler bill; H.R. 3845, the Conyers bill; or S. 1686, the Feingold bill, refer to those bills as introduced.

[2] S. 1686, §101(c)(2).

[3] S. 1692, §2(c).

[4] H.R. 3845, §202.

[5] H.R. 1800, §5.

[6] This report is limited to a discussion of the NSL proposals in the three bills as introduced.

[7] 18 U.S.C. 2709(a), (b) (2000 ed.).

[8] 18 U.S.C. 2709(b)(1) (2000 ed.).

[9] 18 U.S.C. 2709(b)(2) (2000 ed.).

[10] 12 U.S.C. 3414(a)(5) (2000 ed,).

[11] 15 U.S.C. 1681u(a), (b) (2000 ed.).

[12] Id.

[13] 50 U.S.C. 436 (2000 ed.).

[14] Id.

[15] Id.

[16] Thus for example, section 626 of the Fair Credit Report Act, once stated in part that

> The Director or the Director's designee may make such a certification only if [he or she] has determined in writing that – (1) such information is necessary for the conduct of an authorized foreign counterintelligence investigation; and (2) there are specific and articulable facts giving reason to believe that the consumer – (A) is a foreign power . . . or a person who is not United States person . . and is an official of a foreign power; or (b)

is an agent of a foreign power and is engaging or has engaged in an act of international terrorism . . . or clandestine intelligence activities that involve or may involve a violation of criminal statutes of the United States, 15 U.S.C. 168 1u(a) (2000 ed.).

The USA PATRIOT Act redesignated section 626 as section 625 and the amended provision stated that

The Director or the Director's designee in a position not lower that Deputy Assistant Director at Bureau headquarters or Special Agent in Charge of a Bureau field office designated by the Director may make such a certification only if [he or she] has determined in writing that such information is sought for the conduct of an authorized investigation to protect against international terrorism or clandestine intelligence activities, provided that such as investigation of a United Stats person is not conducted solely upon the basis of activities protected by the first amendment to the Constitution of the Untied States, U.S.C. 1681u(a)(2000 ed. Supp.I).

[17] 15 U.S.C. 1681v(a)(2000 ed. Supp. I).

[18] Id.

[19] Sec. 224, P.L. 107-56, 115 Stat. 295 (2001).

[20] P.L. 109-177, 120 Stat. 192 (2006); P.L. 109-178, 120 Stat. 278 (2006), respectively.

[21] E.g., Anti-Terrorism Intelligence Tools Improvement Act of 2003: Hearing Before the Subcomm. on Crime, Terrorism, and Homeland Security, 108th Cong., 2d Sess. 7-8 (2004)(prepared statement of U.S. Ass't Att'y Gen. Daniel J. Bryant).

[22] *Doe v. Ashcroft,* 334 F. Supp.2d 471 (S.D.N.Y. 2004)(First and Fourth Amendment concerns); *Doe v. Gonzales,* 386 F.Supp.2d 66 (D. Conn. 2005)(First Amendment concerns).

[23] 28 U.S.C. 3511.

[24] 28 U.S.C. 3511(c), 18 U.S.C. 1510(e).

[25] 12 U.S.C. 3414((a)(3)(A); 15 U.S.C. 1681v(c)(1), 1681u(d)(1); 18 U.S.C. 2709(c)(1); 50 U.S.C. 436(B)(1).

[26] 28 U.S.C. 3511(b).

[27] P.L. 109-177, §118.

[28] P.L. 109-177, §119.

[29] U.S. Department of Justice, Office of the Inspector General, A Review of the Federal Bureau of Investigation's Use of National Security Letters(IG Report I) (March 2007); A Review of the FBI's Use of National Security Letters: Assessment of Corrective Actions and Examination of NSL Usage in 2006 (IG Report II) (March 2008), both available on Sept. 18, 2009 at http://www.usdoj.gov/oig/special/index.htm.

[30] *Id.* A "U.S. person" is generally understood to mean "a citizen of the United States, an alien lawfully admitted for permanent residence (as defined in section 1 101(a)(2) of title 8), an unincorporated association a substantial number of members of which are citizens of the United States or aliens lawfully admitted for permanent residence, or a corporation which is incorporated in the United States, but does not include a corporation or an association which is a foreign power, as defined in subsection(a)(1), (2), or (3) of this section," 50 U.S.C. 1801.

[31] IG Report I at 49.

[32] *IG Report II* at 65. The Foreign Intelligence Surveillance Act (FISA) authorizes the FBI to apply for court orders in national security cases authorizing electronic surveillance, physical searches, the installation and use of pen registers and trap and trace devices, and access to business records and other tangible property, 50 U.S.C. 1801-1862.

[33] Critics might suggest that these offenses are "possible" in the operation of any convenience store.

[34] IG Report I at 50.

[35] *Id.* at 51.

[36] *Id.* at 65.

[37] Id.

[38] *Smith v. Maryland*, 442 U.S. 735, 745 (1979)

[39] *Richards v. Wisconsin*, 520 U.S. 385, 391 (1997); *Wilson v. Arkansas*, 514 U.S. 927, 936 (1995).

[40] 18 U.S.C. 2702(c).

[41] 18 U.S.C. 2703(c)(2).

[42] 18 U.S.C. 2709(a).

[43] 18 U.S.C. 2707(a).

[44] IG Report I at 90.

[45] *E.g.*, 18 U.S.C. 2709(c)(1). The other NSL statutes have comparable provisions.

[46] Id.

[47] *E.g.*, 12 U.S.C. 3414(a)(5)(D)(iii). The other NSL statutes have comparable provisions.

[48] *E.g*,, 15 U.S.C. 168 1u(d)(4). The other NSL statutes have comparable provisions.

[49] 18 U.S.C. 351 1(b)(2). As explained below, the Second Circuit opinion requires that the provisions in italics here and at the end of the paragraph be understood in the context of First Amendment demands.

[50] 18 U.S.C. 3511(b)(3).

[51] 18 U.S.C. 3511(b)(2), (3).

[52] Id.

[53] 18 U.S.C. 3511(a).

[54] F.R.Crim.P. 17(c)(2).
[55] 2 Wright, Federal Practice and Procedure §275 (Crim. 3d ed. 2000).
[56] United States v. R. Enterprises, Inc., 498 U.S. 292, 301 (1991).
[57] 18 U.S.C. 3511(c).
[58] 18 U.S.C. 1510(e), 3571, 3559.
[59] *John Doe, Inc. v. Mukasey*, 549 F.3d 861, 883-84 (2d Cir. 2008).
[60] *Doe v. Holder*, ____ F. Supp. 2d ____ (S.D.N.Y. Aug. 5, 2009); see also *Doe v. Holder*, ____ F. Supp. 2d ____ (S.D.N.Y. Oct. 20, 2009).
[61] S. 1686, §101(c)(2). The relevant text of the NSL statutes, prior to the effective date of the USA PATRIOT Act and now, is appended.
[62] S. 1692, §2(c).
[63] H.R. 3845, §202.
[64] H.R. 1800, §5.
[65] P.L. 107-56, §505, 115 Stat. 365 (2001).
[66] P.L. 107-56, §358(g), 115 Stat. 327 (2001).
[67] 18 U.S.C. 2709((b), 12 U.S.C. 3414(a)(5)(A), 15 U.S.C. 1681u(a).
[68] 18 U.S.C. 2709((b)(2000 ed.), 12 U.S.C. 3414(a)(5)(A)(2000 ed.), 15 U.S.C. 1681u(a)(2000 ed.).
[69] National Security Letters: The Need for Greater Accountability and Oversight: Hearing Before the Senate Comm. on the Judiciary, 1 10th Cong., 2d sess. (2008)(testimony of Michael J. Woods, former Chief of the FBI's National Security Law Unit), available on Oct. 23, 2009 at [http://judiciary].
[70] P.L. 109-177, 120 Stat. 192 (2006), and P.L. 109-178, 120 Stat. 278 (2006), respectively.
[71] Depending upon one's perspective these provisions may be described as nondisclosure provisions, secrecy provisions, or gag order provisions. The descriptions are used interchangeably without any intended connotations in this report.
[72] 18 U.S.C. 2709((c), 12 U.S.C. 3414(a)(5)(D), 15 U.S.C. 1681u(d).
[73] 15 U.S.C. 168 1v(a). Such agencies would presumably include at a minimum those agencies who are members of the "intelligence community," see e.g., 50 U.S.C. 401a(4)("The term 'intelligence community' includes the following: (A) The Office of the Director of National Intelligence. (B) The Central Intelligence Agency. (C) The National Security Agency. (D) The Defense Intelligence Agency. (E) The National Geospatial-Intelligence Agency. (F) The National Reconnaissance Office. (G) Other offices within the Department of Defense for the collection of specialized national intelligence through reconnaissance programs. (H) The intelligence elements of the Army, the Navy, the Air Force, the Marine Corps, the Federal Bureau of Investigation, and the Department of Energy. (I) The Bureau of Intelligence and Research of the Department of State. (J) The Office of Intelligence and Analysis of the Department of the Treasury. (K) The elements of the Department of Homeland Security concerned with the analysis of intelligence information, including the Office of Intelligence of the Coast Guard. (L) Such other elements of any other department or agency as may be designated by the President, or designated jointly by the Director of National Intelligence and the head of the department or agency concerned, as an element of the intelligence community"). Admittedly, section 168 1v only identifies those who may invoke NSL authority, not necessarily those who have or will exercise that authority.
[74] *IG Report I*, at 80-1, 125; *IG Report II*, at 29-30.
[75] 50 U.S.C. 436(a)(3)(A).
[76] 12 U.S.C. 3414(a)(5)(D); 18 U.S.C. 2709(c); 15 U.S.C. 1681u(d); 15 U.S.C. 1681v(c); 50 U.S.C. 436(b).
[77] Id.
[78] Id.
[79] 18 U.S.C. 3511(b)(1), (2).
[80] 18 U.S.C. 3511(b)(1), (3).
[81] 549 F.3d 861, 883 (2d Cir. 2008).
[82] H.R. 3845, §207; proposed 18 U.S.C. 3511(b). S. 1686, §101; proposed 18 U.S.C. 2709(c); 12 U.S.C. 3414((b); 15 U.S.C. 1681u(b).
[83] H.R. 3845, §207, proposed 18 U.S.C. 3511(b).
[84] S. 1692, §5; proposed 18 U.S.C. 2709(c)(1)(B); 15 U.S.C. 1681u(d)(1)(B); 15 U.S.C. 1681v(c)(1)(B); 12 U.S.C. 3414(a)(5)(D)(i)(II); 50 U.S.C. 436(b)(1)(B). H.R. 3845, §207, proposed 18 U.S.C. 3511(b).
[85] H.R. 1800, §3(d)(5). Most of the amendments in H.R. 1800 and S. 1686 would not apply to 50 U.S.C. 436. S. 1686, §101; proposed 18 U. 18 U.S.C. 2709(c)(1)(B); 15 U.S.C. 1681u(b); 12 U.S.C. 3414(b). S. 1686 would repeal 15 U.S.C. 1681v.
[86] H.R. 1800, §3(d)(5). Most of the amendments in H.R. 1800 and S. 1686 would not apply to 50 U.S.C. 436. S. 1686, §101; proposed 18 U. 18 U.S.C. 2709(c)(1)(B); 15 U.S.C. 1681u(b); 12 U.S.C. 3414(b). S. 1686 would repeal 15 U.S.C. 1681v.
[87] H.R. 1800, §3(d).
[88] S. 1686, §§101, 102; proposed 18 U.S.C. 2709(c)(4); 15 U.S.C. 1681u(b); 12 U.S.C. 3414(b); 18 U.S.C. 3511(b). S. 1686 would repeal 15 U.S.C. 1681v, and most of the amendments in S. 1686 would not apply to 50 U.S.C.

436. S. 1692, §5; proposed 18 U.S.C. 2709(c)(4); 15 U.S.C. 1681u(d)(4); 15 U.S.C. 1681v(c)(4); 12 U.S.C. 3414(a)(5)(D)(iv); 50 U.S.C. 436(b)(4); 18 U.S.C. 3511(b).

[89] S. 1686, §101; proposed 18 U.S.C. 2709(c)(1); 15 U.S.C. 1681u(b); 12 U.S.C. 3414(b). S. 1686 would repeal 15 U.S.C. 1681v, and most of the amendments in S. 1686 would not apply to 50 U.S.C. 436. S. 1692, §5; proposed 18 U.S.C. 2709(c)(1); 15 U.S.C. 1681u(d)(1); 15 U.S.C. 1681v(c)(4); 12 U.S.C. 3414(a)(5)(D)(iv); 50 U.S.C. 436(b)(4); 18 U.S.C. 3511(b).

[90] S. 1686, §102; proposed 18 U.S.C. 351 1(b)(1). S. 1692, §6(b), proposed 18 U.S.C. 351 1(b)(1).

[91] S. 1692, §6(b); proposed 18 U.S.C. 351 1(b)(1). H.R. 3845, §207, proposed 18 U.S.C. 3511(b)(1).

[92] H.R. 1800, §3(d). H.R. 3845, §207, proposed 18 US.C. 351 1(b)(2). S. 1686, §102; proposed 18 U.S.C. 351 1(b)(2). S. 1692, §6(b); proposed 18 U.S.C. 3511(b)(2).

[93] S . 1686, §102; proposed 18 U.S.C. 3511(b)(2).

[94] S. 1686, §102; proposed 18 U.S.C. 351 1(b)(2). S. 1692, §6(b); proposed 18 U.S.C. 351 1(b)(2).

[95] H.R. 1800, §3(d). H.R. 3845, §207, proposed 18 U.S.C. 3511(b)(1). S. 1686, §102; proposed 18 U.S.C. 3511(b)(1).

[96] H.R. 1800, §3(d). H.R. 3845, §207, proposed 18 U.S.C. 3511(b)(4). S. 1686, §102; proposed 18 U.S.C. 3511(b)(4).

[97] S. 1692, §§5, 6(b); proposed 18 U.S.C. 351 1(b)(1) 18 U.S.C. 2709(c)(3); 12 U.S.C. 3414(a)(5)(D)(iii); 15 U.S.C. 1681u(d)(3); 15 U.S.C. 1681v(d)(3), 50 U.S.C. 436(b)(3). Each of the revised NSL statutes would require an agency to terminate a no longer necessary nondisclosure order upon a request for judicial review which seems to confirm that the Leahy bill contemplates recipient requests for judicial review after the passage of time. S. 1692, §5; proposed 18 U.S.C. 2709(c)(4); 12 U.S.C. 3414(a)(5)(D)(iv); 15 U.S.C. 1681u(d)(4); 15 U.S.C. 1681v(d)(4), 50 U.S.C. 436(b)(4).

[98] 18 U.S.C. 3511(a).

[99] Id.

[100] H.R. 1800, §3(e)(1).

[101] 18 U.S.C. 2709 (relevant to an investigation to protect against international terrorism or clandestine intelligence activities); 12 U.S.C. 3414(5)(A)(sought for foreign counterintelligence purposes); 15 U.S.C. 1681u (a)(sought for an investigation to protect against international terrorism or clandestine intelligence activities); 15 U.S.C. 168 1v(a) (necessary for an agency's investigation, activity, or analysis relating to international terrorism); 50 U.S.C. 436(sought for an inquiry or investigation relating to agency employees with access to classified information).

[102] H.R. 1800, §3(a). H.R. 3845, §204.

[103] S. 1686, §101; proposed 18 U.S.C. 2709(b)(1); 12 U.S.C. 3414(b); 1681u(b). S. 1686 would repeal 15 U.S.C. 1681v, and most of the amendments in S. 1686 would not apply to 50 U.S.C. 436.

[104] S. 1692, §7; proposed 18 U.S.C. 2709(b)(1); 15 U.S.C. 1681u(b); 15 U.S.C. 1681v(a); 12 U.S.C. 3414(a)(5)(A); 50 U.S.C. 436(a)(3).

[105] H.R. 1800, §3(c). S. 1686, §101; proposed 18 U.S.C. 2709(b)(3); 12 U.S.C. 3414(b); 15 U.S.C. 1681u(b). S. 1686 would repeal 15 U.S.C. 1681v, and most of the amendments in S. 1686 would not apply to 50 U.S.C. 436.

[106] 50 U.S.C. 1801(h)("'Minimization procedures', with respect to electronic surveillance, means – (1) specific procedures, which shall be adopted by the Attorney General, that are reasonably designed in light of the purpose and technique of the particular surveillance, to minimize the acquisition and retention, and prohibit the dissemination, of nonpublicly available information concerning unconsenting United States persons consistent with the need of the United States to obtain, produce, and disseminate foreign intelligence information; (2) procedures that require that nonpublicly available information, which is not foreign intelligence information, as defined in subsection (e)(1) of this section, shall not be disseminated in a manner that identifies any United States person, without such person's consent, unless such person's identity is necessary to understand foreign intelligence information or assess its importance; (3) notwithstanding paragraphs (1) and (2), procedures that allow for the retention and dissemination of information that is evidence of a crime which has been, is being, or is about to be committed and that is to be retained or disseminated for law enforcement purposes; and (4) notwithstanding paragraphs (1), (2), and (3), with respect to any electronic surveillance approved pursuant to section 1802(a) of this title, procedures that require that no contents of any communication to which a United States person is a party shall be disclosed, disseminated, or used for any purpose or retained for longer than 72 hours unless a court order under section 1805 of this title is obtained or unless the Attorney General determines that the information indicates a threat of death or serious bodily harm to any person").

[107] P.L. 109-177, 120 Stat. 220 (2006).

[108] *IG Report II*, at 64; see also *id.* at 68 n.41 ("In general, information related to intelligence investigations is retained in the FBI's files (either in the paper case file or in the FBI's electronic systems) for 30 years after a case is closed, and information related to criminal investigations is retained for 20 years after a case is closed. After that time, the case information is reviewed, and information that is identified for permanent retention is transferred to the National Archives and Records Administration (NARA) for storage. Any cases not meeting the criteria for permanent retention and transfer to the NARA are destroyed"); *IG Report I*, at 110 ("neither the

Attorney General's NSI Guidelines nor internal FBI policies require the purging of information derived from NSLs in FBI databases, regardless of the outcome of the investigation. Thus, once information is obtained in response to a national security letter, it is indefinitely retained and retrievable by the many authorized personnel who have access to various FBI databases").

[109] IG Report II, at 64.

[110] Reauthorizing the USA PATRIOT Act: Ensuring Liberty and Security: Hearing Before the Senate Comm. on the Judiciary, 11 1th Cong., 1st sess. (2009)(statement of Inspector General Glenn A. Fine).

[111] S. 1686, §101; proposed 18 U.S.C. 2709(d); 12 U.S.C. 3414(b); 15 U.S.C. 1681u(b). S. 1692, §12.

[112] S. 1686, §101; proposed 18 U.S.C. 2709(d); 12 U.S.C. 3414(b); 15 U.S.C. 1681u(b).

[113] H.R. 1800, §6. H.R. 3845, §208.

[114] Id.

[115] H.R. 1800, §3(f). S. 1686, §101; proposed 18 U.S.C. 2709(f); 12 U.S.C. 3414(b); 15 U.S.C. 1681u(b). S. 1686 would repeal 15 U.S.C. 1681v, and most of the amendments in S. 1686 would not apply to 50 U.S.C. 436.

[116] H.R. 3845, §206.

[117] S. 1686, §106.

[118] *The Attorney General's Guidelines for Domestic FBI Operations*, at 12-3 (Sept. 29, 2008), available on Oct. 26, 2009 at http://www.justice.gov/ag/readingroom/guidelines

[119] S. 1686, §106.

[120] *IG Report I*, 92-8, 115-18.

[121] *Id.* at 94-5.

[122] 18 U.S.C. 2702(b)(8), (c)(4).

[123] H.R. 1800, §7. S. 1686, §105.

[124] S. 1686, §105(b).

[125] 18 U.S.C. 2709(e); 15 U.S.C. 1681u(h); 15 U.S.C. 1681v(f).

[126] P.L. 109-177, §118, 120 Stat. 217 (2006), 18 U.S.C. 3511 note.

[127] P.L. 109-177, §119, 120 Stat. 219 (2006).

[128] H.R. 1800, §6(c). S. 1686, §104. S. 1692, §8.

[129] S. 1692, §10. H.R. 3845, §105(b).

In: National Security Letters: Background and Issues. Volume 1 ISBN: 978-1-61668-941-4
Editor: Carolyn D. Hines

Chapter 3

A REVIEW OF THE FEDERAL BUREAU OF INVESTIGATION'S USE OF NATIONAL SECURITY LETTERS*

United States Department of Justice

LIST OF ACRONYMS

ACS	Automated Case Support
ASAC	Assistant Special Agent in Charge
ATAC	Anti-Terrorism Advisory Council
CAU	Communications Analysis Unit
CDC	Chief Division Counsel
CXS	Communications Exploitations Section
CY	Calendar Year
DIDO	Designated Intelligence Disclosure Official
EAD	Executive Assistant Director
EC	Electronic Communication
ECPA	Electronic Communications Privacy Act
EOPS	Electronic Surveillance Operations and Sharing Unit
FBI	Federal Bureau of Investigation
FCRA	Fair Credit Reporting Act
FIG	Field Intelligence Group
FISA	Foreign Intelligence Surveillance Act of 1978
IDW	Investigative Data Warehouse
IIR	Intelligence Information Report
IOB	Intelligence Oversight Board
ITOS	International Terrorism Operations Section

* This is an edited, reformatted and augmented edition of a United States Department of Justice publication, dated March 2007.

JI 1F	Joint Terrorism Task Force
NFIP	National Foreign Intelligence Program
NSI	National Security Investigation
NSL	National Security Letter
NSLB	National Security Law Branch
OGC	Office of the General Counsel
OIG	Office of the Inspector General
OIPR	Office of Intelligence Policy and Review
OLC	Office of Legal Counsel
RFPA	Right to Financial Privacy Act
SAC	Special Agent in Charge
SSA	Supervisory Special Agent
1140S	Terrorist Financing Operations Section
USAO	United States Attorneys' Offices

Executive Summary

In the USA PATRIOT Improvement and Reauthorization Act of 2005 (Patriot Reauthorization Act), Congress directed the Department of Justice (Department) Office of the Inspector General (OIG) to review "the effectiveness and use, including any improper or illegal use, of national security letters issued by the Department of Justice." See Pub. L. No. 109-177, § 119. Four federal statutes contain five specific provisions authorizing the Federal Bureau of Investigation (FBI) to issue national security letters (NSLs) to obtain information from third parties, such as telephone companies, financial institutions, Internet service providers, and consumer credit agencies. In these letters, the FBI can direct third parties to provide customer account information and transactional records, such as telephone toll billing records.

Congress directed the OIG to review the use of NSLs for two time periods - calendar years (CY) 2003 through 2004 and CY 2005 through 2006. The first report is due to Congress on March 9, 2007; the second is due on December 31, 2007.[1] Although we were only required to review calendar years 2003 and 2004 in the first review, we elected to include data from calendar year 2005 as well.

In the Patriot Reauthorization Act, Congress directed the OIG's review to include:

(1) an examination of the use of national security letters by the Department of Justice during calendar years 2003 through 2006;

(2) a description of any noteworthy facts or circumstances relating to such use, including any improper or illegal use of such authority; and

(3) an examination of the effectiveness of national security letters as an investigative tool, including -

(A) the importance of the information acquired by the Department of Justice to the intelligence activities of the Department of Justice or to any other department or agency of the Federal Government;

(B) the manner in which such information is collected, retained, analyzed, and disseminated by the Department of Justice, including any direct access to such information (such as access to "raw data") provided to any other department, agency, or instrumentality of Federal, State, local, or tribal governments or any private sector entity;

(C) whether, and how often, the Department of Justice utilized such information to produce an analytical intelligence product for distribution within the Department of Justice, to the intelligence community . . ., or to other Federal, State, local, or tribal government departments, agencies or instrumentalities;

(D) whether, and how often, the Department of Justice provided such information to law enforcement authorities for use in criminal proceedings . . . .[2]

In this report, we address each of these issues. To examine these issues, the OIG conducted interviews of over 100 FBI employees, including personnel at FBI Headquarters and at the Department. OIG teams also traveled to FBI field offices in New York, Chicago, Philadelphia, and San Francisco where we interviewed over 50 FBI employees. In the field offices, the OIG teams examined a judgmental sample of 77 counterterrorism and counterintelligence investigative cases files and 293 NSL,s issued by those field offices to determine if the NSLs complied with relevant statutes, Attorney General Guidelines, and internal FBI policy.

The OIG also analyzed the FBI's NSL tracking database maintained by the FBI's Office of the General Counsel (FBI-OGC), which is the only database that compiles infot information on NSL usage for the entire FBI. The OGC database is used by the FBI to collect information that the Department is required to report to Congress in semiannual classified reports and, since passage of the Patriot Reauthorization Act, in an annual public report. We performed various tests on the OGC database to assess the accuracy and reliability of the FBI's reports.

This Executive Summary summarizes our full 126-page report of investigation on NSLs, including its main findings, conclusions, and recommendations.

The Appendix to the report contains comments on the report by the Attorney General, the Director of National Intelligence, and the FBI. The Appendix also contains copies of the national security letter statutes in effect prior to the Patriot Reauthorization Act. The classified report also contains a classified appendix.

I. Background on National Security Letters

The Patriot Act significantly expanded the FBI's preexisting authority to obtain information through national security letters.[3] Section 505 of the Patriot Act broadened the FBI's authority by eliminating the requirement that the information sought in an NSL must pertain to a foreign power or an agent of a foreign power. This section of the Patriot Act statute substituted the lower threshold that the information sought must be relevant to an investigation to protect against international terrorism or espionage, provided that the investigation of a United States person is not conducted "solely on the basis of activities protected by the first amendment of the Constitution of the United States." As a consequence of this lower threshold, NSLs may request information about persons other than the subjects of FBI national security investigations so long as the requested information is relevant to an authorized investigation.

Section 505 of the Patriot Act also permits Special Agents in Charge of the FBI's 56 field offices to sign NSLs, a change that significantly expanded approval authority beyond the pre-Patriot Act group of senior FBI Headquarters officials authorized to sign NSLs.

In addition, the Patriot Act added a new authority permitting the FBI to use NSLs to obtain consumer full credit reports in international terrorism investigations pursuant to an amendment to the Fair Credit Reporting Act (FCRA).[4]

NSLs may be issued by the FBI in the course of national security investigations, which are governed by Attorney General Guidelines.[5] The Attorney General's Guidelines for FBI National Security Investigations and Foreign Intelligence Collection (NSI Guidelines) authorize the FBI to conduct investigations concerning threats or potential threats to the national security, including threats arising from international terrorism, espionage, other intelligence activities, and foreign computer intrusions. The NSI Guidelines authorize three levels of investigative activity - threat assessments, preliminary investigations, and full investigations. NSLs are among the investigative techniques that are permitted to be used during national security investigations.

A. The Four National Security Letter Statutes

There are four statutes authorizing the FBI to issue five types of NSLs. We discuss each of these statutes below:

1. The Right to Financial Privacy Act

The Right to Financial Privacy Act (RFPA) was enacted in 1978 "to protect the customers of financial institutions from unwarranted intrusion into their records while at the same time permitting legitimate law enforcement activity."[6] The RFPA requires federal government agencies to provide individuals with advance notice of requested disclosures of personal financial information and affords individuals an opportunity to challenge the request before disclosure is made to law enforcement authorities.[7]

The RFPA NSL statute, enacted in 1986, created an exception to the advance notice requirement that permitted the FBI to obtain financial institution records in foreign counterintelligence cases. Since the Patriot Act, the FBI may obtain financial records upon certification that the information is sought.

> for foreign counterintelligence purposes to protect against international terrorism or clandestine intelligence activities, provided that such an investigation of a United States person is not conducted solely on the basis of activities protected by the first amendment to the Constitution of the United States.[8]

The types of financial information the FBI can obtain through RFPA national security letters include information concerning open and closed checking and savings accounts and safe deposit box records from banks, credit unions, thrift institutions, investment banks or investment companies, as well as transactions with issuers of travelers checks, operators of credit card systems, pawnbrokers, loan or finance companies, travel agencies, real estate companies, casinos, and other entities.

2. The Electronic Communications Privacy Act

The Electronic Communications Privacy Act (ECPA), enacted in 1986, extends statutory protection to electronic and wire communications stored by third parties, such as telephone companies and Internet service providers.[9]

The ECPA NSL statute allows the FBI to obtain "subscriber information and toll billing records information, or electronic communication transactional records" from a "wire or electronic communications service provider" in conjunction with a foreign counterintelligence investigation upon certification that the information sought is

> relevant to an authorized investigation to protect against international terrorism or clandestine intelligence activities provided that such an investigation of a United States person is not conducted solely on the basis on activities protected by the first amendment to the Constitution of the United States.[10]

The types of telephone and e-mail transactional information the FBI can obtain through ECPA national security letters include:

- Historical information on telephone calls made and received from a specified number, including land lines, cellular phones, prepaid phone card calls, toll free calls, alternate billed number calls (calls billed to third parties), and local and long distance billing records associated with the phone numbers (known as toll records);
- Electronic communication transactional records (e-mails), including e-mail addresses associated with the account; screen names; and billing records and method of payment; and
- Subscriber information associated with particular telephone numbers or e-mail addresses, such as the name, address, length of service, and method of payment.[11]

3. The Fair Credit Reporting Act

The Fair Credit Reporting Act (FCRA) was enacted in 1970 to protect personal information collected by credit reporting agencies.[12] As amended by the Patriot Act, the FCRA authorizes two types of national security letters, FCRAu and FCRAv NSLs. The initial FCRA NSL statute, enacted in 1996, authorizes the FBI and certain other government agencies to issue NSLs to obtain a limited amount of information about an individual's credit history: the names and addresses of all financial institutions at which a consumer maintains or has maintained an account; and consumer identifying information limited to name, current address, fonner addresses, places of employment, or former places of employment pursuant to FCRAu NSLs.[13] Since the Patriot Act, the certifying official must certify that the information requested is

> sought for the conduct of an authorized investigation to protect against international terrorism or clandestine intelligence activities, provided that such an investigation of a United States person is not conducted solely upon the basis of activities protected by the first amendment to the Constitution of the United States.[14]

In 2001, the Patriot Act amended the FCRA to add a new national security letter authority, referred to as FCRAv NSLs, which authorizes the FBI to obtain a consumer reporting agency's credit reports and "all other" consumer information in its files.[15] Thus, since the Patriot Act, the FBI can now obtain full credit reports on individuals during national security investigations. The certifying official must certify that the information is "necessary for" the FBI's "investigations of, or intelligence or counterintelligence activities or analysis related to, international terrorism . . . ."[16]

4. The National Security Act

In the wake of the espionage investigation of former Central Intelligence Agency employee Aldrich Ames, Congress enacted an additional NSL authority in 1994 by amending the National Security Act of 1947. The National Security Act NSL statute authorizes the FBI to issue NSLs in connection with investigations of improper disclosure of classified information by government employees.[17] The statute permits the FBI to make requests to financial agencies and other financial institutions and consumer reporting agencies "in order to conduct any authorized law enforcement investigation, counterintelligence inquiry, or security determination."[18]

National Security Act NSLs are rarely used by the FBI.

B. The FBI's Collection and Retention of Information Obtained from National Security Letters

To obtain approval for national security letters, FBI case agents must prepare: (1) an electronic communication (EC) seeking approval to issue the letter (approval EC), and (2) the national security letter itself. The approval EC explains the justification for opening or maintaining the investigation and why the information requested by the NSL is relevant to that investigation.

For field division-initiated NSLs, the Supervisory Special Agent of the case agent's squad, the Chief Division Counsel (CDC), and the Assistant Special Agent in Charge are responsible for reviewing the approval EC and the NSL prior to approval by the Special Agent in Charge. Division Counsel are required to review the NSLs to ensure their legal sufficiency - specifically, the relevance of the information requested to an authorized national security investigation.

The final step in the approval process occurs when the Special Agent in Charge or authorized FBI Headquarters official (the certifying official) certifies that the requested records are relevant to an authorized investigation to protect against international terrorism or clandestine intelligence activities and, with respect to investigations of "U.S. persons," that the investigation is not conducted solely on the basis of activities protected by the First Amendment. After making the required certifications, the official initials the approval EC and signs the national security letter.

During the time period covered by this review, the FBI had no policy or directive requiring the retention of signed copies of national security letters or any requirement to upload national security letters into the FBI's case management system, the Automated Case Support (ACS) system. We also found that the FBI has no uniform system for tracking responses to national security letters, either manually or electronically. Instead, individual case agents are responsible for following up with NSL recipients to ensure timely and complete responses, ensuring that the documents or electronic media provided to the FBI match the requests, analyzing the responses, and providing the documents or other materials to FBI intelligence or financial analysts who also analyze the information.

In some field offices, case agents are required to formally document their receipt of information from NSLs, including the date the information was received; the NSL subject's name, address, and Social Security number; and a summary of the information obtained. This document then is electronically uploaded into ACS. Once the data is available electronically, other case agents throughout the FBI can query ACS to identify information that may pertain to their investigations.

The FBI also evaluates the relationship between NSL-derived information and data derived from other investigative tools that are available in various databases. For example, when communication providers furnish telephone toll billing records and subscriber information on an investigative subject in response to an NSL, the data is uploaded into Telephone Applications, a specialized FBI database that can be used to analyze the calling patterns of a subject's telephone number. The FBI also places NSL-derived information into its Investigative Data Warehouse (IDW), a database that enables users to access, among other data, biographical information, photographs, financial data, and physical location information for thousands of known and suspected terrorists. IDW can be accessed by nearly 12,000 users, including FBI agents and analysts and members of Joint Terrorism Task Forces. Information derived from responses to national security letters that is uploaded into ACS and into Telephone Applications is periodically uploaded to IDW.

II. National Security Letters Issued by the FBI from 2003 through 2005

In this section of the Executive Summary, we first discuss several problems with the FBI's Office of General Counsel National Security Letter database (OGC database) that affect the accuracy of the information in this database. We then present data on the FBI's use of national security letters from 2003 through 2005 based on data derived from the OGC database, the Department's semiannual classified reports to Congress on NSL usage, and our field work.

A. Inaccuracies in the FBI's National Security Letter Tracking Database

During the period covered by our review, the Department was required to file semiannual classified reports to Congress describing the total number of NSL requests issued pursuant to three of the five NSL authorities.[19] In these reports, the Department provided the number of requests for records and the number of investigations of different persons or organizations that generated NSL requests. These numbers were each broken down into separate categories for investigations of "U.S. persons or organizations" and "non-U.S. persons or organizations."

Total Number of NSL Requests. According to FBI data, the FBI issued approximately 8,500 NSL requests in CY 2000, the year prior to passage of the Patriot Act. After the Patriot Act, according to FBI data, the number of NSL requests increased to approximately 39,000 in 2003, approximately 56,000 in 2004, and approximately 47,000 in 2005.

However, we determined that these numbers were inaccurate because of three flaws in the manner in which the FBI records, forwards, and accounts for information about its use of NSLs.

First, we found incomplete or inaccurate information in the OGC database on the number of NSLs issued.[20] We compared the number of NSLs contained in the 77 case files we reviewed during our field work to those recorded in the OGC database and found approximately 17 percent more NSLs in the case files we examined than were recorded in the OGC database.

We also identified the total number of "requests" contained in the NSLs (such as requests in a single NSL for multiple telephone numbers or bank accounts) and compared that to the number of NSL requests recorded in the OGC database for those same national security letters. Overall, we found 22 percent more NSL requests in the case files we examined than were recorded in the OGC database.

Second, we found that the FBI did not consistently enter the NSL approval ECs into ACS in a timely manner. As a result, this information was not in the OGC database when data was extracted for the semiannual classified reports to Congress, and the reports were therefore inaccurate. Although this data subsequently was entered in the OGC database, it was not included in later congressional reports because each report only includes data on NSL requests made in a specific 6-month period.

We determined that from 2003 through 2005 almost 4,600 NSL requests were not reported to Congress as a result of these delays in entering this information into the OGC database. In March 2006, the FBI acknowledged to the Attorney General and Congress that NSL data in the semiannual classified reports may not have been accurate and stated that the data entry delays affected an unspecified number of NSL requests.[21] After the FBI became aware of these delays, it took steps to reduce the impact of the delays to negligible levels for the second half of CY 2005.

Third, when we examined the OGC database, we found incorrect data entries. We discovered a total of 212 incorrect data entries, including blank data fields, typographical errors, and a programming feature that provides a default value of "0" for the number of "NSL requests." Taken together, these factors caused 477 NSL requests to be erroneously excluded from the Department's semiannual classified reports to Congress.

As a result of the delays in uploading NSL data and the flaws in the OGC database, the total numbers of NSL requests that were reported to Congress semiannually in CYs 2003, 2004, and 2005 were significantly understated. We were unable to fully determine the extent of the inaccuracies because an unknown amount of data relevant to the period covered by our review was lost from the OGC database when it malfunctioned. However, by comparing the data reflected in these reports to data in the OGC database for 2003 through 2005, we estimated that approximately 8,850 NSL requests, or 6 percent of NSL requests issued by the FBI during this period, were missing from the database.

Total Number of Investigations of Different U.S. Persons and Non-U.S. Persons. We found other inaccuracies in the OGC database that affect the accuracy of the total number of "investigations of different U.S. persons" or "investigations of different non-U.S. persons" that the Department reported to Congress. These included inaccuracies in the NSL approval ECs from which personnel in FBI-OGC's National Security Law Branch (NSLB) extract U.S. person/non-U.S. person data, as well as incorrect data entries in the OGC database.

Incomplete or inaccurate entries resulted from several factors, including the inability of the OGC database to filter NSL requests for the same person in the same investigation (for example, "John T. Doe" and "J.T. Doe"); failure to account for NSL requests from different FBI divisions seeking information on the same person; and a default setting of "non-U.S. person" for the investigative subject for NSL requests seeking financial records and telephone toll billing/electronic communication transactional records. These errors resulted in the misidentification and understatement of the number of investigations of different U.S. persons that used NSLs.

The problems with the OGC database, including the loss of data because of a computer malfunction, also prevented us from determining with complete accuracy the number of investigations of different U.S. persons and different non-U.S. persons during which the FBI issued NSLs seeking financial records and for telephone toll billing/electronic communication transactional records.

Although we found that the data in the OGC database is not fully accurate or complete and, overall, significantly understates the number of FBI NSL requests, it is the only database that compiles informaation on the FBI's use of NSLs. Moreover, the data indicates the general levels and trends in the FBI's use of this investigative tool. We therefore relied in part on information compiled in the OGC database to respond to questions Congress directed us to answer regarding the FBI's use of NSLs.

B. National Security Letter Requests from 2003 through 2005

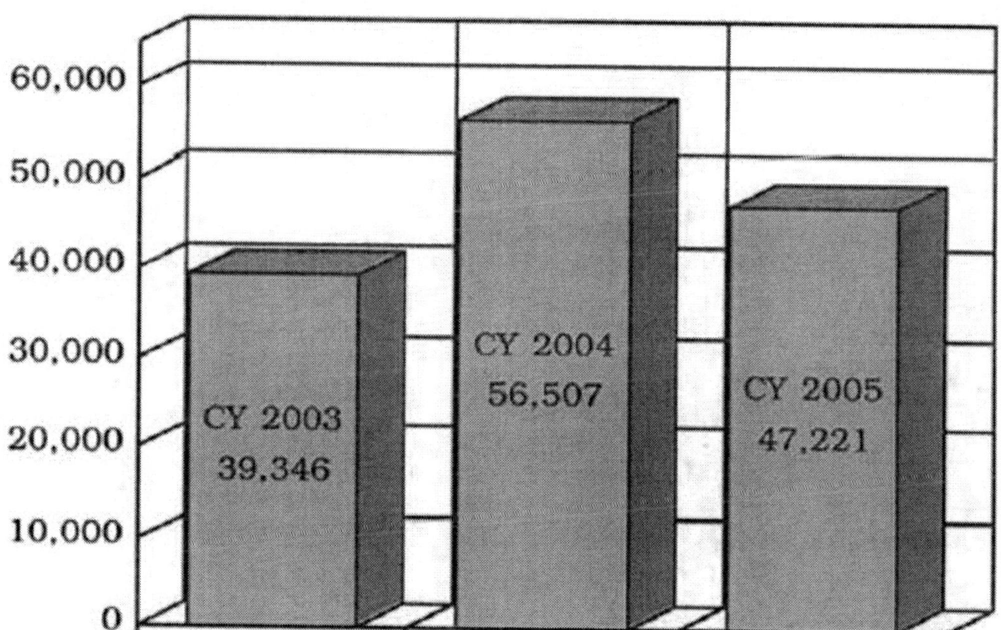

Sources: DOJ semiannual classified NSL reports to Congress and FBIOGC NSL database as of May 2006

Chart 4.1. NSL Requests (2003 through 2005)

1. The Total Number of NSL Requests

From 2003 through 2005, the FBI issued a total of 143,074 NSL requests. These included all requests issued for telephone toll billing records information, subscriber information (telephone or e-mail), or electronic communication transactional records under the ECPA NSL statute; records from financial institutions such as banks, credit card companies, and finance companies under the RFPA authority; requests seeking either financial institution or consumer identifying information (FCRAu) or consumer full credit reports (FCRAv); and requests pursuant to the National Security Act NSL authority.[22] The overwhelming majority of the NSL requests sought telephone toll billing records information, subscriber information (telephone or e-mail), or electronic communication transactional records under the ECPA NSL statute.

Chart 4.1 illustrates the total number of NSL requests issued in calendar years 2003 through 2005.

The number of NSL requests we identified significantly exceeds the number reported in the Department's first public annual report on NSL usage, issued in April 2006, because the Department was not required to include all NSL requests in that report. The Department's public report stated that in CY 2005 the FBI issued 9,254 NSL requests for information relating to U.S. persons, of which there were 3,501 NSLs relating to different U.S. persons. However, this does not include NSL requests under the ECPA NSL authority for telephone and e-mail subscriber information and NSL requests related to "non-U.S. persons," which were reported to Congress in the semiannual classified reports to Congress, or NSL requests not required to be reported to Congress under FCRAv for consumer full credit reports.

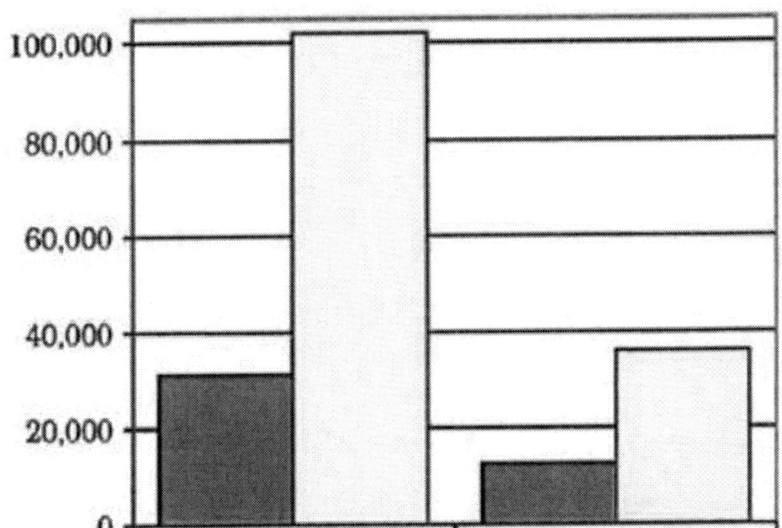

	Counterterrorism	Counterintelligence
NSLs	31,246	12,754
NSL Requests	101,885	35,948

Source: FBI-OGC Database

Chart 1.1. Relationship Between NSLs and NSL Requests (2003 through 2005)

It is also important to note the total number of national security letter *requests* is different from the number of national security *letters,* because one "letter" may include more than one request. That is, during an investigation several national security letters may be issued, and each letter may contain several requests. For example, one letter to a telephone company may request information on seven telephone numbers. As a result, the numbers normally presented in the FBI's classified reports to Congress and in its public report are the number of requests made, not the number of letters issued. In this report, we follow that same approach. However, Chart 1.1 shows the relationship we found between the number of NSLs and NSL requests from 2003 through 2005 in counterterrorism and counterintelligence cases.[23]

2. Types of NSL Requests

As illustrated on Chart 4.2 below, during the 3 years of our review the balance of NSL requests related to investigations of U.S. persons versus non-U.S. persons shifted. The percentage of NSL requests generated from investigations of U.S. persons increased from about 39 percent of all NSL requests in CY 2003 to about 53 percent of all NSL requests in CY 2005.[24]

Our analysis of the FBI's use of NSL authorities during the 3 years also revealed that:

- Approximately 73 percent of the total number of NSL requests issued from 2003 through 2005 were issued in counterterrorism investigations, approximately 26 percent were issued in counterintelligence investigations, and less than 1 percent were issued in foreign computer intrusion cyber investigations;
- Of the 293 NSLs we examined in four field offices, 43.7 percent of the NSLs were issued during preliminary investigations and 56.3 percent were issued during full investigations.

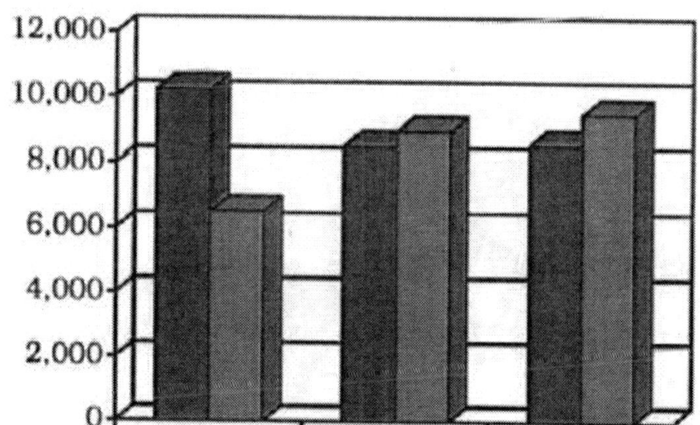

	2003	2004	2005
Non-U.S. Person	10,232	8,494	8,536
U.S. Person	6,519	8,943	9,475

Source: DOJ semiannual classified NSL reports to Congress

Chart 4.2. NSL Requests Reported to Congress Relating to U.S. Persons and non-U.S. Persons (2003 through 2005)

III. The Effectiveness of National Security Letters as an Investigative Tool

The Patriot Reauthorization Act also directed the OIG to review the use and effectiveness of national security letters, including the importance of the information acquired and the manner in which information from national security letters is analyzed and disseminated within the Department, to other members of the intelligence community, and to other entities.

A. The Importance of the Information Acquired from National Security Letters to the Department's Intelligence Activities

FBI Headquarters and field personnel told us that they found national security letters to be effective in both counterterrorism and counterintelligence investigations. Many FBI personnel used terms to describe NSLs such as "indispensable" or "our bread and butter."

FBI personnel reported that the principal objectives for using NSLs are to:

- establish evidence to support Foreign Intelligence Surveillance Act (FISA) applications to the Foreign Intelligence Surveillance Court for electronic surveillance, physical searches, or pen register/trap and trace orders;
- assess communication or financial links between investigative subjects and others;
- collect information sufficient to fully develop national security investigations;
- generate leads for other field divisions, members of Joint Terrorism Task Forces, other federal agencies, or to pass to foreign governments;
- develop analytical products for distribution within the FBI, other Department components, other federal agencies, and the intelligence community;
- develop information that is provided to law enforcement authorities for use in criminal proceedings;
- collect information sufficient to eliminate concerns about investigative subjects and thereby close national security investigations; and
- corroborate information derived from other investigative techniques.

Diagram 5.1 illustrates the key uses of national security letters.

1. Telephone toll billing records and subscriber information, and electronic communication transactional records

FBI agents and officials told us that telephone toll billing records and subscriber information and electronic communication transactional records obtained pursuant to ECPA NSLs enable FBI case agents to connect investigative subjects with particular telephone numbers or e-mail addresses and connect terrorism subjects and terrorism groups with each other. Analysis of subscriber information for telephone numbers and e-mail addresses also can assist in the identification of the investigative subject's family members, associates, living arrangements, and contacts. If the subject's associates are identified, case agents can generate new leads for their squad or another FBI field division, the results of which may complement the information obtained from the original NSL.

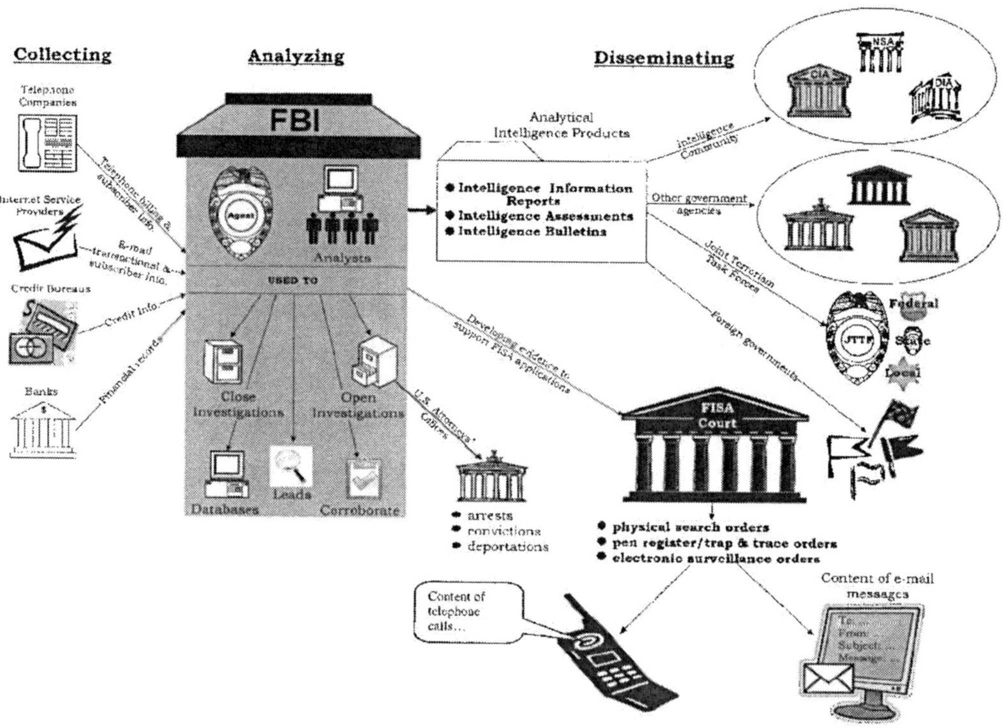

Diagram 5.1. How the FBI Uses National Security Letters

The FBI also informed us that the most important use of ECPA national security letters is to support FISA applications for electronic surveillance, physical searches, or pen register/trap and trace orders. FISA court orders for electronic surveillance may authorize the FBI to collect the content of telephone calls and Internet e-mail messages, information the FBI cannot obtain using NSLs.

2. Financial records

In addition, the FBI noted that NSLs are important tools for obtaining financial records related to suspected terrorists and terrorist organizations. The FBI's ability to track the movement of funds through financial institutions is essential to identify and locate individuals who provide financial support to terrorist operations. For example, transactional data obtained from banks and other financial institutions in response to RFPA national security letters can reveal the manner in which suspected terrorists conduct their operations, whether they are obtaining money from suspicious sources, and identify their spending patterns. Analysis of this data also can reveal the identity of the financial institutions used by the subject; the financial position of the subject; the existence of overseas wire transfers by or to the subject ("pass through" activity); loan transactions; evidence of money laundering; the subject's involvement in unconventional monetary transactions, including accounts that have more money in them than can be explained by ordinary income or the subject's employment; the subject's financial network; and payments to and from specific individuals.

In addition, NSLs issued pursuant to FCRA allow the FBI to obtain information from financial institutions from which an individual has sought or obtained credit and consumer identifying information limited to the subject's name, address and former addresses, places of employment, and former places of employment. The Patriot Act amendment to the FCRA authorizes the FBI to obtain consumer full credit reports, including records of individual accounts, credit card transactions, and bank account activity. Information secured from both types of FCRA NSLs provide information that often is not available from other types of financial records. For example, consumer credit records provide confirming information about a subject (including name, aliases, and Social Security number); the subject's employment or other sources of income; and the subject's possible involvement in illegal activity, such as bank fraud or credit card fraud.

B. Analysis of Information Obtained from National Security Letters

The FBI performs various analyses and develops different types of analytical intelligence products using information obtained from national security letters. In counterterrorism investigations, once the case agent confirms that the response to the NSL matches the request, the most important function of the initial analysis is to determine if the records link the investigative subjects or other individuals whose records are sought to suspected terrorists or terrorist groups. In counterintelligence investigations, the case agent's initial analysis focuses on the subject's network and, in technology export cases, the subject's access to prohibited technologies.

Following the case agent's initial analysis, agents and analysts assigned to the FBI's Field Intelligence Groups (FIGs) and analysts with special expertise in the Headquarters Counterterrorism, Counterintelligence, and Cyber Divisions generate detailed analyses of intelligence information, some of which is derived from NSLs. One of the principal analytical intelligence products generated by FIG analysts are "link analyses" that typically illustrate the telephone numbers, Internet e-mail addresses, businesses, credit card transactions, addresses, places of employment, banks, and other data derived from the NSLs, other investigative tools, and open sources.

Information derived from NSLs also may be used in the development of a variety of written products that are shared with FBI personnel, distributed more broadly within the Department, shared with Joint Terrorism Task Forces, or disseminated to other members of the intelligence community. Among the intelligence products that use information obtained from NSLs are Intelligence Information Reports, which contain raw intelligence obtained from NSLs such as telephone numbers and Internet email accounts; Intelligence Assessments, which are finished intelligence products that provide information on emerging developments and trends; and Intelligence Bulletins, which are finished intelligence products that contain general information on a topic rather than case-specific intelligence.

C. The FBI's Dissemination of Information Obtained from National Security Letters to Other Entities

Attorney General Guidelines and various information-sharing agreements require the FBI to share information with other federal agencies and the intelligence community. In addition, four of the five national security letter authorities expressly permit dissemination of infoi derived from NSLs to other federal agencies if the information is relevant to the authorized responsibility of those agencies and is disseminated pursuant to applicable Attorney General Guidelines.[25]

Pursuant to these statutes and directives, the FBI disseminated information derived from national security letters to other members of the intelligence community and to a variety of federal, state, and local law enforcement agencies during the period covered by our review. However, we could not determine the number of analytical intelligence products containing NSL-derived data that were disseminated from 2003 through 2005 because these products do not reference NSLs as the source of the information. Although none of the FBI or other Department officials we interviewed could estimate how often NSL-derived information was disseminated to other entities, they noted that when analytical intelligence products provided analyses of telephone or Internet communications or financial or consumer credit transactions, the products likely were derived in part from NSLs.

The principal entities outside the Department to whom information derived from NSLs are disseminated are members of the intelligence community and Joint Terrorism Task Forces (JTTFs). JTTFs across the country, composed of representatives of federal, state, and local law enforcement agencies, respond to, investigate, and share intelligence related to terrorist threats. Some designated task force members who obtain the necessary clearances to obtain access to FBI information, are authorized to access information stored in FBI databases such as ACS, Telephone Applications, and IDW which, as noted above, contain information derived from NSLs.

D. Information from National Security Letters Provided to Law Enforcement Authorities for Use in Criminal Proceedings

1. Routine Information Sharing with United States Attorneys' Offices

Following the September 11 terrorist attacks, the Department established several initiatives that required the FBI to share information from its counterterrorism files with prosecutors in United States Attorneys' Offices (USAOs) in order to determine if criminal or other charges may be brought against individuals who are subjects of FBI counterterrorism investigations. As a result, information obtained from NSLs and analytical products derived from this information are routinely shared with terrorism prosecutors, although the source and details of the information may not be readily apparent to the prosecutors.

In addition, Anti-Terrorism Advisory Councils (ATACs), other terrorism prosecutors, and intelligence research specialists in the USAOs who review the FBI's investigative files may see the results of NSLs or the analyses of the information derived from NSLs in the investigative files or through access to the FBI's databases.

2. Providing Information to Law Enforcement Authorities for Use in Criminal Proceedings

Information from national security letters may also be used in criminal proceedings. As noted above, however, information derived from national security letters is not required to be marked or tagged as coming from NSLs when it is entered in FBI databases or when it is shared with law enforcement authorities outside the FBI.

As a result, FBI and DOJ officials told us they could not identify how often information derived from national security letters was provided to law enforcement authorities for use in criminal proceedings. To obtain a rough sense of how often the FBI provided NSL-derived information to federal law enforcement authorities for use in criminal proceedings, we asked

FBI field personnel to identify (1) instances in which they referred targets of national security investigations to law enforcement authorities for prosecution and (2) whether in those instances they shared information derived from national security letters with law enforcement authorities.

The field offices that provided data on such referrals were unable to state in what percentage of these referrals they used NSLs. However, they provided examples of the use of NSLs in these proceedings, including instances in which NSLs were used in a counterintelligence case to obtain information on the subject's role in exporting sensitive U.S. military technology to a foreign country; and in a counterterrorism case in which NSLs generated subscriber information that supported FISA applications for electronic surveillance on the subjects, leading to multiple convictions for conspiracy and providing material support to terrorists.

We learned from the responses that about half of the FBI's field divisions referred one or more counterterrorism investigation targets to law enforcement authorities for possible prosecution from 2003 through 2005. Of the 46 Headquarters and field divisions that responded to our request for infoiination about referral of national security investigation targets, 19 divisions told us that they made no such referrals. Of the remaining 27 divisions, 22 divisions provided details about the type of information they referred and the nature of charges brought against these investigative subjects. In most cases, multiple charges were brought against the subjects, with the most common charges involving fraud (19), immigration (17), and money laundering (17).

IV. Improper or Illegal Use of National Security Letter Authorities

In this section of the Executive Summary, as directed by the Patriot Reauthorization Act, we report our findings on instances of "improper or illegal use" of national security letter authorities, including instances identified by the FBI as well as other instances identified by the OIG.[26]

A. Field Division Reports to FBI-OGC of 26 Possible IOB Violations Involving the Use of National Security Letters

The President's Intelligence Oversight Board (IOB) is directed by Executive Order 12863 to inform the President of any intelligence activities that "may be unlawful or contrary to Executive order or Presidential Directive." This directive has been interpreted by the Department and the IOB during the period covered by our review to include reports of violations of Department investigative guidelines or investigative procedures.[27]

We describe two groups of possible IOB violations related to NSLs that occurred during our review period (2003 through 2005). The first group consists of 26 possible IOB violations that were reported by FBI employees to FBI-OGC. The second group of incidents consists of 22 possible IOB violations which were not reported to FBI-OGC or the IOB that the OIG identified during our review of a sample of 77 investigative files in the 4 field divisions we visited.

1. Possible IOB Violations Identified by the FBI

We determined that from 2003 through 2005, FBI field divisions reported 26 possible IOB violations to FBI-OGC arising from the use of national security letter authorities. The 26 possible IOB violations included:

- Three matters in which the NSLs were signed by the appropriate officials but the underlying investigations were not approved or extended by the appropriate Headquarters or field supervisors.
- Four matters in which the NSLs did not satisfy the requirements of the pertinent NSL statute or the applicable Attorney General Guidelines. In three of these matters, the FBI obtained the information without issuing NSLs. One of these three matters involved acquisition of telephone toll billing records in the absence of investigative authority under the Attorney General's NSI Guidelines. In the fourth matter, the FBI sought and obtained consumer full credit reports in a counterintelligence investigation, which is not permitted by the Patriot Act amendment to the FCRA, 15 U.S.C. § 1681v.
- Nineteen matters in which the NSL recipient provided more information than was requested in the NSL or provided information on the wrong person, due either to FBI typographical errors or errors by recipients of the NSLs. Thirteen of these matters involved requests for telephone toll billing records, 4 involved requests for electronic communication transactional records, and 2 involved requests for telephone subscriber information.

In 15 of the 26 matters identified by the FBI as possible IOB violations, the subject was a "U.S. person," and in 8 of the matters the subject was a "non-U.S. person." In one of the matters, the subject was a presumed "non-U.S. person," in one there was no subject because there was no underlying investigation, and in another the status of the subject could not be determined.

In total, 22 of the 26 possible IOB violations were due to FBI errors, while 4 were due to third-party errors. The FBI errors included typographical errors on the telephone numbers or e-mail addresses listed in the NSLs; telephone numbers that did not belong to the targets of NSLs; receipt of responses to three telephone toll billing record requests when the investigative authority was not properly authorized or had lapsed; receipt of telephone toll billing records and subscriber information from a telephone company employee on nine separate occasions without issuing ECPA national security letters; and a FCRA NSL request for a consumer full credit report in a counterintelligence case. The errors also included instances in which the FBI obtained information without issuing the required NSL, including receipt of telephone toll billing records in the absence of an open national security investigation through informal contact with FBI Headquarters Counterterrorism Division's Communications Analysis Unit without issuing an ECPA NSL and accessing financial records through the use of FISA authorities rather than by issuing an RFPA NSL.

The four third-party errors included the NSL recipient providing prohibited content information (including voice messages) in response to an ECPA NSL for telephone toll billing records; and a third party providing prohibited content information (including e-mail content and images) in response to three ECPA NSLs requesting electronic communication transactional records.

Twenty of the 26 possible IOB violations were timely reported within 14 days of discovery to FBI-OGC in accordance with FBI policy. However, 6 were not reported in a timely fashion, taking between 15 days and 7 months to report. FBI records show that FBI-OGC reported 19 of the 26 possible violations to the IOB and decided not to report the 7 remaining matters.

2. OIG Analysis Regarding Possible IOB Violations Identified by the FBI

Our examination of the 26 possible IOB violations reported to FBI-OGC did not reveal deliberate or intentional violations of NSL statutes, the Attorney General Guidelines, or internal FBI policy. Although the majority of the possible violations - 22 of 26 - arose from FBI errors, most of them occurred because of typographical errors or the case agent's good faith but erroneous belief that the information requested related to an investigative subject.

However, three of the possible IOB violations arising from FBI errors demonstrated FBI agents' unfamiliarity with the constraints on NSL authorities. In one instance, an FBI analyst was unaware of the statutory, Attorney General Guidelines, and internal FBI policy requirements that NSLs can only be issued during a national security investigation and must be signed by the Special Agent in Charge of the field division. In the two other matters, probationary agents erroneously believed that they were authorized to obtain records about investigative subjects - without issuing NSLs - from information derived from FISA electronic surveillance orders. In these instances, it is clear that the agents, and in one instance the squad supervisor, did not understand the interrelationship between FISA authorities and national security letter authorities.

With regard to the FBI's decisions whether to report the possible violations to the IOB, we concurred in FBI-OGC's analysis with one exception. We disagreed with the FBI-OGC decision not to report the possible violation to the IOB related to the FBI's acquisition of telephone toll billing records and subscriber information relating to a "non-U.S. person" from a telephone company employee on nine occasions without issuing an NSL. FBI-OGC reasoned that because the investigative subject was a "non-U.S. person" agent of a foreign power, the only determination it had to reach was whether the FBI's failure to conform to its internal administrative requirements was reportable "as a matter of policy" to the IOB. In light of FBI-OGC's decisions to report at least four other IOB violations that were triggered by NSLs in which the investigative subject or the target of the NSL was a "non-U.S. person," we disagreed with FBI-OGC's determination that this matter should not be reported to the IOB.

B. Additional Possible IOB Violations Arising from National Security Letters Identified by the OIG during Our Field Visits

1. Possible IOB Violations Identified by the OIG

In addition to the 26 possible IOB violations identified by the FBI in this 3-year review period, we found 22 additional possible IOB violations during our review of 77 investigative files in the 4 field offices we visited.

In those 77 files, we reviewed 293 NSLs. We identified 22 NSL-related possible IOB violations that arose in the course of 17 separate investigations. None of these possible violations was reported to FBI-OGC or the JOB. Thus, we found that 22 percent of the investigative files we reviewed (17 of 77) contained one or more possible IOB violations that were not reported to FBI-OGC or the IOB.

The possible IOB violations we identified fell into three categories: improper authorization for the NSL (1), improper requests under the pertinent national security letter statutes (11), and unauthorized collections (10). The possible violations included:

- One NSL for telephone toll billing records was issued 22 days after the authorized period for the investigation had lapsed.
- Nine NSLs involved improper requests under the FCRA. Two of the 9 NSLs issued during one investigation requested consumer full credit reports during a counterintelligence investigation, while the statute authorizes this type of NSL only in international terrorism investigations. The approval ECs for 3 of these 9 NSLs listed FCRAv as the authority for the request but the NSLs included the certification of relevance language either for the RFPA or FCRAu NSL authorities. In addition, 4 of these 9 NSLs were FCRAv requests where the types of records approved by field supervisors differed from the records requested in the NSL.
- Two NSLs referenced the ECPA as authority for the request but sought content infoimation not permitted by the statute. In one instance, the NSL requested information that arguably was content information and associated subscriber information.[28] The second NSL requested financial records associated with two e-mail addresses but requested the information under the ECPA rather than the RFPA, which only authorizes access to financial records.
- Ten NSLs involved the FBI's receipt of unauthorized information. In 4 instances, the FBI received telephone toll billing records or subscriber information for telephone numbers that were not listed in the national security letters. In these instances the provider either erroneously furnished additional records for another telephone number associated with the requested number or made transcription errors when querying its systems for the records. In 4 instances, the FBI received telephone toll billing records information and electronic communication transactional records for longer periods than that specified in the NSL - periods ranging from 30 days to 81 days. One NSL sought subscriber records pursuant to the ECPA, but the recipient provided the FBI with toll billing records. One NSL sought financial institution and consumer identifying information about an individual pursuant to FCRAu. However, the recipient erroneously gave the FBI the individual's consumer full credit report, which is available pursuant to another statute, FCRAv.

Twelve of the 22 possible IOB violations identified by the OIG were due to FBI errors, and 10 were due to errors on the part of third party recipients of the NSLs.[29]

2. OIG Analysis Regarding Possible IOB Violations Identified by the OIG

In the limited file review we conducted of 77 investigative files in 4 FBI field offices, we identified nearly as many NSL-related possible IOB violations (22) as the number of NSL-related possible violations that the FBI identified (26) in reports from all FBI Headquarters and field divisions for the same 3-year period. We found that 22 percent of the investigative files that we reviewed contained at least one possible IOB violation that was not reported to FBI-OGC or the JOB. Because we have no reason to believe that the number of NSL-related possible IOB violations we identified in the four field offices was skewed or disproportionate to the number of possible IOB violations that exist in other offices, our findings suggest that a significant number of NSL-related possible IOB violations throughout the FBI have not been identified or reported by FBI personnel.

Our review did not reveal intentional violations of national security letter authorities, the Attorney General Guidelines, or internal FBI policy. Rather, we found confusion about the authorities available under the various NSL statutes. Our interviews of FBI field personnel and review of e-mail exchanges between NSLB attorneys and Division Counsel indicated that field personnel sometimes confused the two different authorities under the FCRA: the original FCRA provision that authorized access to financial institution and consumer identifying information in both counterterrorism and counterintelligence cases (15 U.S.C. §§ 1681u(a) and (b)), and the Patriot Act provision that amended the FCRA to authorize access to consumer full credit reports in international terrorism investigations where "such information is necessary for the agency's conduct of such investigation, activity or analysis" (15 U.S.C. § 1681v). Although NSLB sent periodic guidance and "all CDC" e-mails to clarify the distinctions between the two NSLs, we found that the problems and confusion persisted.

In addition, we believe that many of the violations occurred because case agents and analysts do not consistently cross check the approval ECs with the text of proposed NSLs or verify upon receipt that the information supplied by the NSLs recipient matches the requests. We also question whether case agents or analysts reviewed the records provided by the NSL recipients to determine if records were received beyond the time period requested or, if they did so, determined that the amount of excess information received was negligible and did not need to be reported.

Our review also found that the FBI did not issue comprehensive guidance describing the types of NSL-related infractions that needed to be reported to FBI-OGC as possible IOB violations. We noted frequent exchanges between Division Counsel and NSLB attorneys about what should and should not be reported as possible IOB violations which we believe showed significant confusion about the reporting requirements. However, the FBI did not issue comprehensive guidance about NSL-related infractions until November 2006, more than 5 years after the Patriot Act was enacted. We believe the lack of guidance contributed to the high rate of unreported possible IOB violations involving national security letters that we found.

As was the case with the NSL-related possible IOBs identified by the FBI, the possible violations identified or reviewed by the OIG varied in seriousness. Among the most serious matters resulting from FBI errors were the two NSLs requesting consumer full credit reports in a counterintelligence case and the NSL requesting educational records from a university, ostensibly pursuant to the ECPA. In these three instances, the FBI misused NSL authorities. Less serious infractions resulting from FBI errors were the seven matters in which three levels of supervisory review failed to detect and correct NSLs that contained incorrect certifications or sought records not referenced in the approval ECs. While the FBI was entitled to obtain the records sought or obtained in these seven NSLs, the lapses in oversight indicate that the FBI should reinforce the need for careful preparation and review of all documentation supporting the use of NSL authorities.

C. Improper Use of National Security Letter Authorities by FBI Headquarters Counterterrorism Division Units Identified by the OIG

We identified two ways in which FBI Headquarters Counterterrorism Division units circumvented the requirements of national security letter authorities or issued NSLs contrary to the Attorney General's NSI Guidelines and internal FBI policy. First, we learned that on over 700 occasions the FBI obtained telephone toll billing records or subscriber information from 3 telephone companies without first issuing NSLs or grand jury subpoenas. Instead, the FBI issued so-called "exigent letters" signed by FBI Headquarters Counterterrorism Division personnel who were not authorized to sign NSLs. The letters stated the records were requested due to "exigent circumstances" and that subpoenas requesting the information had been submitted to the U.S. Attorney's Office for processing and service "as expeditiously as possible." However, in most instances there was no documentation associating the requests with pending national security investigations. In addition, while some witnesses told us that many of the exigent letters were issued in connection with fast-paced investigations, many were not issued in exigent circumstances, and the FBI was unable to determine which letters were sent in emergency circumstances due to inadequate recordkeeping. Further, in many instances after obtaining such records from the telephone companies, the FBI issued NSLs after the fact to "cover" the information obtained, but these after-the-fact NSLs sometimes were issued many months later.

Second, we determined that FBI Headquarters personnel regularly issued national security letters seeking electronic communication transactional records exclusively from "control files" rather than from "investigative files," a practice not permitted under FBI policy. If NSLs are issued exclusively from control files, the NSL approval documentation does not indicate whether the NSLs are issued in the course of authorized investigations or whether the information sought in the NSLs is relevant to those investigations. Documentation of this infounation is necessary to establish compliance with NSL statutes, the Attorney General's NSI Guidelines, and internal FBI policy.

We describe below these practices, how they were discovered, and what actions the FBI took to address the issues.

1. Using "Exigent Letters" Rather Than ECPA National Security Letters

The FBI entered into contracts with three telephone companies between May 2003 and March 2004 to obtain telephone toll billing records or subscriber information more quickly than by issuing ECPA NSLs. The requests for approval to obligate funds for each of these contracts referred to the Counterterrorism Division's need to obtain telephone toll billing data from telephone companies as quickly as possible. The three memoranda stated that:

> Previous methods of issuing subpoenas or National Security Letters (NSL) and having to wait weeks for their service, often via hard copy reports that had to be retyped into FBI databases, is insufficient to meet the FBI's terrorism prevention mission.

The three memoranda also stated that the telephone companies would provide "near real-time servicing" of legal process, and that once legal process was served telephone records would be provided.

The Communications Analysis Unit (CAU) in the Counterterrorism Division's Communications Exploitation Section (CXS) worked directly with telephone company representatives in connection with these contracts. CAU personnel told FBI employees that it expected to receive national security letters or other legal process before it obtained records from the telephone companies.

Using as its model a letter used by the FBI's New York Division to request telephone records in connection with the FBI's criminal investigations of the hijackers involved in the September 11 attacks, CAU issued over 700 exigent letters to the three telephone companies between March 2003 and December 2005 that requested telephone toll billing records or subscriber information.[30] The letters stated:

> Due to exigent circumstances, it is requested that records for the attached list of telephone numbers be provided. Subpoenas requesting this information have been submitted to the U.S. Attorney's Office who will process and serve them formally to [information redacted] as expeditiously as possible.

We determined that, contrary to the provisions of the contracts and the assertions in CAU's briefings that the FBI would obtain telephone records only after it served NSLs or grand jury subpoenas, the FBI obtained telephone toll billing records and subscriber information in response to the exigent letters prior to serving NSLs or grand jury subpoenas. Moreover, CAU officials told us that contrary to the assertion in the exigent letters, subpoenas requesting the information had not been provided to the U.S. Attorney's Office before the letters were sent to the telephone companies.

In total, between March 2003 and December 2005 the FBI issued at least 739 exigent letters to the three telephone companies requesting information on approximately 3,000 different telephone numbers. The exigent letters were signed by CXS Section Chiefs, CAU Unit Chiefs, and subordinate CAU personnel - including intelligence analysts - none of whom was delegated authority to sign NSLs.

CAU personnel told us that many of the exigent letters were generated in connection with significant Headquarters-based counterterrorism investigations as well as investigations in which the FBI provided assistance to foreign counterparts, such as investigations of the July 2005 London bombings, and that some CAU personnel believed some requests were urgent. However, when CAU personnel gave the exigent letters to the three telephone companies, they did not provide to their supervisors any documentation demonstrating that the requests related to pending FBI investigations. This documentation is necessary to establish compliance with the ECPA NSL statute, the NSI Guidelines, and internal FBI policy.

Moreover, when CAU requested telephone records from the three telephone companies pursuant to exigent letters, there sometimes were no open investigations tied to the request. In the absence of pending investigations, CAU sent leads either to the Headquarters Counterterrorism Division or to field offices that were geographically associated with the requests asking them to initiate new investigations from which the after-thefact NSLs could be issued. However, Counterterrorism Division units and field personnel often resisted generating the documentation for these new investigations or declined to act on the leads, primarily for three reasons. First, CAU often did not provide the operating units with sufficient information to justify the initiation of an investigation. Second, on some occasions the documentation CAU supplied to the field divisions did not disclose that the FBI had already obtained the information from the telephone companies.[31] When the field offices learned that the records had already been received, they complained to attorneys in FBI-

OGC's National Security Law Branch (NSLB) that this did not seem appropriate. Third, since Headquarters and field divisions were unfamiliar with the reasons underlying the requests, they believed that the CAU leads should receive lower priority than their ongoing investigations.

NSLB attorneys responsible for providing guidance on the FBI's use of national security letter authorities told us that they were not aware of CAU's practice of using exigent letters until late 2004. When an NSLB Assistant General Counsel learned of the practice at that time, she believed that the practice did not comply with the ECPA NSL statute. For nearly 2 years after learning of the practice, beginning in late 2004, NSLB attorneys counseled CAU officials to take a variety of actions, including: to discontinue use of exigent letters except in true emergencies; obtain more details to be able to justify associating the information with an existing national security investigation or to request the initiation of a new investigation; issue duly authorized NSLs promptly after the records were provided in response to the exigent letters; modify the letters to reference national security letters rather than grand jury subpoenas; and consider opening "umbrella" investigations out of which NSLs could be issued in the absence of another pending investigation. In addition, NSLB offered to dedicate personnel to expedite issuance of CAU NSL requests (as it had done for other high priority matters requiring expedited NSLs). However, CAU never pursued this latter option.

In addition, we found that the FBI did not maintain a log to track whether it issued NSLs or grand jury subpoenas after the fact to cover the records provided in response to the exigent letters, relying instead upon the three telephone companies to track whether NSLs or grand jury subpoenas were later issued. As a result, when we asked the FBI to match NSLs and grand jury subpoenas issued to the three telephone companies with a random sample of the exigent letters, the FBI was unable to provide reliable requests asking them to initiate new investigations from which the after-thefact NSLs could be issued. However, Counterterrorism Division units and field personnel often resisted generating the documentation for these new investigations or declined to act on the leads, primarily for three reasons. First, CAU often did not provide the operating units with sufficient information to justify the initiation of an investigation. Second, on some occasions the documentation CAU supplied to the field divisions did not disclose that the FBI had already obtained the information from the telephone companies.[31] When the field offices learned that the records had already been received, they complained to attorneys in FBI-OGC's National Security Law Branch (NSLB) that this did not seem appropriate. Third, since Headquarters and field divisions were unfamiliar with the reasons underlying the requests, they believed that the CAU leads should receive lower priority than their ongoing investigations.

NSLB attorneys responsible for providing guidance on the FBI's use of national security letter authorities told us that they were not aware of CAU's practice of using exigent letters until late 2004. When an NSLB Assistant General Counsel learned of the practice at that time, she believed that the practice did not comply with the ECPA NSL statute. For nearly 2 years after learning of the practice, beginning in late 2004, NSLB attorneys counseled CAU officials to take a variety of actions, including: to discontinue use of exigent letters except in true emergencies; obtain more details to be able to justify associating the information with an existing national security investigation or to request the initiation of a new investigation; issue duly authorized NSLs promptly after the records were provided in response to the exigent letters; modify the letters to reference national security letters rather than grand jury subpoenas; and consider opening "umbrella" investigations out of which NSLs could be issued in the absence of another pending investigation. In addition, NSLB offered to dedicate personnel to expedite issuance of CAU NSL requests (as it had done for other high priority matters requiring expedited NSLs). However, CAU never pursued this latter option.

In addition, we found that the FBI did not maintain a log to track whether it issued NSLs or grand jury subpoenas after the fact to cover the records provided in response to the exigent letters, relying instead upon the three telephone companies to track whether NSLs or grand jury subpoenas were later issued. As a result, when we asked the FBI to match NSLs and grand jury subpoenas issued to the three telephone companies with a random sample of the exigent letters, the FBI was unable to provide reliable evidence to substantiate that NSLs or other legal process was issued to cover the FBI's receipt of records requested in the sample exigent letters.

We also were troubled that the FBI issued exigent letters that contained factual misstatements indicating that "Eslubpoenas requesting this information have been submitted to the U.S. Attorney's Office who will process and serve them formally . . . as expeditiously as possible."[32] In fact, in examining the documents CAU provided in support of the first 25 of the 88 randomly selected exigent letters, we could not confirm one instance in which a subpoena had been submitted to any United States Attorney's Office before the exigent letter was sent to the telephone companies.

We concluded that, as a consequence of the CAU's use of the exigent letters to acquire telephone toll billing records and subscriber information from three telephone companies without first issuing NSLs or grand jury subpoenas, the FBI circumvented the requirements of the ECPA NSL statute and violated the NSI Guidelines and internal FBI policies. These actions were compounded by the fact that CAU used exigent letters in non-emergency circumstances, failed to ensure that there were duly authorized investigations to which the requests could be tied, and failed to ensure that NSLs were issued promptly after the fact pursuant to existing or new counterterrorism investigations.

In evaluating these matters, it is also important to recognize the significant challenges the FBI was facing during the period covered by our review. After the September 11 terrorist attacks, the FBI implemented major organizational changes to seek to prevent additional terrorist attacks in the United States, such as overhauling its counterterrorism operations, expanding its intelligence capabilities, beginning to upgrade its information technology systems, and seeking to improve coordination with state and local law enforcement agencies. These changes occurred while the FBI and its Counterterrorism Division has had to respond to continuing terrorist threats and conduct many counterterrorism investigations, both internationally and domestically. In addition, the FBI developed specialized operational support units that were under significant pressure to respond quickly to potential terrorist threats. It was in this context that the FBI used exigent letters to acquire telephone toll billing records and subscriber information on approximately 3,000 different telephone numbers without first issuing ECPA national security letters. We also recognize that the FBI's use of so-called "exigent letters" to obtain the records without first issuing NSLs was undertaken without the benefit of advance legal consultation with FBI-OGC.

However, we believe none of these circumstances excuses the FBI's circumvention of the requirements of the ECPA NSL statute and its violations of the Attorney General's NSI Guidelines and internal FBI policy governing the use of national security letters.

2. National Security Letters Issued from Headquarters Control Files Rather Than from Investigative Files

The national security letter statutes and the Attorney General's NSI Guidelines authorize the issuance of national security letters only if the information sought is relevant to an "authorized investigation." Within the FBI, the only types of investigations in which NSLs may be used are national security investigations.

For purposes of conducting its investigations and compiling information obtained from the use of various investigative authorities, agents may seek supervisory approval to establish an "investigative file." The FBI also provides for the establishment of non-investigative files, referred to as "control files" or "repository files," which are used to store information (such as the results of indices searches of the names of individuals who are relevant to FBI investigations) that may never rise to the level of predication necessary to initiate a national security investigation. The FBI's National Foreign Intelligence Program (NFIP) Manual states that control files are not investigative files and are not considered preliminary investigations or full investigations.

Unless national security letters are issued from investigative files, case agents and their supervisors - and internal and external reviewers - cannot determine whether the requests are tied to substantive investigations that have established the required evidentiary predicate for issuing NSLs. As the FBI General Counsel told us, the only way to determine if the information requested in a national security letter is relevant to an authorized investigation is to have an investigative file to which the NSL request can be tied or to have the connection described in the NSL approval EC.

Notwithstanding these policies, we found that in two circumstances the FBI relied exclusively on "control files" rather than "investigative files" to initiate approval for the issuance of many national security letters, in violation of FBI policy. In the first circumstance, from 2003 through 2005, CAU initiated NSL approval memoranda for approximately 300 national security letters in connection with a classified special project from a Headquarters control file. All of the resulting NSLs sought telephone toll billing records, subscriber information, or electronic communication transactional records pursuant to the ECPA NSL statute, but none of the approval ECs referred to the case number of any specific pending FBI investigation.

Since CAU officials are not authorized to sign NSLs, CAU sent leads to field offices to initiate the process to issue NSLs, but CAU met resistance from some field personnel who questioned the adequacy of predication to initiate a national security investigation.[33] To address the problem, the Counterterrorism Division opened a special project control file from which the CAU sought approval from NSLB to issue NSLs for subscriber information.

In December 2006, after considering a number of options that would comply with the ECPA NSL statute, the Attorney General's NSI Guidelines, and internal FBI policy, the FBI initiated an "umbrella" investigative file from which national security letters related to this classified project could be issued.

In the second circumstance, the FBI issued at least six national security letters from 2003 through 2005 solely on the authority of a control files established by the Counterterrorism Division's Electronic Surveillance Operations and Sharing Unit (EOPS) in the Communications Exploitation Section and another control file.[34] The six NSLs sought information from Internet service providers. None of the approval ECs accompanying the requests for these NSLs referred to the case number of any specific pending FBI investigation. Following questions raised by the OIG in this review, the NSLB Deputy General Counsel told us that she has advised the EOPS Unit Chief to discontinue requesting approval of national security letters issued exclusively out of control files.

D. Failure to Adhere to FBI Internal Control Policies on the Use of National Security Letter Authorities

During our field visits, we also examined FBI investigative files to determine whether the field office's use of national security letters violated FBI internal control policies. In our review of the 77 investigative files and 293 national security letters in 4 FBI field offices, we identified repeated failures to adhere to FBI-OGC guidance regarding the documentation necessary for approval of national security letters. Forty-six of the 77 files we examined (60 percent) contained one or more of the following infractions: (1) NSL approval memoranda that were not reviewed and initialed by one or more of the required field supervisors or Division Counsel; (2) NSL approval memoranda that did not contain the required information; and (3) NSLs that did not contain the certifications or other information required by the authorizing statutes.

Approximately 7 percent of the approval memoranda we examined (22 of 293) did not reflect review or approval by one or more of the field supervisors who are required to approve NSL requests. They included failures to document approval by the Special Agents in Charge (4); Assistant Special Agents in Charge (18); Supervisory Special Agents (8); or the Chief Division Counsel or Assistant Division Counsel (3).

Thirty-four percent of the approval memoranda we examined (99 of 293) did not contain one or more of the four elements required by FBI internal policy. Approval memoranda failed to reference the statute authorizing the FBI to obtain the information or cited the wrong statute (16); failed to reference the "U.S. person" or "non-U.S. person" status of the investigative subject (66); failed to specify the type and number of records requested (34); and failed to recite the required predication for the request (7).

Approximately 2 percent of the national security letters we examined (5 of 293) did not include at least one of the required elements, including failures to reference an NSL statute or referencing the wrong statute. In addition, we were unable to comprehensively audit the field divisions' compliance with the requirement that Special Agents in Charge sign national security letters because three of the four divisions we visited did not maintain signed copies of their national security letters. The Special Agent in Charge of the fourth division maintained a control file with copies of all NSLs he signs, but this practice was instituted only during the last year of our review period.

V. Other Noteworthy Fact and Circumstances Related to the FBI's Use of National Security Letters

As directed by the Patriot Reauthorization Act, our report includes "other noteworthy facts and circumstances" related to the FBI's use of national security letters that we found during our review.

A. Using the "Least Intrusive Collection Techniques Feasible"

The NSI Guidelines that were in effect during most of the period covered by our review state:

> Choice of Methods. The conduct of investigations and other activities authorized by these Guidelines may present choices between the use of information collection methods that are more or less intrusive, considering such factors as the effect on the privacy of individuals and potential damage to reputation. As Executive Order 12333 § 2.4 provides, "the least intrusive collection techniques feasible" are to be used in such situations. The FBI shall not hesitate to use any lawful techniques consistent with these Guidelines, even if intrusive, where the degree of intrusiveness is warranted in light of the seriousness of a threat to the national security or the strength of the information indicating its existence. This point is to be particularly observed in investigations relating to terrorism.[35]

However, during our review we found that no clear guidance was given to FBI agents on how to reconcile the limitations expressed in the Attorney General Guidelines, which reflect concerns about the impact on privacy of FBI collection techniques, with the expansive authorities in the NSL statutes.

These issues raise difficult questions that regularly arise regarding the FBI's use of national security letters, such as (1) whether case agents should access NSL information about parties two or three steps removed from their subjects without determining if these contacts reveal suspicious connections; (2) whether there is an evidentiary threshold beyond "relevance to an authorized investigation" that should be considered before financial records or full credit histories are obtained on persons who are not investigative subjects; and (3) whether NSLs are more or less intrusive than other investigative techniques authorized for use during national security investigations, such as physical surveillance. On the other hand, if agents are hindered from using all types of NSLs at early stages of national security investigations, this may compromise the FBI's ability to pursue critical investigations of terrorism or espionage threats or to reach resolution expeditiously that certain subjects do not pose threats.

The impact of the FBI's investigative choices when using national security letters is magnified by three factors. First, the FBI generates tens of thousands of NSLs per year on the authority of Special Agents in Charge, and the predication standard - relevance to an authorized investigation - can easily be satisfied. Second, we found that FBI Division Counsel in field offices have asked NSLB attorneys in FBI Headquarters for ad hoc guidance on application of the "least intrusive collection techniques feasible" proviso, suggesting a need for greater clarity. Third, neither the Attorney General's NSI Guidelines nor internal FBI policies require the purging of information derived from NSLs in FBI databases, regardless of the outcome of the investigation. Thus, once information is obtained in response to a national security letter, it is indefinitely retained and retrievable by the many authorized personnel who have access to various FBI databases.

We recognize that there cannot be one model regarding the use of NSLs in all types of national security investigations, and that the FBI cannot issue definitive guidance addressing when and what types of NSLs should issue at each stage of investigations. The judgment of FBI agents and their supervisors, coupled with review by Chief Division Counsel and Special Agents in Charge or senior Headquarters officials, are critical to ensuring the appropriate use of NSLs and preventing overreaching. However, we believe that the meaning and application of the Attorney General Guidelines' proviso calling for use of the "least intrusive collection techniques feasible" to the FBI's use of national security letter authorities should be addressed in general guidance as well as in the training of special agents, Chief Division Counsel, and all FBI officials authorized to sign NSLs. With the FBI's increasing reliance on national security letters as an investigative technique, such guidance and training would be helpful in assisting FBI personnel in reconciling the important privacy considerations that underlie the Attorney General Guidelines' proviso with the FBI's mission to detect and deter terrorist attacks and espionage threats.

B. Telephone "Toll Billing Records Information"

We found that FBI agents and attorneys frequently have questions regarding the types of records they can obtain when requesting "toll billing records information," a term that is not defined in the ECPA NSL statute. In the absence of a statutory defmition or case law interpreting this phrase, different electronic communication service providers produce different types of information in response to the FBI's ECPA national security letter requests for these records. We found that ongoing uncertainty about the meaning of the phrase "toll billing records information" has generated multiple inquiries by Division Counsel to NSLB attorneys and confusion on the part of various communication providers. In light of this recurring issue, we recommend that the Department consider seeking a legislative amendment to the ECPA to define the phrase "toll billing records information."

C. The Role of FBI Division Counsel in Reviewing National Security Letters

FBI Division Counsel are responsible for identifying and correcting erroneous information in NSLs and NSL approval memoranda, resolving questions about the scope of the NSL statutes, ensuring adequate predication for NSL requests, and providing advice on issues concerning the collection of unauthorized information through national security letters. However, Division Counsel are not in the chain of review or approval for the initiation of national security investigations. Thus, by the time Division Counsel see the first NSL request in an investigation, the investigation has already been approved by a field supervisor and an Assistant Special Agent in Charge, both of whom report to the Special Agent in Charge. Division Counsel also report to the Special Agents in Charge of the field offices in which they work, not to the Office of the General Counsel at FBI Headquarters.

We found that these factors have led some Division Counsel to be reluctant to question the predication for NSL requests or the relevance of the information sought in the NSL to the investigation. The impact of these factors on the independence and aggressiveness of Division Counsels' review of NSLs was manifest in an informal survey of 22 Chief Division Counsel who were asked by a Chief Division Counsel whether they would approve a particular NSL request. Some said that they would have approved the request for reasons other than the merits of the approval documentation. The results of this inquiry led senior attorneys in FBI-OGC's National Security Law Branch to be very concerned that some Chief Division Counsel believe they cannot exercise their independent professional judgment on the use of NSL authorities because they are reluctant to second guess the operational judgments of senior field office officials in their chain of command.

D. The OGC Database Does Not Identify the Targets of National Security Letters When They are Different from the Subjects of the Underlying Investigations

In our evaluation of the use and effectiveness of national security letters, we attempted to analyze information in the OGC database, including the numbers and types of NSL requests issued during the period of our review. One of the most significant Patriot Act expansions of NSL authorities was the lower predication standard of "relevance" to an authorized investigation. In lieu of requiring individualized suspicion about an investigative subject, the FBI is now permitted to obtain records on other individuals, so long as the information is relevant to an authorized investigation. However, we found that the OGC database does not capture information on whether the target of the NSL is the subject of the underlying investigating or another individual. As a result, because the target of an NSL is frequently not the same person as the subject of the underlying investigation, the FBI does not know and cannot estimate the number of NSL requests relating to persons who are not investigative subjects.

In 2006, the FBI modified its guidance to require, with the exception of NSLs seeking subscriber information pursuant to the ECPA NSL statute, that agents indicate in the NSL approval EC whether the request is for a person other than the subject of the investigation or in addition to that subject, and to state the U.S. person or non-U.S. person status of those individuals.

In light of the Patriot Act's expansion of the FBI's authority to collect information about individuals who are not subjects of its investigations, we believe the OGC database should contain this information so that the issue is subject to internal and external oversight.

VI. OIG Conclusions and Recommendations

Our review found that the FBI's use of national security letters has grown dramatically since enactment of the Patriot Act in October 2001. The FBI issued approximately 8,500 NSL requests in CY 2000, the last full year prior to passage of the Patriot Act. After the Patriot Act, the number of NSL requests increased to approximately 39,000 in 2003, approximately 56,000 in 2004, and approximately 47,000 in 2005. During the period covered by our review, the FBI issued a total of 143,074 NSL requests pursuant to national security letter authorities. The overwhelming majority of the NSL requests sought telephone toll billing records information, subscriber information (telephone or e-mail), or electronic communication transactional records under the ECPA NSL statute.

Most NSL requests (about 73 percent) occurred during counterterrorism investigations. About 26 percent of all NSL requests were issued during counterintelligence investigations, and less than 1 percent of the requests were generated during foreign computer intrusion cyber investigations. In addition, the use of national security letters in FBI counterterrorism investigations increased from approximately 15 percent of investigations opened during 2003 to approximately 29 percent of the counterterrorism investigations opened during 2005.

We found that the use of NSL requests related to "U.S. persons" and "non-U.S. persons" shifted during our 3-year review period. The percentage of requests generated from investigations of U.S. persons increased from about 39 percent of all NSL requests issued in 2003 to about 53 percent of all NSL requests during 2005.

It is important to note that these statistics, which were obtained from the FBI electronic database that tracks NSL usage, understate the total number of national security letter requests. We found that the OGC database is inaccurate and does not include all national security letter requests issued by the FBI. Because of inaccuracies in the OGC database, we compared data in this database to a sample of investigative files in four FBI field offices that we visited. Overall, we found approximately 17 percent more national security *letters* and 22 percent more national security letter *requests* in the case files we examined in four field offices than were recorded in the OGC database. As a result, we believe that the total number of NSL requests issued by the FBI is significantly higher than the FBI reported.

We also found the OGC database did not accurately reflect the status of investigative targets and that the Department's semiannual classified reports to Congress on NSL usage were also inaccurate. Specifically, the data provided in the Department's semiannual classified reports regarding the number of requests for records, the number of different persons or organizations that were the subjects of investigations in which records were requested, and the status of those individuals as "U.S. persons or organizations" and "non-U.S. persons or organizations" were all inaccurate. We found that 12 percent of the case files we examined did not accurately report the status of the target of the NSL as being a U.S. person or a non-U.S. person. In each of these instances, the FBI database indicated that the subject was a non-U.S. person while the approval memoranda in the investigative file indicated the subject was a U.S. person or a presumed U.S. person.

With respect to the effectiveness of national security letters, FBI Headquarters and field personnel told us that they believe NSLs are indispensable investigative tools that serve as building blocks in many counterterrorism and counterintelligence investigations. National security letters have various uses, including obtaining evidence to support FISA applications for electronic surveillance, pen register/trap and trace devices, or physical searches; developing communication or financial links between subjects of FBI investigations and between those subjects and others; providing evidence to initiate new investigations, expand national security investigations, or enabling agents to close investigations; providing investigative leads; and corroborating information obtained by use of other investigative techniques.

FBI agents and analysts also use information obtained from national security letters, in combination with other information, to prepare analytical intelligence products for distribution within the FBI and to other Department components, and for dissemination to other federal agencies, Joint Terrorism Task Forces, and other members of the intelligence community. We found that information derived from national security letters is routinely shared with United States Attorneys' Offices pursuant to various Departmental directives requiring terrorism prosecutors and intelligence research specialists to be familiar with FBI counterterrorism investigations. However, because information derived from national security letters is not marked or tagged as such, it is impossible to determine when and how often the FBI provided information derived from national security letters to law enforcement authorities for use in criminal proceedings.

We determined that information obtained from national security letters is routinely stored in the FBI's Automated Case Support (ACS) system, Telephone Applications, IDW, and other databases. FBI personnel and Joint Terrorism Task Force members who have the appropriate clearances to use these databases would therefore have access to information obtained from national security letters.

Our review also examined instances of "improper or illegal use" of national security letters. First, our review examined possible national security letter violations that the FBI was required to report to the President's Intelligence Oversight Board (IOB). The FBI identified 26 possible violations involving the use of national security letter authorities from calendar years 2003 through 2005, of which 19 were reported to the IOB. These 19 involved the issuance of NSLs without proper authorization, improper requests under the statutes cited in the national security letters, and unauthorized collection of telephone or Internet e-mail transactional records. Of these 26 possible violations, 22 were the result of FBI errors, while 4 were caused by mistakes made by recipients of the national security letters.

Second, in addition to the violations reported by the FBI, we reviewed documents relating to national security letters in a sample of FBI investigative files in four FBI field offices. In our review of 77 FBI investigative files, we found that 17 of these files - 22 percent - contained one or more violations relating to national security letters that were not identified by the FBI. These violations included infractions that were similar to those identified by the FBI and considered as possible IOB violations, but also included instances in which the FBI issued national security letters for different information than what had been approved by the field supervisor. Based on our review and the significant percentage of files that contained unreported violations (22 percent), we believe that a significant number of NSL violations are not being identified or reported by the FBI.

Third, we identified many instances in which the FBI obtained telephone toll billing records and subscriber information from 3 telephone companies pursuant to more than 700 "exigent letters" signed by personnel in the Counterterrorism Division without first issuing national security letters. We concluded that the FBI's acquisition of this information circumvented the requirements of the ECPA NSL statute and violated the Attorney General's Guidelines for FBI National Security Investigations and Foreign Intelligence Collection (NSI Guidelines) and internal FBI policy. These actions were compounded by the fact that the FBI used the exigent letters in non-emergency circumstances, failed to ensure that there were duly authorized investigations to which the requests could be tied, and failed to ensure that NSLs were issued promptly after the fact pursuant to existing or new counterterrorism investigations. In addition, the exigent letters inaccurately represented that the FBI had already requested subpoenas for the information when, in fact, it had not.

Fourth, we determined that in two circumstances during 2003 though 2005 FBI Headquarters Counterterrorism Division generated over 300 national security letters from "control files" rather than from "investigative files" in violation of FBI policy. In these instances, FBI agents did not generate and supervisors did not approve documentation demonstrating that the factual predicate required by the Electronic Communications Privacy Act, the Attorney General's NSI Guidelines, and internal FBI policy had been established. When NSLs are issued from control files rather than from investigative files, internal and external reviewers cannot determine whether the requests are tied to investigations that established the required evidentiary predicate for issuing the national security letters.

Fifth, we examined FBI investigative files in four field offices to determine whether FBI case agents and supervisors adhered to FBI policies designed to ensure appropriate supervisory review of the use of national security letter authorities. We found that 60 percent of the investigative files we examined contained one or more violations of FBI internal control policies relating to national security letters. These included failures to document supervisory review of national security letter approval memoranda and failures to include required information such as the authorizing statute, the status of the investigative subject, or the number or types of records requested in NSL approval memoranda. Moreover, because the FBI has no policy requiring the retention of signed copies of national security letters, we were unable to conduct a comprehensive audit of the FBI's compliance with its internal control policies and the statutory certifications required for national security letters.

Our review also describes several other "noteworthy facts or circumstances" identified in the review. For example, we found that the FBI has not provided clear guidance describing how case agents and supervisors should apply the Attorney General Guidelines' requirement to use the "least intrusive collection techniques feasible" in their use and sequencing of national security letters. In addition, we found confusion among FBI attorneys and communication providers over the meaning of the phrase "telephone toll billing records information" in the ECPA NSL statute. We also saw indications that some Chief Division Counsel and Assistant Division Counsel are reluctant to provide an independent review of national security letter requests because these attorneys report to the Special Agents in Charge whose field supervisors have already approved the underlying investigation.

Finally, in evaluating the FBI's use of national security letters it is important to note the significant challenges the FBI was facing during the period covered by our review and the major organizational changes it was undergoing. Moreover, it is also important to recognize that in most cases the FBI was seeking to obtain information that it could have obtained properly if it had it followed applicable statutes, guidelines, and internal policies. We also did not find any indication that the FBI's misuse of NSL authorities constituted criminal misconduct.

However, as described above, we found that the FBI used NSLs in violation of applicable NSL statutes, Attorney General Guidelines, and internal FBI policies. In addition, we found that the FBI circumvented the ECPA NSL statute when it issued over 700 "exigent letters" to obtain telephone toll billing records and subscriber information from three telephone companies without first issuing NSLs. Moreover, in a few other instances, the FBI sought or obtained information to which it was not entitled under the NSL authorities when it sought educational records through issuance of an ECPA NSL, when it sought and obtained telephone toll billing records in the absence of a national security investigation, when it sought and obtained consumer full credit reports in counterintelligence investigations, and when it sought and obtained financial records and telephone toll billing records without first issuing NSLs.

Based on our review, we believe the FBI needs to ensure that all national security letters are issued in accord with applicable statutes, guidelines, and policies. Therefore, to address the issues identified in our report we recommend that the FBI:

1. Require all Headquarters and field personnel who are authorized to issue national security letter to create a control file for the purpose of retaining signed copies of all national security letters they issue.
2. Improve the FBI-OGC NSL tracking database to ensure that it captures timely, complete, and accurate data on NSLs and NSL requests.
3. Improve the FBI-OGC NSL tracking database to include data reflecting NSL requests for information about individuals who are not the investigative subjects but are the targets of NSL requests.
4. Issue additional guidance to field offices that will assist in identifying possible IOB violations arising from use of national security letter authorities, such as (a) measures

to reduce or eliminate typographical and other errors in national security letters so that the FBI does not collect unauthorized information; (b) best practices for identifying the receipt of unauthorized information in the response to national security letters due to third-party errors; (c) clarifying the distinctions between the two NSL authorities in the Fair Credit Reporting Act (15 U.S.C. §§ 1681u and 1681v); and (d) reinforcing internal FBI policy requiring that NSLs must be issued from investigative files, not from control files.

5. Consider seeking legislative amendment to the Electronic Communications Privacy Act to define the phrase "telephone toll billing records information."
6. Consider measures that would enable FBI agents and analysts to (a) label or tag their use of information derived from national security letters in analytical intelligence products and (b) identify when and how often infonnation derived from NSLs is provided to law enforcement authorities for use in criminal proceedings.
7. Take steps to ensure that the FBI does not improperly issue exigent letters.
8. Take steps to ensure that, where appropriate, the FBI makes requests for information in accordance with the requirements of national security letter authorities.
9. Implement measures to ensure that FBI-OGC is consulted about activities undertaken by FBI Headquarters National Security Branch, including its operational support activities, that could generate requests for records from third parties that the FBI is authorized to obtain exclusively though the use of its national security letter authorities.
10. Ensure that Chief Division Counsel and Assistant Division Counsel provide close and independent review of requests to issue national security letters.

We believe that these recommendations, if fully implemented, can improve the accuracy of the reporting of the FBI's use of national security letters and ensure the FBI's compliance with the requirements governing their use.

1. INTRODUCTION

In the Patriot Reauthorization Act, enacted in 2006, Congress directed the Department of Justice (Department) Office of the Inspector General (OIG) to review "the effectiveness and use, including any improper or illegal use, of national security letters issued by the Department of Justice."[36] The Act required the OIG to conduct reviews of the use of national security letters for two separate time periods.[37] This report describes the results of the first OIG review of the FBI's use of national security letters (NSLs), covering calendar years (CY) 2003 through 2005.[38]

I. Provisions of the USA Patriot Act and Reauthorization Act

In October 2001, in the wake of the September 11 terrorist attacks, Congress passed the USA PATRIOT Act.[39] Section 505 of the Patriot Act expanded four existing statutes (the "national security letter statutes") that authorized the Federal Bureau of Investigation (FBI) to use national security letters to obtain certain specified types of info' illation from third parties for use in authorized counterintelligence, counterterrorism, and foreign computer intrusion cyber investigations. As part of the Patriot Act legislation, Congress enacted a fifth NSL authority permitting the FBI to use national security letters to obtain consumer full credit reports in international terrorism investigations.

National security letters, which are written directives to provide information, are issued by the FBI directly to third parties, such as telephone companies, financial institutions, Internet service providers, and consumer credit agencies, without judicial review. In these letters, the FBI can direct third parties to provide customer account information and transactional records, such as telephone toll billing records.[40]

The national security letter authorities expanded by the Patriot Act were originally scheduled to sunset on December 31, 2005, but were temporarily extended by Congress until it finalized a reauthorization bill. Congress passed the reauthorization bill in early 2006, and on March 9, 2006, the President signed into law the Patriot Reauthorization Act, which, among other things, reauthorized the five national security letter authorities.

In the Patriot Reauthorization Act, Congress directed the OIG's review to include:

(1) an examination of the use of national security letters by the Department of Justice during calendar years 2003 through 2006;
(2) a description of any noteworthy facts or circumstances relating to such use, including any improper or illegal use of such authority; and
(3) an examination of the effectiveness of national security letters as an investigative tool, including -
    (A) the importance of the information acquired by the Department of Justice to the intelligence activities of the Department of Justice or to any other department or agency of the Federal Government;
    (B) the manner in which such information is collected, retained, analyzed, and disseminated by the Department of Justice, including any direct access to such information (such as access to "raw data") provided to any other department, agency, or instrumentality of Federal, State, local, or tribal governments or any private sector entity;
    (C) whether, and how often, the Department of Justice utilized such information to produce an analytical intelligence product for distribution within the Department of Justice, to the intelligence community . . ., or to other Federal, State, local, or tribal government departments, agencies or instrumentalities;
    (D) whether, and how often, the Department of Justice provided such information to law enforcement authorities for use in criminal proceedings; . . . .[41]

According to the Patriot Reauthorization Act, the OIG's first report on the FBI's use of national security letters is due to Congress on March 9, 2007.

I. Methodology of the OIG Review

In this review, the OIG conducted interviews of over 100 FBI employees, including personnel at FBI Headquarters in the Office of the General Counsel (FBI-OGC), Counterterrorism Division, and Counterintelligence Division, and personnel in four field divisions. We also interviewed officials in the Department's Criminal Division and National Anti-Terrorism Advisory Council Coordinators. We also attended background briefings regarding national security letters and the databases in which information derived from national security letters is stored and analyzed. We examined over 31,000 FBI documents from FBI Headquarters operational and support divisions and four field divisions pertaining to national security letters. Among the documents we analyzed were Headquarters guidance memoranda; correspondence; and reports by the FBI's Inspection Division, FBI-OGC, and Office of Professional Responsibility. In addition, we analyzed documents from the Department's Office of Legislative Affairs that included testimony, memoranda, and hearing transcripts regarding the oversight and reauthorization of the Patriot Act, including provisions affecting national security letter authorities and semiannual classified reports to Congress on the FBI's use of national security letter authorities.

OIG teams also examined FBI case files that contained national security letters and conducted interviews at four FBI field divisions in May and June 2006: Chicago, New York, Philadelphia, and San Francisco. These field divisions were selected from among the eight field divisions that issued the most national security letter requests during the period of our review, from 2003 through 2005. At the four field divisions, we conducted interviews of 52 FBI personnel, including an Assistant Director in Charge, Special Agents in Charge, Acting Special Agents in Charge, Assistant Special Agents in Charge, supervisory special agents overseeing counterterrorism and counterintelligence squads, Chief Division Counsel and Assistant Division Counsel, special agents, intelligence analysts, and intelligence research specialists.

Also at the four field divisions, we examined a judgmental sample of 77 counterterrorism and counterintelligence investigative case files. Those files contained approximately 800 requests for information under four of the five national security letter authorities. Of that total, we reviewed up to 5 national security letters in each investigative file, for a total of 293 national security letters issued from January 1, 2003, through December 31, 2005. We reviewed those documents to determine whether the national security letters were issued in accordance with the relevant statutes, Attorney General Guidelines, and FBI policies. With regard to these national security letters, we reviewed documentation pertaining to case initiations, authorizations, delivery to the designated recipients, the recipients' production of documents and electronic media in response to the letters, retention of that information, and the analysis and dissemination of the information within the Department, to the intelligence community, and to others.

The OIG also analyzed the FBI-OGC's National Security Letter Database (OGC database), which the FBI uses for collecting information necessary to compile the Department's semiannual classified reports to Congress on NSL usage and, since passage of the Patriot Reauthorization Act, to compile the Department's annual public report on NSL usage. During the period of our review, the Department was directed to file semiannual classified reports to Congress reflecting the number of "NSL requests" the FBI made pursuant to three of the five national security letter authorities (see Chart 1.1). We also analyzed this

OGC database to assess the accuracy and reliability of the FBI's reports. We compared the OGC database entries to the documentation of the use of these authorities in the field divisions' investigative case files and performed other tests. These tests revealed significant errors in the OGC database, which we describe in Chapter Four. However, although we recognize the limitations of the OGC database, we used data from the OGC database for some of our analysis because it is the only source of centralized data on the FBI's use of NSLs.

CHART 1.1. RELATIONSHIP BETWEEN NSLS AND NSL REQUESTS (2003 THROUGH 2005)

In this report, we often refer to the number of national security letter *requests* rather than the number of national security *letters* because one "letter" may include more than one request. That is, during an investigation several national security letters may be issued, and each letter may contain several requests. For example, one letter to a telephone company may request information on seven telephone numbers. As a result, the numbers normally presented in the FBI's classified reports to Congress and in its public report are the numbers of requests made, not the number of letters issued. In this report, we follow that same approach. This chart shows the relationship we found between the number of investigations, NSLs, and NSL requests from 2003 through 2005 by counterterrorism and counterintelligence cases. Fewer than one percent of all NSL requests during this period were issued in foreign computer intrusion cyber investigations.

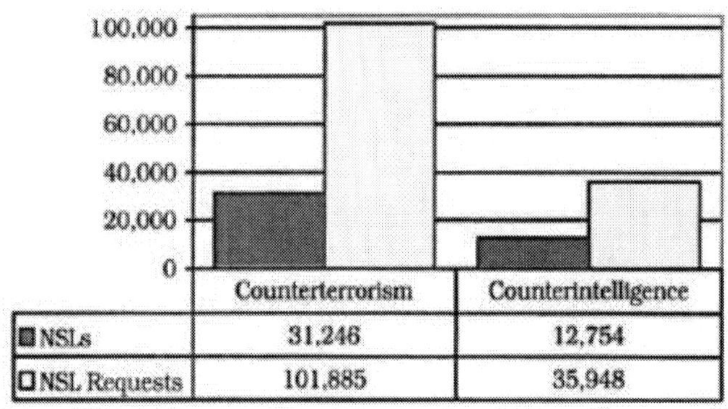

Source: FBI-OGC Database

*The NSL request totals on this chart are less than the NSL requests noted above because they do not include NSL requests issued in connection with cyber investigations or the total number of NSL requests that were lost due to a malfunction of the OGC database.

During this review, we also distributed an e-mail questionnaire to the counterintelligence and counterterrorism squads in the FBI's 56 domestic field offices to attempt to determine the types of analytical products the FBI developed based on national security letters; the manner in which national security letter-derived information was disseminated within the Department, to other members of the intelligence community, and to others; and the occasions when such information was provided to law enforcement authorities for use in criminal proceedings.

II. Organization of the Report

This report is divided into eight chapters. Following this introduction, Chapter Two provides background on the use of national security letters, the Attorney General Guidelines which govern the FBI's conduct of national security investigations, and the roles of several FBI Headquarters divisions and components involved in the approval and operational use of national security letters.

Chapter Three describes the manner in which the FBI collects information by issuing national security letters and how it retains the information in investigative case files, shared computer drives, and databases.

Chapter Four presents data on the FBI's use of national security letters from 2003 through 2005. This information is based on data derived from the OGC database, the Department's semiannual classified reports to Congress on NSL usage, and our field work.

Chapter Five addresses other issues the Patriot Reauthorization Act directed the OIG to review regarding the use and effectiveness of national security letters, including the importance of the information acquired and the manner in which information from national security letters is analyzed and disseminated within the Department, to other members of the intelligence community, and to other entities.

Chapter Six reports our findings on instances of improper or illegal use of national security letter authorities, including instances identified by the FBI, as well as other instances identified by the OIG.

Chapter Seven reports other noteworthy facts or circumstances identified in the review, including the interpretation of the Attorney General Guidelines' requirement to use the "least intrusive collection techniques feasible" with regard to the use of national security letters; uncertainty about the types of telephone toll billing records the FBI may obtain pursuant to an Electronic Communications Privacy Act (ECPA) national security letter; the review by Division Counsel of NSL requests; the issuance of NSLs from control files rather than investigative files, in violation of FBI policy; the FBI's use of "certificate letters" rather than Right to Financial Privacy Act (RFPA) national security letters to obtain records from Federal Reserve Banks; and the FBI's failure to include in the OGC database information reflecting the use of NSLs to obtain information on individuals who are not subjects of FBI investigations.

Chapter Eight contains a summary of our conclusions and our recommendations.

The Appendix to the report contains comments on the report by the Attorney General, the Director of National Intelligence, and the FBI. The Appendix also contains copies of the national security letter statutes in effect prior to the Patriot Reauthorization Act. The classified report also contains a classified appendix.

2. Background

In this chapter we describe the five national security letter authorities and the Attorney General Guidelines that govern their use. We also describe the roles of FBI Headquarters divisions and field components in issuing and using these letters in national security investigations.

I. Background on National Security Letters

Over the last 20 years, Congress has enacted a series of laws authorizing the FBI to obtain certain types of information from third parties in terrorism, espionage, and classified information leak investigations without obtaining warrants from the Foreign Intelligence Surveillance Court or approval from another court.[42] These include five statutory provisions that authorize the FBI to obtain customer and consumer transactional information from communications providers, financial institutions, and consumer credit agencies by issuing national security letters (NSLs).[43] All but one of these provisions - the statute allowing access to consumer full credit reports in international terrorism investigations - predated the October 2001 passage of the Patriot Act. The authorizing statutes in effect prior to the Patriot Act required certification by a senior FBI Headquarters official that the FBI had "specific and articulable facts giving reason to believe that the customer or entity whose records are sought is a foreign power or agent of a foreign power" as defined in the Foreign Intelligence Surveillance Act of 1978.[44]

A. The Patriot Act

The September 11 attacks prompted a reevaluation of the law enforcement and intelligence tools that were available to detect and prevent terrorist attacks. Among the topics Congress and the Department of Justice considered was the use of national security letters.[45] The Department reported in Congressional testimony that “in many cases, counterintelligence and counterterrorism investigations suffer substantial delays while waiting for NSLs to be prepared, returned from Headquarters, and served.”[46]

The Patriot Act significantly expanded the FBI's preexisting authority to obtain information through national security letters. Section 505 of the Patriot Act broadened the FBI's authority by:

- Eliminating the requirement that the information sought in an NSL must pertain to a foreign power or an agent of a foreign power and substituting the lower threshold that the information requested be relevant to or sought for an investigation to protect against international terrorism or espionage, provided that the investigation of a United States person is not conducted "solely on the basis of activities protected by the first amendment of the Constitution of the United States";
- Permitting, as a consequence of this lower threshold, national security letters to request information from communication providers, financial institutions, and consumer credit agencies about persons other than the subjects of FBI national security investigations so long as the requested information is relevant to an authorized investigation; and
- Permitting Special Agents in Charge of the FBI's 56 field offices to sign national security letters, thus significantly expanding approval authority beyond senior FBI Headquarters officials.[47]

In addition to expanding preexisting NSL authorities, the Patriot Act added a new NSL authority permitting the FBI and certain other federal government agencies to use NSLs to obtain access to consumer full credit reports in international terrorism investigations pursuant to an amendment to the Fair Credit Reporting Act (FCRA).[48] Prior to this amendment, the FBI could use FCRA NSLs only to obtain basic financial institution and consumer-identifying information about the person's bank accounts, places of employment, and addresses.[49]

The Patriot Act did not alter existing provisions in the statutes barring recipients of national security letters from disclosing their receipt of the letters and from disclosing the records provided. These so-called "gag order" provisions prohibited NSL recipients from challenging NSLs in court. Similarly, NSL authorities prior to the Patriot Act did not provide an express mechanism by which the FBI could enforce an NSL in court if a recipient refused to comply. The Patriot Act also did not include any express enforcement mechanism.

The pre-Patriot Act statutes required the FBI to provide classified semiannual reports to Congress disclosing summary information about national security letter usage.[50] The Patriot Act continued to require classified reports to Congress on the FBI's use of its NSL authorities.

B. Types of Information Obtained by National Security Letters

The type of information the FBI can obtain through national security letters includes:

Telephone and e-mail Information

- Historical information on telephone calls made and received from a specified number, including land lines, cellular phones, prepaid phone card calls, toll free calls, alternate billed number calls (calls billed to third parties), and local and long distance billing records associated with the phone numbers (known as toll records);
- Electronic communication transactional records (e-mails), including e-mail addresses associated with the account; screen names; and billing records and method of payment; and
- Subscriber information associated with particular telephone numbers or e-mail addresses, such as the name, address, length of service, and method of payment.

Financial Information

- Financial information such as information concerning open and closed checking and savings accounts and safe deposit box records from banks, credit unions, thrift institutions, investment banks or investment companies, as well as transactions with issuers of travelers checks, operators of credit card systems, pawnbrokers, loan or finance companies, travel agencies, real estate companies, casinos, and other entities.

Consumer Credit Information

- Names and addresses of all financial institutions at which a consumer maintains or has maintained an account;
- Identifying information respecting a consumer . . . limited to name, address, former addresses, places of employment, or former places of employment; and
- Consumer reports of a consumer and all other information in a consumer's file (full credit reports).

C. The Patriot Reauthorization Act

The Patriot Reauthorization Act reauthorized all of the provisions that were subject to lapse or "sunset" in the original Patriot Act (with some modification), including the five NSL authorities.[51] One of the modifications required the Department to issue, in addition to its semiannual classified reports, annual public reports that disclose certain data on the FBI's national security letter requests. The public report must include the aggregate number of NSL requests issued pursuant to the five NSL statutes including, for the first time, data on the use of the full credit report authority established pursuant to the Fair Credit Reporting Act, the only new NSL authority enacted by the Patriot Act.

The Department's first public annual report pursuant to the Patriot Reauthorization Act on the use of NSL authorities was issued on April 28, 2006.[52] The report stated that during calendar year 2005, federal government agencies issued 9,254 "NSL requests" involving 3,501 different "United States persons."[53]

II. The Four National Security Letter Statutes

The following is a brief overview of the four statutes authorizing the FBI to issue five types of national security letters.

A. The Right to Financial Privacy Act

The Right to Financial Privacy Act (RFPA) was enacted in 1978 "to protect the customers of financial institutions from unwarranted intrusion into their records while at the same time permitting legitimate law enforcement activity."[54] The RFPA requires federal government agencies to provide individuals with advance notice of requested disclosures of personal financial information and gives individuals an opportunity to challenge the request before disclosure is made to law enforcement authorities.[55]

The first NSL statute was passed in 1986 as an amendment to the RFPA. It created an exception to the advance notice requirement by permitting the FBI to obtain financial institution records in foreign counterintelligence cases. Before the Patriot Act, the FBI could issue RFPA NSLs upon certification of

> specific and articulable facts giving reason to believe that the customer or entity whose records are sought is a foreign power or an agent of a foreign power. . . .[56]

Since the Patriot Act, the FBI may obtain financial records upon certification that the information is sought

> for foreign counterintelligence purposes to protect against international terrorism or clandestine intelligence activities, provided that such an investigation of a United States person is not conducted solely on the basis of activities protected by the first amendment to the Constitution of the United States.[57]

In December 2003, Congress amended the RFPA to expand the definition of "financial institutions" to which NSLs could be issued, including entities such as rental car companies, automobile dealerships, credit unions, issuers of travelers' checks, pawnbrokers, and real estate companies.[58]

The FBI can disseminate information derived from the RFPA national security letters only in accordance with the Attorney General Guidelines governing national security investigations and can disseminate such information to other federal agencies only if the information is clearly relevant to the authorized responsibilities of those federal agencies.[59]

B. The Electronic Communications Privacy Act

In 1986, Congress enacted the Electronic Communications Privacy Act (ECPA), which extended statutory protection to electronic and wire communications stored by third parties such as telephone companies and Internet Service Providers.[60] The statute restricted the government's access to live telephone transactional data, such as the telephone numbers that a particular telephone number calls or received (known as "pen register" and "trap and trace" data). The ECPA required the government to obtain a court order for which it must certify the relevance of the information to an ongoing criminal investigation.[61] The statute requires that subjects of government requests for these records be given advance notice of the requested disclosure and an opportunity to challenge the request.

However, the ECPA allowed the FBI to obtain "subscriber information and toll billing records information, or electronic communication transactional records" from a "wire or electronic communications service provider" in conjunction with a foreign counterintelligence investigation. Before the Patriot Act, the FBI could obtain ECPA NSLs upon certification of

> specific and articulable facts giving reason to believe that the person or entity to whom the information sought pertains is a foreign power or an agent of a foreign power. . . .[62]

Since the Patriot Act, the FBI must certify that the information sought is

> relevant to an authorized investigation to protect against international terrorism or clandestine intelligence activities provided that such an investigation of a United States person is not conducted solely on the basis on activities protected by the first amendment to the Constitution of the United States.[63]

In 1993, Congress expanded the ECPA NSL authority by permitting access to the subscriber and toll billing records of additional persons, such as those who were in contact with agents of a foreign power.[64] Congress amended the ECPA again in 1996 by defining "toll billing records" to expressly include "local and long distance toll billing records."[65]

Recipients of ECPA NSLs were prohibited until the Patriot Reauthorization Act from disclosing to any person that the FBI had sought or obtained the requested information.[66]

The FBI may disseminate information obtained from ECPA NSLs to other federal agencies "only if such information is clearly relevant to the authorized responsibilities of such agency."[67]

The ECPA permits access only to "subscriber and toll billing records information" or "electronic communication transactional records," as distinguished from the content of telephone conversations or e-mail communications.[68]

C. The Fair Credit Reporting Act

The Fair Credit Reporting Act (FCRA), as amended by the Patriot Act, authorizes two types of national security letters, FCRAu and FCRAv NSLs. The FCRA was enacted in 1970 to protect personal information collected by credit reporting agencies.[69] The FCRA prohibits the disclosure of information collected for the purpose of establishing eligibility for credit, insurance, employment, and other related purposes.

However, Congress amended the FCRA in 1996 to authorize the FBI (and certain other government agencies) to issue national security letters to obtain a limited amount of information about an individual's credit history: the names and addresses of all financial institutions at which a consumer maintains or has maintained an account pursuant, referred to as FCRAu NSLs; and consumer identifying information limited to name, address, former addresses, places of employment and former places of employment.[70] Before the Patriot Act, the FBI could obtain FCRA NSLs upon certification that

> (1) such information is necessary for the conduct of an authorized foreign counterintelligence investigation; and
> (2) there are specific and articulable facts giving reason to believe that the consumer -
> (A) is a foreign power or a person who is not a United States person and is an official of a foreign power; or
> (B) is an agent of a foreign power and is engaging or has engaged in an act of international terrorism or clandestine intelligence activities that involve or may involve a violation of criminal statutes of the United States.[71]

Since the Patriot Act, the FBI must certify that the information is

> sought for the conduct of an authorized investigation to protect against international terrorism or clandestine intelligence activities, provided that such an investigation of a United States person is not conducted solely upon the basis of activities protected by the first amendment to the Constitution of the United States.[72]

In 2001, the Patriot Act amended the FCRA to add a new national security letter authority (FCRAv). The Patriot Act amendment to the FCRA authorizes the FBI and other government agencies that investigate or analyze international terrorism to obtain a consumer reporting agency's credit reports and "all other" consumer information in its files in accordance with the following provision:

> (A) consumer credit agency shall furnish a consumer credit report of a consumer and all other information in a consumer's files to a government agency authorized to conduct investigations of, or intelligence or counterintelligence activities or analysis related to, international terrorism when presented with a written certification by such government agency that such information is necessary for the agency's conduct or such investigation, activity or analysis.[73]

This NSL authority is available to the FBI only in connection with international terrorism investigations. Until the Patriot Reauthorization Act, recipients of FCRA NSLs were prohibited from disclosing to any person that the FBI had sought or obtained the requested information.

D. The National Security Act

In 1994, in the wake of the espionage investigation of former Central Intelligence Agency employee Aldrich Ames, Congress enacted an additional NSL authority by amending the National Security Act of 1947. The amendment authorized NSLs to be issued in connection with investigations of improper disclosure of classified information by government employees.[74]

The statute permits the FBI to make requests to financial agencies and other financial institutions and consumer reporting agencies "in order to conduct any authorized law enforcement investigation, counterintelligence inquiry, or security determination."[75] Prior to the Patriot Reauthorization Act, recipients of National Security Act NSLs, like recipients of RFPA and ECPA NSLs, were prohibited from disclosing to any person that the FBI had sought or obtained the requested information, with some exceptions.

National Security Act NSLs are rarely used by the FBI.[76]

III. The Attorney General's Guidelines for FBI National Security Investigations and Foreign Intelligence Collection

National security letters may be issued by the FBI in connection with national security investigations, which are governed by Attorney General Guidelines.

During the time period covered by this report, calendar years 2003 through 2005, the Attorney General Guidelines for national security investigations were revised. From January 1, 2003, through October 31, 2003, investigations of international terrorism or espionage were governed by the Attorney General Guidelines for FBI Foreign Intelligence Collection and Foreign Counterintelligence Investigations (FCI Guidelines) (March 1999). Effective October 31, 2003, these investigations were conducted pursuant to the Attorney General's Guidelines for FBI National Security Investigations and Foreign Intelligence Collection (NSI Guidelines).[77]

A. Levels of Investigative Activity under the FCI Guidelines (January 1, 2003 - October 31, 2003)

The FCI Guidelines authorized two levels of investigative activity: preliminary inquiries and full investigations. The FCI Guidelines identified the basis or "predicate" for opening each type of investigation as well as the authorized techniques permitted at each stage. Full foreign counterintelligence investigations permitted the FBI to gather information and conduct activities

> to protect against espionage and other intelligence activities, sabotage, or assassinations conducted by, for or on behalf of foreign powers, organizations or persons, or international terrorist activities . . . .[78]

The FCI Guidelines did not permit the FBI to use national security letters during preliminary inquiries, only during full investigations. However, following the September 11 attacks, the Attorney General authorized the use of NSLs during preliminary inquiries with prior approval by the Attorney General and the FBI Director.[79]

B. Levels of Investigative Activity under the NSI Guidelines (October 31, 2003)

The NSI Guidelines issued on October 31, 2003, which remain in effect today, authorize the FBI to conduct investigations concerning threats or potential threats to the national security, including threats arising from international terrorism, espionage, other intelligence activities, and foreign computer intrusions. The NSI Guidelines authorize three levels of investigative activity - threat assessments, preliminary investigations, and full investigations - and prescribe the investigative techniques available during each investigative stage.

Threat Assessments: Under the NSI Guidelines, the FBI is authorized to conduct threat assessments

[80]

The NSI Guidelines do not permit the FBI to issue national security letters during a threat assessment.

Preliminary Investigations: Under the NSI Guidelines, a preliminary investigation (previously known as a "preliminary inquiry") can be initiated or "opened" by certain Headquarters officials or by a field office with the approval of certain field supervisors. A preliminary investigation can be opened when there is information or an allegation indicating the existence of one of several identified circumstances. In preliminary investigations, FBI agents are authorized to employ the activities and techniques permitted to be used during threat assessments as well as certain other investigative techniques, including the issuance of national security letters.[81]

Full Investigations: Under the NSI Guidelines, full investigations may be opened when there are "specific and articulable facts giving reason to believe that a threat to the national security may exist."[82] During these investigations, FBI agents are authorized to employ the activities and techniques permitted to be used during threat assessments and preliminary investigations, as well as certain other investigative techniques.[83] National security letters are permitted to be used during full investigations.

The NSI Guidelines also provide guidance concerning the selection of authorized techniques during different investigative stages:

> Choice of Methods. The conduct of investigations authorized by these Guidelines may present choices between the use of information collection methods that are more or less intrusive, considering such factors as the effect on the privacy of individuals and potential damage to reputation. As Executive Order 12333 § 2.4 provides, "the least intrusive collection

techniques feasible" are to be used in such situations. It is recognized, however, that the choice of techniques is a matter of judgment. The FBI shall not hesitate to use any lawful techniques consistent with these Guidelines, even if intrusive, where the degree of intrusiveness is warranted in light of the seriousness of a threat to the national security or the strength of the information indicating its existence. This point is to be particularly observed in investigations relating to terrorism.[84]

IV. The Role of FBI Headquarters and Field Offices in Issuing and Using National Security Letters

We describe below the responsibilities of Headquarters and field divisions assigned to conduct or support the FBI's investigative and intelligence activities in national security investigations.

A. FBI Headquarters

During most of the period of this review, three FBI Headquarters divisions were responsible for supervising the FBI's counterterrorism, counterintelligence, and cyber programs: the Counterterrorism Division, Counterintelligence Division, and Cyber Division. These programs were implemented through the counterterrorism, counterintelligence, and cyber squads in the FBI's 56 domestic field divisions and through the establishment of operational support sections within the Headquarters divisions.

1. Counterterrorism Division

The division's mission is to identify and disrupt potential terrorist plots, freeze terrorist finances, share information with law enforcement and intelligence partners world-wide, and provide strategic and operational threat analysis to the intelligence community. Agents assigned to counterterrorism squads use information derived from national security letters to analyze non-content telephone and Internet communications, financial records, financial institution and consumer-identifying information, and consumer full credit reports.

2. Counterintelligence Division

The division's mission involves counterproliferation, counterespionage, and protection of critical national assets. Agents assigned to counterintelligence squads use information obtained from national security letters to analyze non content telephone and Internet communications, financial records, and financial institution and consumer-identifying information.

3. Cyber Division

The division's mission is to protect the United States against cyber-based attacks and high technology crimes. Its agents provide support for computer-related counterterrorism and counterintelligence investigations with an international nexus, including foreign computer intrusion cyber investigations.

4. Directorate of Intelligence

The directorate's mission is to meet current and emerging national security and criminal threats by assuring that the FBI proactively targets threats to the United States; providing useful, appropriate, and timely information and analysis; and building and sustaining FBI-wide intelligence policies and capabilities. The directorate has no officials who are authorized to sign national security letters. However, during the period covered by our review the field-based Field Intelligence Groups, which report to this directorate, performed significant analytical work on data derived from national security letters in support of the FBI's counterterrorism, counterintelligence, and cyber programs. The directorate also serves as the FBI's primary liaison for dissemination and receipt of intelligence information outside the FBI and has the final review authority over intelligence products to be disseminated outside the FBI, including information derived from national security letters.

5. Office of the General Counsel (FBI-OGC)

The National Security Law Branch (NSLB) of FBI-OGC provides legal advice, guidance, and training on the FBI's use of national security letter authorities; collects data on NSL usage from Headquarters and field divisions for purposes of preparing the Department's required reports to Congress; prepares NSLs for the signatures of the General Counsel, the Deputy General Counsel for NSLB, and certain Headquarters officials; provides technical support regarding retention and dissemination of NSL-derived information; identifies, evaluates, and corrects misuse of NSL authorities; evaluates possible Intelligence Oversight Board (IOB) violations reported by field and Headquarters personnel and reports some of these matters to the President's Foreign Intelligence Oversight Board; and develops legislative proposals and responds to congressional requests for information about the FBI's use of its NSL authorities.

B. FBI Field Divisions

The FBI's 56 field divisions have counterterrorism, counterintelligence, and cyber squads that investigate cases related to national security threats or potential threats. Field supervisors are authorized to initiate counterterrorism, counterintelligence, and cyber investigations, and Special Agents in Charge are authorized to sign national security letters. Additional FBI and non-FBI field personnel who are responsible for reviewing and analyzing information obtained through national security letters are:

1. Chief Division Counsel

Chief Division Counsel (CDCs) in all 56 FBI field divisions report to the Special Agents in Charge of the field division and are responsible for reviewing all national security letters prepared for the signature of the Special Agent in Charge. CDCs in large field divisions sometime delegate this authority to Assistant Division Counsel. The responsible Chief Division Counsel or Assistant Division Counsel examines approval documents and the draft national security letters for legal sufficiency, corrects errors, seeks additional information when needed, and forwards the approval package to the Special Agent in Charge. CDCs also provide training to agents serving on counterterrorism, counterintelligence, and cyber squads, provide advice on how to address legal issues arising from the use of NSL authorities, and assist case agents in reporting possible IOB violations arising from the use of these authorities to FBI-OGC.

2. Field Intelligence Groups

Field Intelligence Groups (FIG) were established in all 56 field divisions by October 2003. They include special agents, intelligence analysts, language analysts, and special surveillance groups. FIG personnel conduct intelligence analyses, direct the collection of information to fill intelligence gaps, and are responsible for disseminating intelligence products to internal and external customers, including state and local law enforcement. FIG personnel analyze information derived from national security letters, often relating it to other cases within the field division and other field divisions. The intelligence directorate's Field Oversight Unit develops, supports, and provides oversight of the FIGs, which are managed in each field division by an Assistant Special Agent in Charge.

3.THE FBI'S COLLECTION AND RETENTION OF INFORMATION OBTAINED FROM NATIONAL SECURITY LETTERS

In this chapter we describe the process by which FBI agents obtain approval to issue national security letters. We also describe the manner in which the FBI obtains information through national security letters from third parties and retains such information in FBI Headquarters and field divisions.

I. The FBI's Process for Collecting Information through National Security Letters

According to our interviews of FBI personnel, case agents conducting counterintelligence, counterterrorism, or foreign computer intrusion cyber investigations who need telephone or e-mail transactional activity, subscriber information, financial transactions, or credit information relevant to their investigations first assess the most effective investigative technique available at a particular stage of the investigation. For example, if the facts developed indicate a nexus to possible criminal activity, agents can ask the United States Attorney's Office to open a grand jury investigation, which allows prosecutors to issue federal grand jury subpoenas to obtain third party records.[85] If there is a criminal nexus, prosecutors often prefer to use grand jury subpoenas because they generally can obtain grand jury subpoenas quickly and recipients respond more promptly to grand jury subpoenas than they do to NSLs. However, issuance of a grand jury subpoena risks public disclosure that the government is conducting a national security investigation. As a result, agents often consider alternative investigative techniques, such as national security letters, which avoid public disclosure of the existence of an investigation.

To obtain approval within the FBI to issue national security letters, FBI agents must determine that information available pursuant to one of the national security letter authorities is relevant to an authorized investigation to protect against international terrorism or clandestine intelligence activities and, with respect to an investigation involving a "U.S. person," is "not solely conducted on the basis of activities protected by the First Amendment."[86] Case agents assigned to counterterrorism, counterintelligence, or cyber squads are responsible for preparing the documentation necessary to secure approval to issue a national security letter. Case agents are encouraged to check FBI databases, such as the Automated Case Support (ACS) system and Telephone Applications, a specialized application storing telephone record data, to determine whether the information they need has previously been obtained by the FBI or is available through public search engines or commercial databases.

FBI administrative policy, set forth in the partially classified National Foreign Intelligence Program (NFIP) Manual and on NSLB's Intranet website, requires that case agents prepare two documents to obtain an NSL: (1) an electronic communication (EC) seeking supervisory approval for the national security letter and (2) the national security letter itself.

1. *Electronic Communication (Approval EC)*

The EC used to obtain approval of national security letters serves four functions. It:

- documents the predication for the national security letter by stating why the information was relevant to an authorized investigation;
- documents the approval of the national security letter by appropriate personnel;
- includes information needed to fulfill congressional reporting requirements; and
- transmits copies of the request to the FBI-OGC; FBI Headquarters Counterterrorism, Counterintelligence, or Cyber Division; and, when the recipient is not located in the field division issuing the national security letter, the field division that is asked to serve the national security letter.

During the period covered by our review, NSLB attorneys developed eight standard formats for the approval ECs that included routine elements common to all NSL requests, data elements needed for congressional reporting, and descriptions of the elements that were to be included in the national security letter package. NSLB modified the standard formats as national security letter statutes were revised and internal FBI administrative policy changed.

As discussed in Chapter Two, the Patriot Act lowered the predication standard for national security letters from "specific and articulable facts giving reasons to believe that the person or entity to whom the information sought pertains is a foreign power or an agent of a foreign power" to "relevan[ce] to an authorized investigation to protect against international terrorism or clandestine intelligence activities." The standard form used during the period covered by this review required that case agents provide justification for opening or maintaining the investigation and "briefly state the relevance of the requested records to the investigation."[87]

To enable the FBI to collect data for its semiannual congressional reporting requirements, the following information also is required to be included in the approval EC: (1) for RFPA financial record NSLs, ECPA toll billing and electronic communication transactional records NSLs, and FCRA NSLs, the investigative subject's status as a "U.S. person" or "non-U.S. person"; (2) the type of national security letter issued; and (3) a list of the individual telephone numbers, e-mail addresses, account numbers, or other records for which information is sought.[88]

For field division-initiated national security letters, the Supervisory Special Agent of the case agent's squad, the Chief Division Counsel, and the Assistant Special Agent in Charge are responsible for reviewing the approval EC and the national security letter prior to approval by the Special Agent in Charge. Division Counsel are required to review the national security letters to ensure their legal sufficiency - specifically, the relevance of the information requested to an authorized national security investigation.

The final step in the approval process occurs when the Special Agent in Charge or authorized FBI Headquarters official (the certifying official) initials the approval EC and signs the national security letter.[89] For national security letters generated by Headquarters, there is a parallel requirement for generating the approval paperwork for the signature of specially designated Headquarters officials.[90] Accordingly, the approval EC includes an "approved by" section that reflects the names of the reviewing and approving officials, who enter their initials on the hard copy of the document.

Field personnel in the four field offices we visited during the review told us that it takes from two to five days to obtain approval to issue NSLs. However, if there is no Special Agent in Charge in place in a field office, NSLs must be sent to another field office for approval by another Special Agent in Charge. Several Special Agents in Charge and Acting Special Agents in Charge told us that this has led to delays of as long as two weeks in securing approval to issue NSLs.

The approval EC also includes directions, known in FBI parlance as "leads," to other FBI offices for actions that these offices are directed to take regarding the national security letter. Leads are "set" electronically through the FBI's ACS computer system when the approval ECs are uploaded into the system. FBI personnel are responsible for checking ACS periodically to determine whether leads have been assigned to them. Leads also may be sent in hard copy via the FBI's interoffice mail delivery system. The initiating field office also includes a lead to NSLB that instructs it to record the appropriate information needed to fulfill congressional reporting requirements and an informational lead notifying the Counterterrorism, Counterintelligence, or Cyber Division of the national security letter.

A case agent from the field office squad initiating the national security letter (the "office of origin") hand carries the letter to the designated recipient if it is located in the field division. If the NSL recipient is located in another field division, the office of origin sets a lead to the field office where the recipient is located with instructions to personally deliver the national security letter to the recipient.

2. *The National Security Letter*

A national security letter is the operative document that directs a third party to provide specific records. Although the internal documentation supporting the approval of national security letters is classified, neither the letters themselves nor the information provided to the FBI in response to the letters is classified.

As mentioned previously, during the period covered by our review NSLB developed and posted on its Intranet web site eight standard formats or models for the different types of national security letters that request the following categories of information, each of which was derived from one of the four statutory national security letter authorities in the Electronic Communications Privacy Act (items 1 - 4), the Right to Financial Privacy Act (item 5), or the Fair Credit Reporting Act (items 6, 7 and 8):

1. Telephone subscriber information;
2. Telephone toll billing records;
3. Electronic (e-mail) subscriber information;

4. Electronic communication transactional records;
5. Financial records;
6. Identity of fmancial institutions;
7. Consumer identifying information; and
8. Credit reports.

National security letters typically are addressed to an established point of contact at the entity possessing the records. For major national communication providers and other routine recipients of national security letters, NSLB posts a list of known points of contact on its Intranet website.

The first paragraph of the national security letter identifies the statutory authority for the request and the types of records requested. For example, a national security letter under the Fair Credit Reporting Act would reference 15 U.S.C. § 1681u(a) as the statutory authority and would request the names and addresses of all financial institutions at which a particular consumer maintains or has maintained an account. The letters also provide the identifying information for the specific individual (such as name, address, date of birth, or social security number), telephone number, or e-mail/Internet Protocol address, and specify a precise time period for which information is requested.

The national security letter also contains a statutorily required certification that the requested records are relevant to an authorized investigation to protect against international terrorism or clandestine intelligence activities and, with respect to investigations of "U.S. persons," that the investigation is not conducted solely on the basis of activities protected by the First Amendment.

In conformity with the non-disclosure provisions in the NSL statutes, the next paragraph of the letter notifies the recipient that no officer, employee, or agent of the entity may disclose that the FBI sought or obtained the requested information or records. The last paragraph instructs the recipient to provide the records personally to an FBI representative at the field division that served the national security letter.

National security letters also may include an attachment that explains the specific types of records that the FBI is requesting or that the recipient may deem to be responsive. For example, attachments to the Electronic Communications Privacy Act and Right to Financial Privacy Act national security letters list the types of information that the recipient might consider to be "toll billing records information" or a "financial record."

The FBI's practices regarding the delivery methods and designated response times noted in the NSLs evolved during the period covered by our review. In response to delays encountered by the personal delivery requirement, NSLB concluded that FBI personnel could, with minimal risk, use certain delivery services to deliver national security letters, such as the U.S. Postal Service or restricted delivery options offered by private delivery services.[91]

Some FBI agents complained to NSLB that failure to designate a due date or "return date" in the body of the NSL led to delayed responses by some recipients, which sometimes compromised time-sensitive investigations. NSLB concluded that there was no legal restriction against including a return date (much as a grand jury subpoena or administrative subpoena includes a specified "return date").

Headquarters and field personnel in the four field divisions we visited told us that there is no FBI policy or directive requiring the retention of signed copies of national security letters or any requirement to upload national security letters into ACS. We found that the FBI has no uniform system for tracking responses to national security letters, either manually or electronically.[92] Instead, individual case agents are responsible for following up with NSL recipients to ensure timely and complete responses. Case agents are also responsible for ensuring that the documents or electronic media provided to the FBI match the requests, both as to content and time period; analyzing the responses; and, depending upon the type of records, providing the documents or other materials to FBI intelligence or financial analysts who also analyze the information received.

II. The FBI's Retention of Information Obtained from National Security Letters

FBI case agents who obtain information from national security letters retain the information in different ways and in a variety of formats. The FBI has not issued general guidance regarding the retention of this infoimation. The manner in which case agents retain the information depends upon the NSL type, the size and format of the response, and the manner in which the data is to be analyzed.

The case agents and squad supervisors we interviewed told us that they prefer to receive responses in electronic format for ease of storage and analysis. However, case agents and squad supervisors told us that the majority of the responses to all types of national security letters during the period covered by our review were delivered in hard copies.[93] Field personnel told us that some major telephone companies provide telephone toll billing records and subscriber information in electronic format.

After inventorying the hard copy response to confirm that the information received matches the information requested in the NSL, the case agents generally prepare and upload an EC into ACS that documents receipt of the information. If the responsive records are relatively small in volume, the records are placed in the investigative case file or in a sub-file created to store information derived from NSLs. If the response to the NSL is voluminous, such as hundreds of pages of toll billing records or bank records, the documents are placed in centralized storage and the case agent completes a tracking form noting where the data is located.

If the response to the NSL is in an electronic format, such as a computer diskette, either the case agent or analyst initially reviews the response to confirm that the response matches the request and prepares the EC documenting receipt of the records. For example, the EC documenting receipt of ECPA telephone toll billing records or e-mail subscriber information states that the telephone number or e-mail address did or did not belong to the investigative subject or other target of the NSL. The case agent, data clerk, or analyst then provides the computer diskette or other electronic medium to an intelligence assistant or analyst, who is responsible for uploading the data into the pertinent database, such as the Telephone Applications database.[94]

Once an EC is uploaded into ACS documenting receipt of the response to an NSL, authorized users of ACS may access the EC's contents. During the period covered by our review, there were approximately 29,000 authorized accounts issued for FBI personnel permitting them to access ACS, and approximately 5,000 accounts issued for non-FBI persormel.[95] The vast majority of the non-FBI account holders were officers serving on task forces, such as the Joint Terrorism Task Forces, the Foreign Terrorist Tracking Task Force, and the National Joint Terrorism Task Force. The remaining accounts were provided to staff in organizations such as the Department of Homeland Security, the Terrorist Screening Center, and the National Counterterrorism Center.

Raw data derived from national security letters or the analysis developed from the raw data are often used to create spreadsheets that are stored on the computer hard drives of Headquarters or field office personnel. As we discuss in Chapter Five, case agents and analysts told us that they generate these types of spreadsheets to establish communication and financial networks between investigative subjects and others. In addition, Headquarters and field offices have shared or "networked" computer drives that permit all case agents, analysts, and support personnel on a particular squad or a larger universe of users in the field office or Headquarters division to access them. In such cases, raw NSL data or the analytical products derived from this data are retained on these shared drives.

If a field or Headquarters supervisor determines that a more formal analytical intelligence product, such as an Intelligence Information Report or Intelligence Bulletin, should use information from NSLs and be shared with other members of the intelligence community or others, analysts on the field-based Field Intelligence Groups or the Headquarters Directorate of Intelligence prepare these products.[96] Electronic versions of these products are stored on field and Headquarters hard drives and, if a decision is made by the Directorate of Intelligence to disseminate them, are uploaded into the databases that are accessed by FBI and non-FBI personnel with authorized accounts.

We learned that the FBI's retention practices regarding information received in response to NSLs in excess of what was requested, whether due to FBI or third-party error, varies. If a field case agent determines that the NSL recipient provided more information than was requested, the case agent is responsible for notifying the Chief Division Counsel (CDC) and sequestering the information. However, we found that FBI-OGC did not issue guidance to all CDCs as to the mechanics of sequestering this information until November 2005. Instead, FBI-OGC provided ad hoc guidance to field agents or Division Counsel who contacted FBI Headquarters with questions.[97]

In our review, we learned of instances in which the excess records were destroyed, returned to the NSL recipient, or sequestered and given to the Chief Division Counsel. However, in other instances we found that case agents retained the information and sought approval to issue a new NSL to cover the excess information. Case agents and supervisors in the four field offices we visited told us that infonnation provided in excess of what was requested in the NSL was not uploaded into ACS or other FBI databases.[98]

As noted above, the principal FBI databases that contain raw data derived from national security letters are ACS and a specialized application for telephone data. ACS is the FBI's centralized case management system. NSL data is periodically downloaded from ACS and Telephone Applications into the FBI's Investigative Data Warehouse (IDW), a centralized repository for intelligence and investigative data with advanced search capabilities.[99] Raw data derived from national security letters also is retained in various classified databases operated by the FBI and other members of the intelligence community.

4. National Security Letter Requests Issued by the FBI from 2003 through 2005

In this Chapter, we describe the FBI's use of national security letters during calendar years 2003 through 2005. In Section I, we discuss several problems with the FBI-OGC National Security Letter database (OGC database) that affect the accuracy of the information in this database. In Section II, while noting the limitations of the OGC database, we present data on the FBI's NSL usage that we developed from the Department's semiannual classified reports to Congress, the OGC database, and our examination of investigative files in four FBI field offices.

I. Inaccuracies in the FBI's National Security Letter Tracking Database

During the period covered by our review, the Department was required to file semiannual classified reports to Congress describing the total number of NSL requests issued pursuant to three of the five NSL authorities.[100] In these reports, the Department provided the number of requests for records and the number of investigations of different persons or organizations that generated NSL requests. These numbers were each broken down into separate categories for investigations of "U.S. persons or organizations" and "non-U.S. persons or organizations."[101] The data in the reports were drawn from the OGC database that was developed specifically to collect infonnation for the Department's semiannual classified reports to Congress. The OGC database is the only centralized repository of data reflecting the FBI's use of national security letter authorities.

However, as we describe below, several flaws with internal reporting by the FBI, as well as structural problems with the OGC database, affect the accuracy of the data and therefore the accuracy of the reports to Congress.[102]

Total Number of NSL Requests. We identified three flaws in the manner in which the FBI records, forwards, and accounts for information about its use of NSLs that affect the accuracy of the FBI's database and reports to Congress on the number of NSL requests issued. They are (1) incomplete or inaccurate information on NSLs issued; (2) field office delays in entering information into ACS, which impedes NSLB's ability to extract and compile data on NSL usage in a timely fashion; and (3) incorrect data in the OGC database.

1) *Incomplete or inaccurate infoimation on NSLs issued:* During our examination of 293 NSLs in 77 investigative case files, we compared the documents in the case files to the data recorded in the OGC database. We first examined whether NSLs contained in the case files were recorded in the OGC database, and whether the NSLs recorded in the OGC database were contained in the case files. We found that 31 of the 77 case files contained NSLs that were not recorded in the OGC database, and 8 of the case files did not contain NSLs that were recorded in the OGC database. Overall, there were approximately 17 percent more NSLs in the case files we examined than were recorded in the OGC database.

We also identified the total number of "requests" (such as several requests in an NSL for individual telephone numbers or bank accounts) in 212 of the 293 NSLs and compared that to the number of NSL requests recorded in the OGC database for those same national security letters.[103] We found 30 of the 212 NSLs in which the number of NSL requests in the letters differed from the number of NSL requests recorded in the OGC database: 21 contained more NSL requests (194 actual NSL requests versus 36 recorded in the OGC database) and 9 contained fewer NSL requests (18 actual NSL requests versus 38 recorded in the OGC database). Overall, we found 22 percent more NSL requests in the case files we examined than were recorded in the OGC database.

2. *Field delays in entering NSL information:* NSLB relies exclusively on the NSL approval ECs to extract information for entry into the OGC database. From 2003 through 2005, some FBI special agents or FBI support personnel in the field did not enter the approval ECs into ACS, the FBI's electronic case management system, in a timely manner. As a result, this information was not in the OGC database when data was extracted for the semiannual reports to Congress. Although this data was subsequently entered in the OGC database, it was not included in later congressional reports because each report only includes data on NSL requests made in a specific 6-month period.

   We determined that from 2003 through 2005 almost 4,600 NSL requests were not reported to Congress as a result of these delays in entering this information into the OGC database.[104] In March 2006, the FBI acknowledged to the Attorney General and Congress that NSL data in the semiannual classified reports may not have been accurate and stated that the data entry delays affected an unspecified number of NSL requests. The FBI indicated that the final numbers of NSL requests may "change slightly should additional data be subsequently reported. . . ."[105] After the FBI became aware of these delays, it took steps to reduce the impact of the delays to negligible levels for the second half of CY 2005.

3. *Incorrect data entries in the OGC database:* During our review of the OGC database, we discovered a total of 212 incorrect data entries that caused 477 NSL requests to be erroneously excluded from the Department's semiannual classified reports to Congress. In some cases, the data fields for relevant dates were blank (153 entries affecting 403 NSL requests). In other cases, typographical errors in entering the relevant dates (for example, entering "12/31/203" instead of "12/31/2003") produced entries that were not captured in the reports (59 entries affecting 74 NSL requests). In addition, we determined that the OGC database is programmed to provide a default value of "0" for the number of "NSL requests." Entering a record with a "0" entry for NSL requests - which sometimes occurred - is an error, as every NSL generates at least one NSL request. We confirmed that the OGC database includes some records that erroneously indicate "0" items were requested in the NSLs, and thus the database understates the number of NSL requests for those records.

   As a result of the delays in uploading NSL data and the flaws in the OGC database, the total numbers of NSL requests that were reported to Congress semiannually in CYs 2003, 2004, and 2005 were significantly understated. However, we were unable to fully determine the extent of the inaccuracies because an unknown amount of data relevant to the period covered by our review was lost from the OGC database when it malfunctioned. Based on our analysis of the database and the semiannual classified reports to Congress, the most significant amount of data was lost in 2004. Nonetheless, by comparing the data reflected in the these reports to data in the OGC database for 2003 through 2005, we estimated that approximately 8,850 NSL requests, or 6 percent of NSL requests issued by the FBI during this period, were missing from the database.[106]

Total Number of Investigations of Different U.S. Persons and Different non-U.S. Persons. In addition to inaccuracies regarding the total number of NSL requests, we found other inaccuracies in the OGC database that affect the accuracy of the total number of "investigations of different U.S. persons" and "investigations of different non-U.S. persons" that the Department reported to Congress. These included (1) inconsistencies among the NSL approval ECs in the same investigation from which NSLB extracts U.S. person/non-U.S. person data; and (2) incorrect tabulations and data entries in the OGC database. The following are examples of some of these inaccuracies:

1. During investigations, individuals' names may be identified and included in approval ECs in a number of different ways (for example, "John Doe," "Doe, John," "John T. Doe," "J.T. Doe"). The OGC database does not have filters that would enable the FBI to identify NSL requests for the same person in the same investigation.[107]
2. During an investigation, different FBI divisions may generate NSLs seeking information on the same person. Even though these NSLs involve the same person, they are counted separately, resulting in an overstatement of the total number of investigations of different persons. In addition, typographical errors in entries for the requesting offices contribute to the overstatement of these totals.

During our review we found that another default setting in the OGC database results in an understatement of the number of different U.S. persons who were the targets of investigations in which certain types of NSLs were issued. Specifically, we found that from 2003 through 2005, the OGC database contained a default setting of "non-U.S. person" for the investigative subject related to NSL requests for RFPA and ECPA toll billing/electronic communication transactional records. As a result, known or presumed U.S. persons could be misidentified if the default setting was not corrected during entry, resulting in an understatement of the number of investigations of different U.S. persons that used the NSLs. The misidentification and understatement of that number was confirmed in our review of case files in four field offices, during which we identified 26 of 212 approval ECs (12 percent) in which there was a discrepancy regarding the U.S. person status between the OGC database and the case file. All of the instances involved U.S. persons who were erroneously identified in the OGC database as non-U.S. persons. We identified no instances in which non-U.S. persons were erroneously identified as U.S. persons.

In a May 10, 2006, memorandum to the Attorney General, the FBI reported that data in the first annual public report on NSL usage concerning the total number of "different U.S. persons" who were subjects of investigations in which requests for RFPA and ECPA toll billing/electronic communication transactional records were issued in CY 2005 may not be accurate.[108] The FBI explained that the data "could include instances in which one targeted individual was counted more than once" due to limitations of the OGC database. However, in addition to the inaccuracy in the public report disclosed by the FBI, our review of the OGC database, the semiannual classified reports to Congress, and the investigative files in four FBI field offices showed that all of the classified semiannual reports to Congress for 2003 through 2005 contained similar inaccuracies regarding the number of "investigations of different U.S. persons" and "investigations of different non-U.S. persons" that generated NSL requests for RFPA and ECPA toll billing/electronic communication transactional records.

The problems with the OGC database, including the loss of data from the OGC database because of a computer malfunction, also prevented us from determining with complete accuracy the number of investigations of different U.S. persons and different non-U.S. persons during which the FBI issued NSLs for financial records and NSLs for toll billing/electronic communication transactional records.

II. National Security Letter Requests from 2003 through 2005

In this section, we describe the FBI's use of NSLs from 2003 through 2005 as documented in the OGC database. As discussed above, the data in the OGC database is not fully accurate or complete and, overall, significantly understates the number of FBI NSL requests. However, it is the only database that compiles information on the FBI's use of NSLs. Moreover, the data indicates the general levels and trends in the FBI's use of this investigative tool.

From 2003 through 2005, the FBI issued a total of 143,074 NSL "lists (see Chart 4.1, next page).[109] Of that number, requests (or percent) were made pursuant to the three NSL statutes that are included in the Department's semiannual classified reports to Congress (RFPA, ECPA, and FCRAu). In addition, although the data was not required to be reported to Congress, the OGC database showed that the FBI issued NSL requests for consumer full credit reports (FCRAv) during the same period. FBI records show that.

The number of ECPA NSL requests increased in CY 2004, and then decreased in CY 2005. We determined that the spike in CY 2004 occurred because of the issuance of 9 NSLs in one investigation that contained requests for subscriber information on a total of 11,100 separate telephone numbers. If those nine NSLs are excluded from CY 2004, the number of NSL requests would show a moderate, but steady increase over the three years.[110] The overwhelming majority of the NSL requests sought telephone toll billing records information, subscriber information (telephone or e-mail), or electronic communication transactional records under the ECPA NSL statute. The used NSL requests, accounting for approximately percent of the total, sought records from financial institutions such as banks, credit card com anies, and finance companies under the authority. The remaining percent of the NSL requests were issued pursuant to the NSL authorities seeking either financial institution or consumer identifying: information.[111]

Chart 4.1 illustrates the total number of NSL requests issued in calendar years 2003 through 2005.

Chart 4.2 (next page) depicts the number of NSL requests relating to investigations of non-U.S. persons and U.S. persons from 2003 through 2005. As shown in Chart 4.2, during the 3 years of our review the balance of NSL requests related to investigations of U.S. persons versus non-U.S. persons shifted. In CY 2003, NSL requests predominantly involved investigations of non-U.S. persons, but by CY 2005 the majority of NSL requests were generated from investigations of U.S. persons. However, the number of NSL requests for information generated from investigations of U.S. persons increased by almost 3,000 from 2003 to 2005, while the number of requests generated from investigations of non-U.S. persons decreased by about 1,700. As a result, the percentage of NSL requests generated from investigations of U.S. persons increased from about 39 percent of all NSL requests in CY 2003 to about 53 percent of all NSL requests in CY 2005.[112]

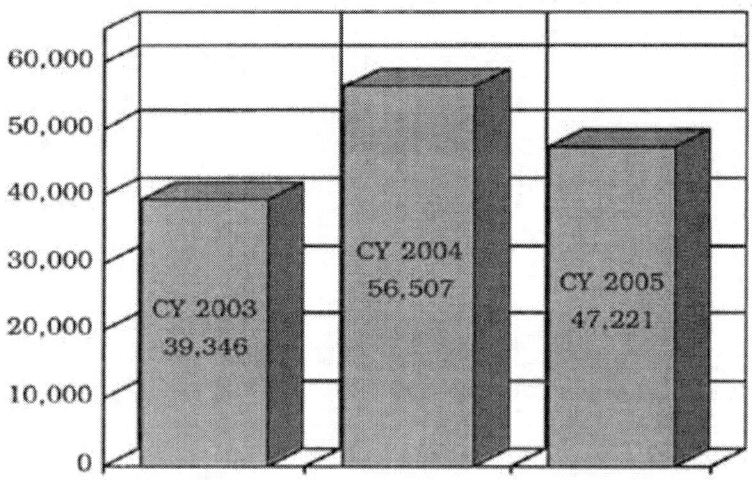

Sources: DOJ semiannual classified NSL reports to Congress and FBI-OGC NSL database as of May 2006

Chart 4.1. NSL Requests (2003 through 2005)]

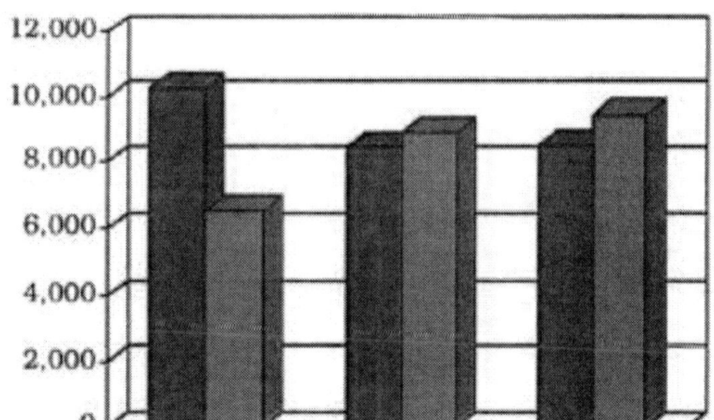

	2003	2004	2005
Non-U.S. Persons	10,232	8,494	8,536
U.S. Persons	6,519	8,943	9,475

Source: DOJ semiannual classified NSL reports to Congress

Chart 4.2. NSL Requests Reported to Congress Relating to U.S. Persons and non-U.S. Persons (2003 through 2005)

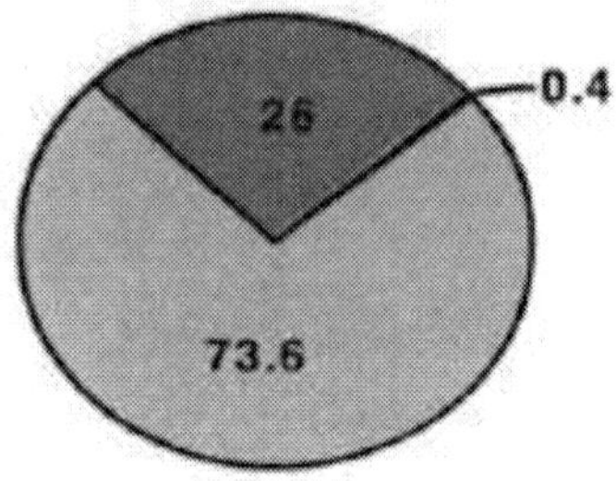

Source: FBI-OGC NSL database as of May 2006

Chart 4.3 NSL Requests in Counterterrorism, Counterintelligence, and Foreign Cyber Investigations (2003 through 2005) (U)

NSL Requests Issued During Counterterrorism, Counterintelligence, and Foreign Computer Intrusion Cyber Investigations: The following charts present the number of NSL requests issued from 2003 through 2005 for different types of investigations.

As shown in Chart 4.3, the majority of NSL requests issued from 2003 through 2005 were issued during counterterrorism investigations. Overall, about 73 percent of the total number of NSL requests issued from 2003 through 2005 were in counterterrorism investigations, and about 26 percent were issued in counterintelligence investigations. Less than 1 percent of the requests were issued in foreign computer intrusion cyber investigations.

We also observed that the use of NSLs in counterterrorism investigations increased between CY 2003 and CY 2005.[113] Chart 4.4 shows the total number of counterterrorism investigations and the number of such investigations in which NSL requests were issued. As shown in Chart 4.4, during the three ears the total number of counterterrorism investigations decreased (from , but the number of such investigations in which one or more NSLs were used increased from in CY 2003 to in CY 2005.[114] As a percentage, the use of NSLs in counterterrorism investigations almost doubled during the three years, from 15 percent of the counterterrorism investigations open during CY 2003 to 23 percent during CY 2004 and then to 29 percent in CY 2005. Overall, one or more NSLs were used in about 19 percent of all the counterterrorism investigations that were open at any point from 2003 through 2005.

The FBI's Use of National Security Letters in Different Investigative Stages: As discussed in Chapter Three, one of the most significant changes to the FBI's authority to issue national security letters occurred when the Attorney General issued the NSI Guidelines on October 31, 2003, permitting NSLs to be issued during preliminary investigations. Prior to that time, with limited exceptions, NSLs could be issued only during full investigations. Although the OGC database does not capture the investigative stage at which NSL authority was used, we recorded that information in the 293 NSLs we examined during our field visits. Chart 4.5 illustrates the type of investigation and the investigative stage during which each of the 293 NSLs we examined was issued. Overall, of the 293 NSLs we examined, 77 percent were issued in counterterrorism investigations, 23 percent were issued in counterintelligence investigations, 43.7 percent of the NSLs were issued during preliminary investigations, and 56.3 percent were issued during full investigations.

Sources: FBI-OGC NSL database as of May 2006 and Counterterrorism Division

Chart 4.4. Counterterrorism Investigations With One or More National Security Letters (2003 through 2005) [The chart below is classified SECRET]

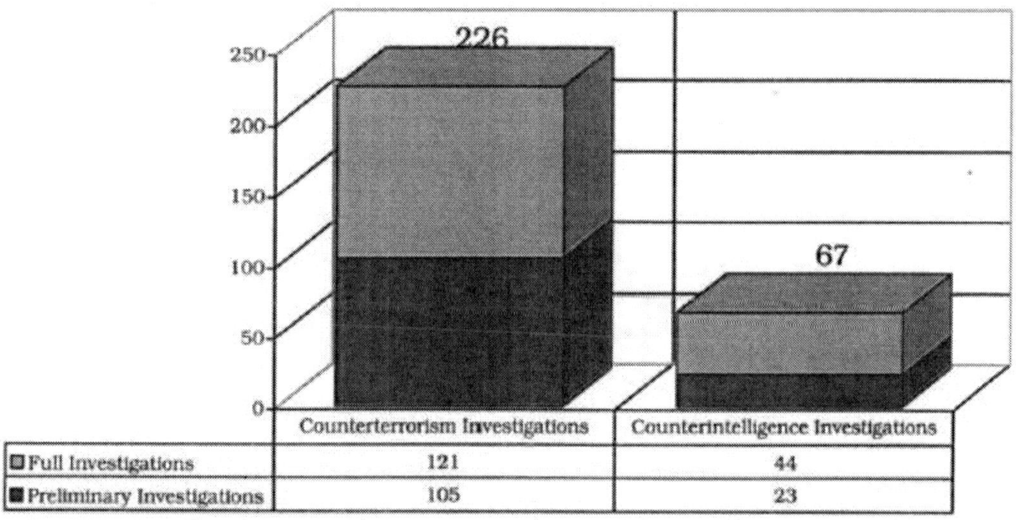

Source: Chicago, New York, Philadelphia, and San Francisco FBI Field Division investigative files

Chart 4.5. NSL Requests During Preliminary and Full Investigations Identified in Files Reviewed by the OIG (2003 through 2005)

5. The Effectiveness of National Security Letters as an Investigative Tool

III. Introduction

Along with other requirements for OIG review, Congress also directed the OIG to include in our review an examination of the effectiveness of national security letters as an investigative tool, including:

- the importance of information acquired by national security letters to the Department's intelligence activities;
- the manner in which the information acquired from national security letters is collected, retained, analyzed, and disseminated by the Department of Justice, including any direct access to such information provided to any other department, agency, or instrumentality of federal, state, local, or tribal governments or any private sector entity;
- whether and how often the FBI used information obtained from national security letters to produce an "analytical intelligence product" for distribution to, among others, the intelligence community; and whether and how often the FBI provided information obtained from national security letters to law enforcement authorities for use in criminal proceedings.

In this chapter, we address the effectiveness of national security letters as an investigative tool, the manner in which information from national security letters is analyzed and disseminated, and how national security letter-derived information is used.[115] First, we briefly describe how national security letters were used prior to the Patriot Act and what FBI personnel told us about their effectiveness during that period. Next, we describe their use after the Patriot Act, including how national security letters are used to develop information on terrorist or espionage threats. We then describe the various types of FBI analytical intelligence products that use information obtained from national security letters, and how these products are shared within the Department and among other federal agencies. We also discuss how NSL-derived information is disseminated to Joint Terrorism Task Forces and the intelligence community, among others. Next, we address whether and how often the FBI provides information derived from national security letters to law enforcement authorities for use in criminal proceedings.

IV. The Effectiveness of National Security Letters Prior to the Patriot Act

FBI personnel we interviewed who were involved in the use of national security letters prior to the Patriot Act told us that before 2001 NSLs were used infrequently in both counterterrorism and counterintelligence cases. They attributed their infrequent use to several reasons, chief of which was the delay in obtaining approval of the letters. Prior to passage of the Patriot Act, FBI field personnel were not authorized to issue national security letters, and there were significant delays in obtaining Headquarters approval. Because of the lengthy process required to obtain national security letters, FBI personnel said NSLs generally were not viewed as an effective investigative tool.[116]

FBI personnel cited three additional reasons for the ineffectiveness of national security letters in the pre-Patriot Act period. First, under the Attorney General Guidelines in effect at the time, national security letters could be used only during certain phases of investigations. Second, prior to the Patriot Act agents could seek national security letters for telephone and electronic communication transactional records from telephone companies and Internet service providers, records from financial institutions, and information from credit bureaus only upon demonstrating "specific and articulable facts" giving reason to believe that the subject was an "agent of a foreign power" or, in the case of requests for subscriber information, had been in contact with such an agent.[117] FBI officials told us that this predication standard limited the utility of NSLs as an investigative tool.[118]

Several counterterrorism officials cited a third factor for the limited value of national security letters prior to the Patriot Act: the FBI's limited analytical resources to exploit the information received. In the absence of specialized analytical expertise, the FBI relied almost exclusively on case agents to analyze information obtained through national security letters. As we describe below, the FBI's increased analytical capabilities in recent years has changed the perspective of FBI personnel on the use and effectiveness of national security letters.

The former Deputy General Counsel for the FBI-OGC's National Security Law Branch who was responsible for approving national security letters in the late 1990s told us that he considered approximately 300 NSL approval memoranda annually, each of which sought approval of one or more NSLs.[119] He stated that it was necessary to spend significant effort going back and forth with field personnel to evaluate whether there was sufficient evidence to establish the statutory predication that the NSLs related to agents of a foreign power.[120] He noted that the approval process could take as long as one year (an estimate confirmed by other field personnel we interviewed), and because of that FBI case agents would sometimes "give up" and withdraw their requests.

Notwithstanding these limitations, some FBI officials stated that national security letters occasionally were effectively used prior to the Patriot Act. For example, a counterterrorism official in a large FBI field division noted that national security letters were used successfully to identif associates of.

However, FBI field and Headquarters personnel who have worked with national security letters before and after the Patriot Act believed that their use and effectiveness has significantly increased after the Patriot Act was enacted. For example, one senior counterterrorism official noted that prior to the Patriot Act, counterterrorism investigations were conducted, then closed, when agents could not identify information associating the investigative subject with a terrorist threat. Since the Patriot Act, counterterrorism investigations are closed after the FBI has evaluated info illation from national security letters, in conjunction with other investigative techniques, which enables the FBI to conclude with a higher level of confidence that the subject poses no terrorism threat. We provide other illustrations of NSLs' use and effectiveness in the sections that follow.

V. The Effectiveness of National Security Letters as an Investigative Tool in 2003 through 2005

As discussed in Chapter Two, the Patriot Act amendments to national security letter authorities eliminated the requirement that the information sought pertain to a foreign power or an agent of a foreign power, substituting the lower evidentiary threshold that the information sought is relevant to an authorized national security investigation. The amendments also authorized Special Agents in Charge of FBI field divisions to sign national security letters, authority previously extended to only a handful of FBI Headquarters officials. In addition, in October 2003, the Attorney General issued revised Guidelines authorizing the FBI to use national security letters in preliminary investigations, not just in full investigations.[121] Taken together, these three expansions of the FBI's national security letter authorities resulted in significantly greater use of national security letters in counterterrorism, counterintelligence, and foreign computer intrusion cyber investigations.

A. The Importance of the Information Acquired from National Security Letters to the Department's Intelligence Activities

National security letters are one of several investigative techniques available to FBI agents in conducting counterterrorism, counterintelligence, and foreign computer intrusion cyber investigations. Many field agents and Headquarters officials we interviewed said it is difficult to isolate the effectiveness of national security letters in the context of a particular case. They stated that the value of a particular national security letter emerges only over the life of the case.

Nonetheless, in our review of 77 counterterrorism and counterintelligence case files and almost 300 national security letters issued in those cases, and in over 100 interviews of Headquarters and field personnel, we developed information about the importance of national security letters in these investigations during calendar years 2003 through 2005.

FBI Headquarters and field personnel told us that they found national security letters issued pursuant to the Electronic Privacy Communications Act (ECPA), the Right to Financial Privacy Act (RFPA), and the two authorities in the Fair Credit Reporting Act (FCRA) to be effective in both counterterrorism and counterintelligence investigations, many calling them "indispensable" or "our bread and butter."

1. Principal Uses of National Security Letters

FBI personnel reported that they use national security letter authorities to accomplish one or more of the following objectives:

- Establish evidence to support FISA applications for electronic surveillance, physical searches, or pen register/trap and trace orders;
- Assess communication or financial links between investigative subjects or others;
- Collect information sufficient to fully develop national security investigations;
- Generate leads for other field divisions, members of Joint Terrorism Task Forces, or other federal agencies, or to pass to foreign governments;
- Develop analytical products for distribution within the FBI, other Department components, other federal agencies, and the intelligence community;
- Develop information that is provided to law enforcement authorities for use in criminal proceedings;
- Collect information sufficient to eliminate concerns about investigative subjects and thereby close national security investigations; and
- Corroborate information derived from other investigative techniques.

Diagram 5.1 illustrates these key uses of national security letters.

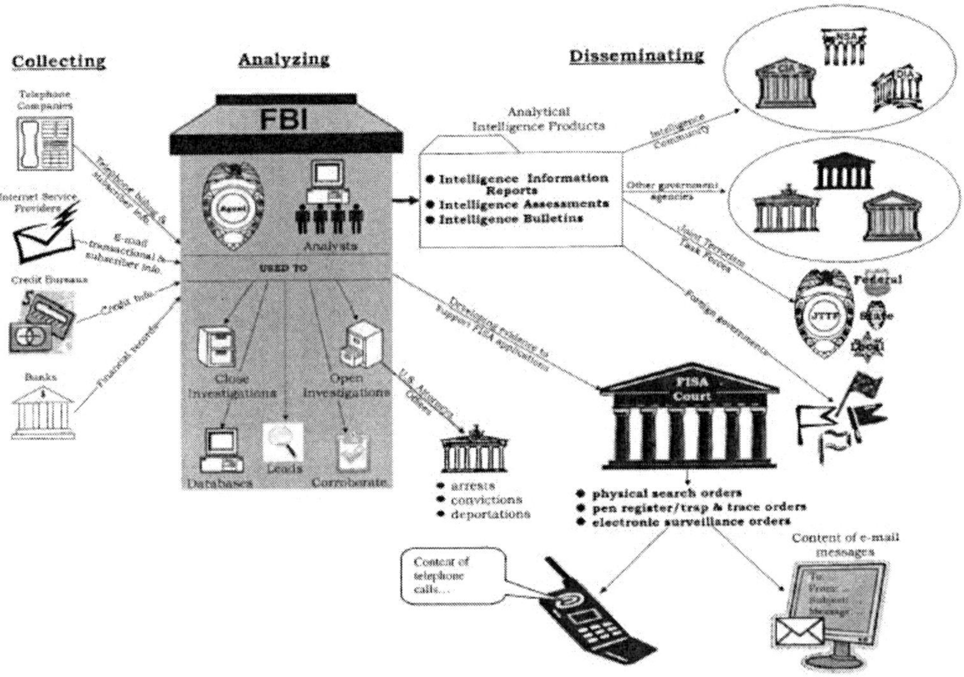

Diagram 5.1. How the FBI Uses National Security Letters

2. The Value of Each Type of National Security Letter

While details concerning the FBI's use of national security letters in particular investigations are classified, our examination of investigative files and interviews of case agents and supervisors assigned to counterintelligence and counterterrorism squads revealed that information obtained from ECPA, RFPA, and FCRA national security letters has contributed significantly to many counterterrorism and counterintelligence investigations. We describe specific examples of the importance of information obtained from the use of each type of national security letter authority below.

a. Telephone toll billing records, subscriber information, and electronic communication transactional records

In counterterrorism investigations, telephone toll billing records and subscriber information and electronic communication transactional records obtained pursuant to ECPA national security letters enables FBI case agents to connect investigative subjects with particular telephone numbers or e-mail addresses. It also allows the FBI to connect terrorism subjects and terrorism groups with each other. Analysis of subscriber information obtained from national security letters for particular telephone numbers and e-mail addresses also can assist in the identification of the investigative subject's family members, associates, living arrangements, and contacts. If the subject's associates are identified, case agents can generate new leads for their squad or another FBI field division, the results of which may complement the information obtained from the original national security letter.

Many Headquarters officials as well as case agents and supervisors in the four field offices we visited told us that the most important use of ECPA national security letters is to support FISA applications for electronic surveillance, physical searches, or pen register/ trap and trace orders. For example, to obtain FISA orders the FBI must establish ECPA national security letters for subscriber information routinely are used to confirm this required element and to otherwise develop evidence to support orders from the FISA Court. FISA court orders for electronic surveillance may authorize the FBI to collect the content of communications, information the FBI cannot obtain using NSLs.

The following text box provides examples of the use of ECPA national security letters in counterterrorism and counterintelligence investigations.

USE OF TELEPHONE TOLL BILLING RECORDS AND SUBSCRIBER INFORMATION OBTAINED BY NATIONAL SECURITY LETTERS IN COUNTERTERRORISM AND COUNTERINTELLIGENCE CASES

- Through national security letters, an FBI field office obtained telephone toll billing records and subscriber information about an investigative subject in a counterterrorism case. The information obtained identified the various telephone numbers with which the subject had frequent contact. Analysis of the telephone records enabled the FBI to identify a group of individuals residing in the same vicinity as the subject. The FBI initiated investigations on these individuals to determine if there was a terrorist cell operating in the city.
- FBI agents told us that national security letters were critical in a counterintelligence investigation that led to a conviction of a representative of a foreign power. The subject owned a company in the United States and traveled to a foreign country at the behest of a foreign intelligence service. In addition, the subject had been collecting telephone records and passing the records to a foreign intelligence officer located in the United States. Through toll billing records obtained from national security letters, the FBI was able to demonstrate that the foreign country's U.S.-based intelligence officer was in contact with the subject.
- After learning from the intelligence community that a suspected terrorist was using a particular telephone number and e-mail account, an FBI field division obtained telephone toll billing and subscriber information on the accounts. The NSLs identified that the subject was in touch with an individual who had been convicted of federal charges.
- In a counterintelligence investigation, telephone toll records obtained through national security letters revealed that, contrary to an FBI source's denials, the source was continuing to contact a foreign intelligence officer by telephone.

In counterintelligence investigations, analysis of telephone and Internet transactional records obtained through national security letters also is valuable, enabling the FBI to identify a subject's contacts with an agent of a foreign power and with individuals who may be in a osition to provide access to prohibited technologies.

b. Financial records

Financing is critical to terrorist organizations, and the FBI's ability to track the movement of funds through financial institutions is essential to identify and locate individuals who provide financial support to terrorist operations. For example, transactional data obtained from banks and other financial institutions in response to RFPA national security letters can reveal the manner in which suspected terrorists conduct their operations, whether they are obtaining money from suspicious sources, and their spending patterns. Analysis of this data can also reveal the identity of the financial institutions used by the subject; the financial position of the subject; the existence of overseas wire transfers by or to the subject ("pass through" activity); loan transactions; evidence of money laundering; the subject's involvement in unconventional monetary transactions, including accounts that have more money in them than can be explained by ordinary income or the subject's employment; the subject's financial network; and payments to and from specific individuals. However, analysis of financial records in counterterrorism investigations may be complex and time-consuming because investigative subjects often engage in legitimate businesses that disguise their terrorist affiliations.

USE OF FINANCIAL RECORDS OBTAINED BY NATIONAL SECURITY LETTERS IN COUNTERTERRORISM INVESTIGATIONS

- The FBI conducted a multi jurisdictional counterterrorism investigation of convenience store owners in the United States who allegedly sent funds to known Hawaladars (persons who use the Hawala money transfer system in lieu of or parallel to traditional banks) in the Middle East. The funds were transferred to suspected Al Qaeda affiliates. The possible violations committed by the subjects of these cases included money laundering, sale of untaxed cigarettes, check cashing fraud, illegal sale of pseudoephedrine (the precursor ingredient used to manufacture methamphetamine), unemployment insurance fraud, welfare fraud, immigration fraud, income tax violations, and sale of counterfeit merchandise.
  The FBI issued national security letters for the convenience store owners' bank account records. The records showed that two persons received millions of dollars from the subjects and that another subject had forwarded large sums of money to one of these individuals. The bank analysis identified sources and recipients of the money transfers and assisted in the collection of information on targets of the investigation overseas.
- The subject of a counterterrorism investigation was allegedly involved in narcotics trafficking. When analysis of telephone records revealed that an individual was in telephone contact with the subject, the FBI issued RFPA NSLs for that individual's bank account records. Examination of the bank records revealed no significant ties to the subject and in the absence of any information linking this individual to terrorist activities, further investigation was terminated.

FBI case agents and supervisors of counterintelligence cases told us that RFPA national security letters have provided vital information in their investigations. For example, NSL-derived information has demonstrated investigative subjects' access to unexplained sources of income, transactions with foreign government officials, and acquisition of prohibited technologies.

The text box provides examples of the use of the RFPA national security letters in two counterterrorism investigations.

c. Consumer credit records

The original FCRA NSL statute authorizes the FBI to obtain information about financial institutions from which an individual has sought or obtained credit and consumer identifying information limited to the subject's name, current address and former addresses, places of employment, and former places of employment. The Patriot Act amendment to the FCRA now authorizes the FBI to obtain through national security letters consumer full credit reports, including records of individual accounts, credit card transactions, and bank account activity. Information secured from both types of FCRA national security letters assist case agents because they provide information that often is not available from other types of financial records. For example, consumer credit records provide confirming information about a subject (including name, aliases, and Social Security number); the subject's employment or other sources of income; and the subject's possible involvement in illegal activity, such as bank fraud or credit card fraud. The supervisor of a counterterrorism squad told us that FCRA NSLs enable the FBI to see "how their investigative subjects conduct their day-to-day activities, how they get their money, and whether they are engaged in white collar crime that could be relevant to their investigations."

The following text box provides examples of the use of both types of FCRA national security letters in counterintelligence and counterterrorism investigations.

USE OF CONSUMER CREDIT BUREAU RECORDS OBTAINED BY NATIONAL SECURITY LETTERS IN COUNTERINTELLIGENCE AND COUNTERTERRORISM INVESTIGATIONS

- During a counterintelligence investigation, the FBI issued an FCRA NSL seeking financial institution and consumer identifying information about an investigative subject who the FBI was told had been recruited to provide sensitive information to a foreign power. The information obtained from the NSL assisted the FBI in eliminating concerns that the subject was hiding assets or laundering funds or that he had received covert payments from the foreign power.
- In the aftermath of Hurricane Katrina, many subjects of a major FBI counterterrorism investigation moved from areas affected by the disaster. To assist in locating these subjects, the FBI served FCRA NSLs for updated credit card information on the subjects. The information revealed the subjects' credit card activity in a major U.S. city and several foreign countries.
- The FBI initiated an investigation of an individual who was identified during the arrest of a known terrorist in a foreign country. After obtaining a credit card number used by the subject, the FBI served an NSL to obtain a consumer full credit report. The report showed that the subject had relocated to another U.S. city. The FBI's investigation was transferred to the FBI division in that city.

B. Analysis of Information Obtained from National Security Letters

The FBI performs various analyses and develops different types of analytical intelligence products using information from national security letters.

1. Types of Analysis

The review of information derived from national security letters is initially performed by the case agents who sought the national security letters. In counterterrorism investigations, once the case agents confirm that the response to the national security letter matches the request, the most important function of the initial analysis is to determine if the records link the investigative subjects or other individuals whose records are sought to suspected terrorists or terrorist groups. In counterintelligence investigations, the case agent's initial analysis focuses on the subject's network and, in technology export cases, the subject's access to prohibited technologies.

In some field offices, case agents are required to formally document their receipt of information from national security letters, including the date the information was received; the subject's name, address, and Social Security number; and a summary of the information obtained. This document then is electronically uploaded into the FBI's principal investigative database, the Automated Case Support (ACS) system. Once the data is available electronically, other case agents can query ACS to identify information obtained from national security letters that may pertain to their investigations.

After the case agent's initial analysis, analysts assigned to counterterrorism, counterintelligence, or cyber squads in the FBI's field divisions can use the NSL-derived information. The Counterterrorism and Counterintelligence Divisions in FBI Headquarters also conduct communication and financial analyses of NSL-derived information from different national security investigations.

Beginning in mid-2003, FBI field offices established Field Intelligence Groups (FIGs) as part of the Counterterrorism Division's Office of Intelligence. These squads later were moved to the FBI's Directorate of Intelligence. The FIG squads are staffed principally with intelligence analysts, language analysts, physical surveillance specialists, and field agents. FIG squads generate detailed analyses of intelligence information, some of which is derived from national security letters.

The FBI also evaluates the relationship between NSL-derived infoimation and data derived from other investigative tools that are available in various databases. For example, when communication providers furnish telephone toll billing records and subscriber information on an investigative subject in response to a national security letter, the data is uploaded into Telephone Applications, a specialized database that can be used to analyze the calling patterns of a subject's telephone number.

The FBI also places NSL-derived information into Investigative Data Warehouse (IDW), a database that enables users to access, among other data, biographical information, photographs, financial data, and physical location information for thousands of known and suspected terrorists. This FBI database contains over 560 million FBI and other agency records; information obtained from state, local and foreign law enforcement agencies; and open source data. The database can be accessed by nearly 12,000 users, including FBI agents and analysts and members of Joint Terrorism Task Forces.[122] Information derived from national security letters that is uploaded into ACS and into the Telephone Applications database is periodically uploaded to IDW.

FBI policy requires that case agents in counterterrorism investigations conduct a financial analysis of the investigative subject's financial activities. Some large FBI field divisions have dedicated squads, such as terrorist financing squads, to assist agents in analyzing the financial aspects of the subject. These squads may include specialists from outside of the FBI, such as the Defense Criminal Investigative Service or the Internal Revenue Service, who provide expertise in specific financial areas.

Like telephone call analysis, a review of financial records obtained through national security letters may show in a counterintelligence case that the subject is in contact with a foreign embassy or other foreign establishment or with other individuals known to be involved in intelligence activities. This analysis may reveal the names of people who have access to bank accounts, funds that have been transferred in and out of the accounts, and where the funds were transferred.

"Link analysis" is one of the principal analytical intelligence products generated by FIG analysts that rely on information derived from all types of national security letters used by the FBI during the period covered by our review Link charts illustrate the telephone numbers, Internet e-mail addresses, businesses, credit card transactions, addresses, places of employment, banks, and other data derived from the NSLs, as well as information derived from other investigative tools and open sources. FBI agents and analysts develop link analyses in both counterterrorism and counterintelligence investigations, often integrating the results of multiple NSLs on the subjects of multiple FBI investigations.

Analytical intelligence products based on info' illation obtained from national security letters integrate communication and financial information on particular investigative subjects and their associates. For example, national security letter-derived data reflecting telephone activity on a cluster of dates may correspond with wire transfer information obtained from national security letters served on financial institutions. In one such example, this type of information was integrated to support investigations of a threat to a major U.S. city. FIG analysts combined related information from different investigations throughout the FBI to identify contacts and financial transactions between subjects of the investigation.

2. Formal Analytical Intelligence Products

Information derived from national security letters may also be used in the development of a variety of written products that are shared with FBI personnel, distributed more broadly within the Department, shared with Joint Terrorism Task Forces, or disseminated to other members of the intelligence community.

However, FBI counterintelligence and counterterrorism personnel told us that FBI practice and policy discourage reference to the source of the information discussed in these products in order to protect the FBI's sources and methods. Nonetheless, field personnel we interviewed, including intelligence analysts and financial analysts, told us that the following types of analytical products frequently contain information derived from national security letters, particularly if they are based on information derived from FISA authorities (electronic surveillance, physical searches, or pen register/trap and trace devices). As noted above, one of the most important uses of national security letters is to develop evidence to support FISA applications. Since FISA applications for electronic surveillance must contain evidence

The following are examples of FBI analytical intelligence products that use information obtained from NSLs.

- **Intelligence Information Reports**

An Intelligence Information Report (IIR) contains "raw intelligence," which may include information from only one source or one area that has not been fully "vetted" or verified. Headquarters and field personnel told us that FBI analysts sometimes use raw data obtained from national security letters - such as telephone numbers or Internet e-mail account information - in preparing IIRs. For example, if the initial analysis of telephone toll records and subscriber information reveals important ties between a known terrorist and others, the analyst may generate an IIR quickly if the geographic location of the subject is known. In this circumstance, the IIR would be based on telephone toll billing records information combined with information derived from other investigative tools, such as physical surveillance. Rather than taking time to verify the information, the analyst may determine that it is important to issue an IIR to alert other FBI divisions, state and local law enforcement authorities, and other members of the intelligence community of the raw intelligence. Similarly, if NSLs accessing bank records show that a subject being investigated for espionage has used certain techniques, the FBI would consider communicating a description of these techniques in an HR.

FIG analysts prepare the IIRs, which are uploaded into an FBI database and distributed to all FBI personnel, to allow other offices to connect information in their files to the information in the IIR. The IIRs also are sent to the Criminal Investigative, Counterterrorism, Counterintelligence, and Cyber divisions at FBI Headquarters where a determination is made whether to distribute them more broadly in the intelligence community. In addition, IIRs involving criminal matters may be sent to other law enforcement agencies. One FIG supervisor of a large field office we visited during the review stated that his office published 700 IIRs in CY 2005, the majority generated by the division's counterintelligence squads. Overall, the FBI has generated over 20,000 IIRs from September 2001 to September 2006.[123]

- **Intelligence Assessments**

An Intelligence Assessment is a finished intelligence product developed by the FIGs that provides information on developing crime problems and emerging developments and trends regarding national security threats. Unlike an IIR that contains raw data, Intelligence Assessments use empirical data, known intelligence information, and information from national security letters to draw conclusions and recommendations. These recommendations can provide direction to specific FBI squads or programs.

Intelligence Assessments are prepared for all FBI investigative programs, including counterterrorism and counterintelligence, and for special events. Intelligence analysts we interviewed told us that while they use information obtained through national security letters to help create Intelligence Assessments, they do not attribute information in the assessment to NSLs. For example, intelligence analysts told us that in developing various Intelligence Assessments they used multiple NSLs to assess threats to a major U.S. city, risks associated with terrorists' use of certain weapons of mass destruction, the presence of foreign intelligence officers in major U.S. cities, and efforts by foreign intelligence officers to target corporate officials in order to influence U.S. policy. The assessmentsrelied in part on information developed from ECPA, RFPA, and FCRA national security letters.

- **Intelligence Bulletins**

An Intelligence Bulletin is a fmished intelligence product that contains general information on a subject or topic as opposed to case-specific intelligence that would be included in an IIR. Intelligence Bulletins generally are prepared by agents or analysts serving on the FIG squads and may be distributed within the Department, to law enforcement authorities, or to other members of the intelligence community.

Intelligence analysts we interviewed told us that while they use information obtained through national security letters to help create Intelligence Bulletins, they do not attribute information in the Bulletins to NSLs. Examples of Intelligence Bulletins that relied on NSI - derived information include products describing bulk purchases of cell phones, developments in the leadership of terrorist groups in U.S. cities, the potential for terrorist recruitment using the Internet, and manufacturers of component parts for explosives being used in Iraq.

C. The FBI's Dissemination of Information Obtained from National Security Letters to Other Entities

Attorney General Guidelines and various information-sharing agreements require the FBI to share information with the intelligence community.[124] For example, the Attorney General's Guidelines for FBI National Security Investigations and Foreign Intelligence Collection (NSI) Guidelines provide:

> The general principle reflected in current laws and policies is that information should be shared as consistently and fully as possible among agencies with relevant responsibilities to protect the United States and its people from terrorism and other threats to the national security, except as limited by specific constraints on such sharing. Under this general principle, the FBI shall provide information expeditiously to other agencies in the Intelligence Community, so that these agencies can take action in a timely manner to protect the national security in accordance with their lawful functions.[125]

In addition, four of the five national security letter authorities expressly permit dissemination of information derived from national security letters to other federal agencies if the information is relevant to the authorized responsibility of those agencies and is disseminated pursuant to the applicable Attorney General Guidelines.[126]

Pursuant to these statutes and directives, the FBI disseminated information derived from national security letters to other members of the Intelligence Community and to a variety of federal, state, and local law enforcement agencies during the period covered by our review. According to the FBI officials we interviewed, the nature and extent of dissemination depended upon several factors, including the importance and specificity of the information and whether the NSL data was integrated into formal analytical intelligence products. However, we could not determine the number of analytical intelligence products containing NSL-derived data that were disseminated from 2003 through 2005 because these products do not reference NSLs as the source of the information.[127] Although none of the FBI or other Department officials we interviewed could estimate how often NSL-derived information was disseminated to other entities, they noted that when analytical intelligence products provided analyses of telephone or Internet communications or financial or consumer credit transactions, the products likely were derived in part from NSLs.

Based on our interviews of Headquarters and field personnel and a questionnaire distributed to counterterrorism and counterintelligence squads in Headquarters and field divisions, we learned that the principal entities outside the Department to whom information derived from national security letters was disseminated were members of the intelligence community and Joint Terrorism Task Forces.

Department Components: The NSI Guidelines authorize the FBI to share information obtained through intelligence activities conducted under the Guidelines with other components of the Department of Justice.[128] Information derived from national security letters is shared with United States Attorneys' Offices (described below), the Drug Enforcement Administration, the Federal Bureau of Prisons, and other Department components, including components whose personnel serve on Joint Terrorism Task Forces, such as prosecutors and intelligence research specialists.

Joint Terrorism Task Forces: Joint Terrorism Task Forces (JTTFs) are composed of representatives of federal, state, and local law enforcement agencies who respond to leads, investigate, make arrests, provide security for special events, and collect and share intelligence related to terrorist threats.[129] Some task force members are designated Task Force Officers, some of whom obtain the necessary clearances to obtain access to FBI information, including information derived from national security letters and other investigative techniques. These Task Force Officers also are authorized to access information stored in FBI databases such as ACS, the specialized application for telephone data, and IDW which, as noted above, contain information derived from NSLs. Task Force Officers who obtain the required security clearances and sign access agreements are issued accounts to access these databases (with the exception of case information to which access was restricted due to special sensitivities). Consequently, Task Force Officers with approved user accounts are able to access databases that house raw data derived from NSLs. In addition, Task Force Officers have access to formal analytical products derived, at least in part, from national security letters and other information. However, Task Force Officers are not permitted to share this information with their host agencies unless specifically authorized in memoranda of understanding between the FBI and the host agency.

Other Federal Agencies: The Attorney General's NSI Guidelines authorize the FBI to share information obtained through intelligence activities conducted under the Guidelines with other federal law enforcement agencies and the Department of Homeland Security.[130] Since many federal agencies are represented on JITtes, the JTIFs are a significant information-sharing mechanism for information derived from national security letters as well as other investigative techniques.[131] In addition, several FBI field divisions told us that they disseminated information derived from NSLs to the Department of Energy and the Department of Commerce in connection with counterintelligence investigations.

During our site visits to four FBI field offices, we reviewed examples of documented dissemination of IIRs, Intelligence Bulletins, and Intelligence Assessments to other federal agencies. For example, case agents on counterintelligence squads disseminated NSL-derived information to the Commerce Department's Export Control Agency to identify products on an export control list. Case agents on counterterrorism squads disseminated NSL-derived information to the Immigration and Customs Enforcement branch in the Department of Homeland Security related to the investigation of potential immigration charges.

Members of the Intelligence Community: The NSI Guidelines authorize the FBI to share information covered by various memoranda of understanding with members of the intelligence community.[132] Consequently, FBI analytical products that contain information from national security letters are disseminated to other members of the intelligence community. FBI field offices told us that they disseminated information derived from national security letters to the Central Intelligence Agency, National Reconnaissance Office, Defense Intelligence Agency, Naval Criminal Investigative Service, Air Force Office of Special Investigations, and the National Security Agency. As noted above, these analytical products normally do not reference the source of the information used to produce the product.

Private Sector Entities: Together with threat information derived from other investigative tools, information from national security letters is included in threat advisories that are communicated to private sector entities. FBI officials in the four divisions we visited during the review told us that they brief members of the private sector on terrorist threats or other threats associated with special events, such as the Olympics or the World Series. These briefings may advise the security officials of private companies of the nature of the threat, but they do not communicate details of pending investigations or what investigative tools were used to identify and assess the severity of the threat.

Foreign Governments: The NSI Guidelines authorize the FBI to share information obtained through intelligence activities under the Guidelines, which include information from national security letters, with foreign authorities under specified circumstances when the dissemination is in the interest of the United States.[133] Information derived from national security letters can also generate leads that are passed on to foreign government counterparts.

Dissemination of information to foreign governments during most of the period covered by our review was handled by the Designated Intelligence Disclosure Officials (DID()) within the Directorate of Intelligence at FBI Headquarters.[134] Personnel in several field offices told us that they proposed the dissemination of information derived from national security letters to foreign governments from 2003 through 2005. For example, the Directorate of Intelligence approved the request of an FBI field division to provide information to a foreign intelligence service about the possible association of two non-U.S. telephone numbers to terrorist activities and to request assistance in obtaining subscriber information about the two telephone numbers.

D. Information from National Security Letters Provided to Law Enforcement Authorities for Use in Criminal Proceedings

Information from national security letters most often is used for intelligence purposes rather than for criminal investigations. In some instances, however, NSL-derived information, when combined with other information, is useful in criminal investigations and prosecutions. However, our review could not determine how often that occurs because the FBI does not maintain such records, and NSL-derived information is not specifically labeled as such when it is provided to law enforcement authorities.

In this section, we describe the ways in which the FBI provides information derived from NSLs to law enforcement authorities both through routine information sharing with United States Attorneys' Offices (USAOs) and in connection with specific criminal investigations and prosecutions. We also give specific examples of instances in which the FBI provided law enforcement authorities information derived from national security letters that was used in criminal proceedings.

1. Routine Information Sharing with United States Attorneys' Offices

Information obtained from national security letters and analytical products derived from this information are routinely shared with prosecutors in the USAOs, although the source and details of the information may not be readily apparent to the prosecutors. The information is shared with USAOs to determine if criminal or other charges may be brought against individuals who are subjects of FBI counterterrorism investigations.[135]

In November 2002, the Attorney General directed the United States Attorneys and the Criminal Division to review counterterrorism intelligence investigative files to determine whether they contained information that would support criminal proceedings. In June 2004, the Deputy Attorney General directed the United States Attorneys to identify all open full field FBI counterterrorism investigations that the USAOs or the local FBI field offices believed may relate to certain current threats. In consultation with FBI field offices, the USAOs were directed to determine "if there exists a potential criminal disruption option by identifying any criminal charges that appear to be available now or could be available imminently with additional investigation."[136]

Through such routine interactions with the FBI, terrorism prosecutors are familiar with the progress of counterterrorism investigations being conducted in their districts. While it would be unlikely that FBI case agents would need to attribute the fruits of their investigative activities to particular investigative techniques - such as national security letters - in routine briefings terrorism prosecutors may learn that national security letters were used and, in significant briefings, likely learn of the fruits of the technique. In addition, ATACs, other terrorism prosecutors, and intelligence research specialists in the USAOs who review the FBI's investigative files may see the results of NSLs or the analyses of the information derived from NSLs in the investigative files or through access to the FBI's databases.[137]

In the course of these file reviews, terrorism prosecutors and intelligence research specialists assigned to the USAOs may identify gaps in the data collected from all investigative techniques, including NSLs, and may suggest that additional NSLs be issued to fill these gaps. For example, if an analyst learns that the subject has received funds from a foreign country, the analyst may suggest to the case agent that RFPA NSLs be issued to obtain financial records about the subject. If the subject is suspected of money laundering or violations of the Export Control Act, the analyst may suggest that the agent issue FCRA NSLs to learn more about the subject's consumer credit transactions.

2. Providing Information to Law Enforcement Authorities for Use in Criminal Proceedings

When criminal prosecutions are pursued, information from national security letters may also be used in criminal proceedings. Information derived from national security letters may produce evidence for the prosecution's case in chief, for example by identifying communications or financial networks indicative of criminal conspiracy or material support for terrorism.[138] It may also provide evidence that persuades the subject to cooperate with the government and provide information on other terrorists or other illegal activity. As noted above, however, information derived from national security letters is not required to be marked or tagged as coming from NSLs when it is entered in FBI databases or when it is shared with law enforcement authorities outside the FBI. Moreover, when sharing intelligence with lawenforcement authorities, FBI agents do not typically refer to the investigative technique that was used to gather information.

As a result, FBI and DOJ officials told us they could not identify how often information derived from national security letters was provided to law enforcement authorities for use in criminal proceedings.[139] However, we attempted in another way to obtain a rough sense of how often the FBI provided NSL-derived information to federal law enforcement authorities for use in criminal proceedings by collecting information that is indicative of such use. Specifically, we asked FBI field personnel to identify instances in which they referred targets of national security investigations to law enforcement authorities for prosecution and whether in those instances they shared information derived from national security letters with law enforcement authorities.[140] We learned from the responses that in addition to the routine sharing of information noted above, about half of the FBI's field divisions referred one or more counterterrorism investigation targets to law enforcement authorities for possible prosecution from 2003 through 2005.[141] Of the 46 Headquarters and field divisions that responded to our request for information about referral of national security investigation targets, 19 divisions told us that they made no such referrals. Of the remaining 27 divisions, 22 divisions provided details about the type of information they referred and the nature of charges brought against these investigative subjects. In most cases, multiple charges were brought against the subjects, with the most common charges involving fraud (19), immigration (17), and money laundering (17).

We also asked FBI field offices to identify examples from the referrals to law enforcement authorities of the particular matters in which information from national security letters was used in criminal prosecutions.[142] Although the field offices that provided data on such referrals were unable to state in what percentage of these referrals they used NSLs, they provided examples of the use of NSLs in these proceedings, such as the following:

a.Counterintelligence Case No. 1

A counterintelligence investigation focused on the possible involvement of the subject in exporting sensitive U.S. military technology to a foreign country. Multiple national security letters were issued to obtain information that enabled the FBI to identify the subject's role in exporting these technologies. The FBI shared the NSL-derived information with the Internal Revenue Service, which led to the initiation of a grand jury that returned money laundering charges against the subject. The FBI also shared the NSL-derived information with the Department of Homeland Security and the Department of Commerce Office of Export

Enforcement. The FBI's investigation led to guilty pleas for 22 violations of the Arms Export Control Act and brokering the export of sensitive technologies without the required government licensing approval.

b. Counterterrorism Case No. 1

Information provided to the FBI from the intelligence community suggested that a high-value detainee who was to be incarcerated at Guantanamo Bay had used an e-mail account. The FBI issued national security letters to obtain e-mail transactional information about the user's e-mail account, which led to additional national security letters seeking telephone toll records and subscriber information on the subject and the subject's friends and associates. Information derived from one of the national security letters established a connection between the subject and the subject of another FBI investigation. The latter individual was later convicted of providing material support to terrorism.

c. Counterterrorism Case No. 2

An FBI field office issued national security letters to ascertain the investigative subject's financial dealings. The information from the national security letters suggested bank fraud activity. A federal grand jury was convened, and grand jury subpoenas were issued to obtain financial records for use in the criminal trial. The investigative subject and his wife were convicted of bank fraud, making false statements, and conspiracy.

d. Counterterrorism Case No. 3

An FBI field division used information from, national security letters in an investi sation of individuals accused of being members of .

VI. Conclusion

FBI Headquarters and field personnel told us that they believe national security letters are indispensable investigative tools that serve as building blocks in many counterterrorism and counterintelligence investigations. In further addressing the question of the effectiveness of NSLs, we considered the investigative and analytical objectives for using NSLs. Headquarters and field personnel told us that the principal objective of the most frequently used type of NSL - ECPA NSLs seeking telephone toll billing records, electronic communication transactional records, or subscriber information (telephone and e-mail) - is to develop evidence to support applications for FISA orders. NSLs also are used in counterterrorism and counterintelligence investigations to determine how and when subjects are communicating with others, their sources of funds and means of transferring funds, and how they are financing their activities. FBI agents and analysts use information derived from NSLs to determine if further investigation is warranted; to generate leads for other field offices, Joint Terrorism Task Forces, or other federal agencies; and to corroborate information developed from other investigative techniques.

The FBI generates a variety of analytical intelligence products using information derived from NSLs, including Intelligence Information Reports, Intelligence Assessments, and Intelligence Bulletins. Information derived from NSLs is stored in various FBI databases, shared within the Department and with Joint Terrorism Task Forces, and disseminated to other federal agencies and the intelligence community. The FBI also provides infoi ination from NSLs to law enforcement authorities for use in criminal proceedings.

6. Improper or Illegal Use of National Security Letter Authorities

The Patriot Reauthorization Act also directed the OIG to describe any "improper or illegal use" of the FBI's authorities to issue national security letters. In this chapter, we report our findings on improper or illegal use of the authorities that were identified by the FBI, as well as instances we discovered during our review of a sample of FBI investigative files. We also describe other uses of national security letter authorities in which FBI field personnel deviated from internal FBI policies related to NSLs that are designed to ensure appropriate FBI supervisory review and compliance with statutory authorities and Attorney General Guidelines.

In the course of our review, we identified a variety of instances in which the FBI used national security letters contrary to statutory limitations, Attorney General Guidelines, or internal FBI administrative guidance or policies. In addition to these incidents, we identified certain practices where the legality or propriety of the use of national security letters was unclear due to inadequate FBI recordkeeping practices that did not generate an audit trail that would enable us to determine if the letters were duly authorized. For example, FBI Headquarters has no policy requiring the retention of signed copies of national security letters issued by the FBI or signed copies of FBI requests for the same types of information without using an NSL, and three of the four field offices we visited did not maintain signed copies of these letters and other requests. This made it impossible for us to determine whether national security letters were signed by appropriate FBI officials, to confirm the precise information requested in the letters, or to determine the number and nature of the other types of requests.[143]

The instances of improper or illegal use of NSL authorities generally fell into the following categories:

- Issuing national security letters when the investigative authority to conduct the underlying investigation had lapsed;
- Obtaining telephone toll billing records and e-mail subscriber information concerning the wrong individuals;
- Obtaining information that was not requested in the national security letter;
- Obtaining information beyond the time period referenced in the national security letter;
- Issuing Fair Credit Reporting Act (FCRA) national security letters seeking records that the FBI was not authorized to obtain through an NSL in the pending investigation under the referenced statute, such as issuing FCRAv consumer full credit report national security letters in counterintelligence investigations;
- Issuing improper requests under the statute referenced in the NSL, such as issuing an ECPA national security letter seeking an investigative subject's educational records,

including applications for admission, emergency contact information, and associations with campus organizations;

- Obtaining telephone toll billing records by issuing "exigent letters" signed by a Counterterrorism Division Unit Chief or subordinate personnel rather than by first issuing duly authorized national security letters pursuant to the ECPA NSL statute; and
- Issuing national security letters out of "control files" rather than from "investigative files" in violation of FBI policy.

In Section I, we discuss incidents triggered by the use of NSLs that were reported by field agents to the FBI's Office of the General Counsel (FBI-OGC) as possible violations of intelligence authorities that should be reported to the Intelligence Oversight Board (IOB). In Section II, we discuss similar types of incidents and other incidents that were not reported by FBI personnel to FBI-OGC but were identified by the OIG during our site visits to four field divisions. In Section III, we discuss the improper or illegal uses of national security letter authorities that we identified were committed by FBI Headquarters Counterterrorism Division personnel. In Section IV, we describe instances identified by the OIG in which we found that FBI employees failed to adhere to internal controls on the exercise of national security letter authorities.

In evaluating these matters, it is important to recognize that in most cases the FBI was seeking to obtain information that it could have obtained properly if it had it followed applicable statutes, guidelines, and internal policies. We also did not find any indication that the FBI's misuse of NSL authorities constituted criminal misconduct.

I. Possible IOB Violations Arising from National Security Letters Identified by the FBI

The OIG issued a report in March 2006 pursuant to Section 1001 of the Patriot Act, which included an evaluation of the FBI's process for reporting possible violations involving intelligence activities in the United States to the IOB.[144] Among the types of possible IOB violations summarized in the report were instances in which the FBI may have improperly utilized national security letter authorities.[145]

In this section, we briefly summarize the FBI's procedures for reporting possible IOB violations to FBI-OGC and the manner in which FBI-OGC decides whether to report the possible violations to the IOB. We then describe the possible IOB violations regarding the use of national security letter authorities that were reported to FBI-OGC from 2003 through 2005; FBI-OGC's decisions whether to report the possible violations to the JOB; and other possible IOB violations involving national security letters that were not reported to FBI-OGC but that the OIG identified in the course of this review.

A. The IOB Process for Reporting Possible Violations of Intelligence Activities in the United States

Executive Order 12863 designates the IOB as a standing committee of the President's Foreign Intelligence Advisory Board and directs the IOB to inform the President of any activities that "may be unlawful or contrary to Executive order or Presidential Directive." This directive has been interpreted by the Department and the IOB during the period covered by our review to include reports of violations of Department investigative guidelines or investigative procedures.

The FBI has developed an internal process for the self-reporting of possible IOB violations to FBI-OGC. During the period covered by our review, FBI-OGC issued 2 guidance memoranda describing the process by which FBI personnel were required to report possible IOB violations to FBI-OGC within 14 days of discovery. The reports were to include a description of the status of the subjects of the investigative activity, the legal authority for the investigation, the potential violation, and the date of the incident. FBI-OGC then reviewed the report, prepared a written opinion as to whether the matter should be sent to the IOB, and prepared the written communication to the IOB for those matters it decided to report.

The following sections describe two groups of possible IOB violations related to NSLs that occurred during our review period (2003 through 2005).

The first group consists of 26 possible JOB violations that were reported by FBI employees to FBI-OGC. The second group of incidents consists of 22 possible JOB violations that the OIG identified during our review of a sample of 77 investigative files in the 4 field divisions we visited. We found that 17 files (22 percent) had one or more possible IOB violations. In total, the 17 files had 22 possible violations. To our knowledge, none of these 22 possible IOB violations was reported to FBI-OGC, and none was reported by FBI-OGC to the I0B.[146]

B. Field Division Reports to FBI-OGC of 26 Possible IOB Violations Involving the Use of National Security Letters

1. Possible IOB Violations Identified by the FBI

We determined that from 2003 through 2005, FBI field divisions reported 26 possible IOB violations to FBI-OGC arising from the use of national security letter authorities. Table 6.1 summarizes these matters, followed by an additional description and our analysis.

Nature of Possible IOB Violation and the NSL Statute at Issue: As noted in Table 6.1, these 26 possible IOB violations involved a variety of issues:

- In three matters, the NSLs were signed by the appropriate officials but the underlying investigations were not approved or extended by the appropriate Headquarters or field supervisors.
- In four matters, the NSLs did not satisfy the requirements of the pertinent national security letter statute or the applicable Attorney General Guidelines. In three of these matters, the FBI obtained the information without issuing national security letters. One of these three matters involved receipt of information when there was no open national security investigation. In the fourth matter, the FBI issued national security letters seeking consumer full credit reports in a counterintelligence investigation, which is not permitted by FCRAv.
- In 19 matters, the NSL recipient provided more information than was requested in the NSL or provided information on the wrong person due either to FBI

typographical errors or errors by recipients of the NSLs. Thirteen of these matters involved requests for telephone toll billing records, 4 involved requests for electronic communication transactional records, and 2 involved requests for telephone subscriber information.

Status of Investigative Subject and Target of NSL: FBI agents are required to include in their reports to FBI-OGC the status of the subject of the investigation as a "U.S. person" or a "non-U.S. person."[147] We also attempted to determine if the subject of the investigation in these 26 matters reported as possible IOB violations was the same as the target of the NSL.

Table 6.1. Summary of 26 Possible IOB Violations Triggered by Use of National Security Letters Reported to FBI-OGC (2003 through 2005)

Category of Possible IOB Violation	Number of Possible IOB Violations Reported to FBI-OGC		Number of Possible Violations Reported to the IOB
	FBI Error	Third Party Error	
Improper Authorization			
Issuing ECPA national security letter without obtaining required FBI Headquarters authorization to extend investigation after one year	1	0	1
Issuing ECPA national security letter without obtaining requi-red SAC approval to initiate a national security investigation	1	0	1
Issuing RFPA national security letter without obtaining required approval to extend investigation	1	0	1
Improper Request Under Pertinent National Security Letter Statute			
Obtaining ECPA toll billing and RFPA financial records without first issuing national security letters	3	0	2
Issuing FCRA national security letter requesting consumer full credit report in a counterintelligence case	1	0	1
Unauthorized Collection			
Obtaining ECPA telephone subscriber information not relevant to an authorized national security investigation	2	0	1
Obtaining ECPA e-mail transactional information not relevant to an authorized national security investigation	1	3	4
Obtaining ECPA telephone toll billing records not relevant to an authorized national security investigation	12	1	8
Total FBI or Third Party Errors	**22**	**4**	
Total Possible IOB Violations	**26**		**19**

- In 15 of the matters, the subject of the investigation was a "U.S. person," and in 8 of the matters the subject was a "non-U.S. person."[148]
- In 19 of the matters, the NSLs sought information about the subject of the underlying national security investigation; 2 NSLs sought information on a target other than the subject of the investigation; 1 NSL sought information on both the subject and a non-subject; 1 NSL was issued during a threat assessment (at which stage there is no subject); and 3 NSL targets could not be determined.

Source of the Error In total, 22 of the 26 possible IOB violations were due to FBI errors, while 4 were due to third-party errors. The 22 possible JOB violations due to FBI error were:

- Receipt of financial records through use of FISA authorities rather than by issuing an RFPA NSL;
- Receipt of telephone toll billing records from a telephone company without first issuing an ECPA NSL;
- Eight NSLs containing typographical errors (seven on the telephone numbers listed in the NSLs and one on the e-mail address listed in the NSL);
- Four NSLs concerning telephone numbers that responses to the NSLs revealed were no longer associated with the investigative subjects;
- An ECPA NSL requesting telephone toll billing records that was issued after the investigative authority had lapsed;
- Receipt of responses to two telephone toll billing record requests after the investigative authority had lapsed;
- A request for telephone toll billing records of an individual whose name was similar to that of the investigative subject;
- A request for financial records after the authority for the underlying investigation had lapsed;
- A request for telephone toll billing records during a criminal investigation before the Special Agent in Charge had approved conversion of the investigation to a counterterrorism investigation;
- Receipt of telephone toll billing records during a threat assessment through informal contact with FBI Headquarters Counterterrorism Division's Communications Analysis Unit; and
- A FCRA request for a consumer full credit report in a counterintelligence case.

The four third-party errors were:

- The NSL recipient providing prohibited content information (including facsimile images) in response to an ECPA NSL for telephone toll billing records; and
- The NSL recipient providing prohibited content information (including e-mail content and images) in response to three ECPA NSLs requesting electronic communication transactional records.

The following text box provides an example of a possible IOB violation.

POSSIBLE IOB VIOLATION NO. 1

In June 2004, during a file review of an authorized national security investigation of a foreign intelligence officer who was the target of a FISA court-authorized electronic surveillance order, a squad supervisor determined that a probationary case agent had on one occasion telephonically accessed the bank account of the investigative subject using information derived from the electronic surveillance order. The probationary agent had obtained the subject's bank account and personal identification number (PIN) to telephonically access the subject's bank account transactions and balance but did so without seeking approval to issue a national security letter for the records. The probationary agent had been assigned to a counterintelligence squad for 16 months at the time of the incident.

The squad supervisor told the probationary agent that the FBI was required to issue a national security letter under the RFPA before obtaining financial records in a foreign counterintelligence investigation. The agent indicated unfamiliarity with the statutory requirement. The agent was verbally counseled, and the squad supervisor promptly reported the matter to FBI-OGC as a possible IOB violation and to the FBI's Inspection Division and Office of Professional Responsibility. A RFPA national security letter later was issued to obtain the subject's financial records, including the information that was improperly obtained from FISA-derived information.

FBI-OGC determined that the matter should be reported to the IOB even if the agent was unaware that the agent was acting in contravention of the RFPA and internal FBI policy. The Inspection Division's Internal Investigations Section determined that the incident was indicative of a performance issue that did not warrant further investigation.

The following text box provides an example of the FBI's acquisition of telephone toll billing records in the absence of an active national security investigation.

POSSIBLE IOB VIOLATION NO. 2

In August 2005, a field division sent a lead to another field office concerning three suspicious telephone calls originating from the second division's jurisdiction. An intelligence analyst in the second division, under the supervision of a new Supervisory Analyst, requested via e-mail that the Counterterrorism Division's Communications Analysis Unit (CAU) "run" three numbers through its databases. CAU agreed to do so and also offered to obtain telephone toll billing records from a telephone company with the understanding that the requesting division would later prepare a national security letter to the telephone companies to cover the records obtained. The intelligence analyst agreed to the arrangement.

The same day, the intelligence analyst telephoned the Primary Relief Supervisor of a Resident Agency within the division regarding the lead on the suspicious calls. According to the field division's report to FBI-OGC, the intelligence analyst inferred that the telephone numbers were requested in the course of an ongoing substantive investigation by the first field division. The intelligence analyst requested that the Primary Relief Supervisor initiate the drafting of approval documents for the national security letter, but the intelligence analyst did not tell the Primary Relief Supervisor that he had already requested the records from CAU. About a week later, CAU sent the requested records to the intelligence analyst.

Because CAU had committed to the telephone company that it would furnish a national security letter after the fact to cover the records, the receiving division considered issuing a national security letter from its control file. However, the division's Chief Division Counsel, following consultation with the National Security Law Branch, determined that a national security letter could not be issued from its control file absent prior approval.

FBI-OGC concluded that the FBI's acquisition of the telephone toll billin records constituted a violation of the ECPA national security letter statute.

Reporting and Remedial Actions: Twenty of the 26 possible IOB violations were timely reported within 14 days of discovery to FBI-OGC in accordance with internal FBI policy. However, 6 were not reported in a timely fashion, taking between 15 days and 7 months to report.

We identified the remedial action that was taken regarding the 26 possible violations.

- In the 19 matters that involved unauthorized collection of information not relevant to an authorized national security investigation, field office documentation stated that the information was retrieved and segregated, reviewed no further, and sometimes forwarded to FBI-OGC for final disposition.[149] If the information had been uploaded or disseminated, FBI records showed that it was removed from the relevant databases and the disseminated information retrieved and segregated with the original information.
- In three of the matters that involved improper requests under pertinent national security letter statutes, field office documentation stated that the records received either were destroyed or sealed or that NSLs were issued for the requested records to cover the time period in question. In the fourth matter, one of the three NSLs was returned unexecuted when the FBI office that was to deliver the letter discovered the error and sent it back to the initiating office. Information from the NSL that had been disseminated to a foreign counterintelligence Task Force Officer was returned to the FBI without being used. The information inappropriately obtained from two NSLs was sealed and sent to FBI-OGC.
- In the three matters that involved improper authorization, field division documentation stated that the field division was instructed to cease further investigative activity in the investigation that was improperly extended without FBI headquarters authorization; an EC was sent to FBI Headquarters requesting approval to extend the investigation for six months; and the case agent submitted appropriate documentation to change the case designation to a counterterrorism case.

FBI-OGC decisions: FBI records show that FBI-OGC reported 19 of the 26 possible violations to the JOB. The FBI-OGC decided that the 7 remaining matters were not reportable to the IOB for the following reasons:

- In one of the matters, the FBI obtained telephone toll billing records on an investigative subject who was a "non-U.S. person" without issuing NSLs. The FBI-OGC decision stated that "only violations of the AG Guidelines which are designed to safeguard the rights of U.S. persons are required to be reported to the IOB."[150] The FBI-OGC decision memorandum noted that if the subject of the national security letter had been a "U.S. person" the matter would likely constitute a reportable IOB violation.
- In four matters, the FBI obtained telephone toll billing records or subscriber information that identified the telephone numbers with the investigative subjects. When the case agents reviewed the responses to the NSLs, they discovered that the telephone numbers were not associated with the investigative subjects. The FBI-OGC decisions stated that in each instance there was an authorized investigation for which NSLs were an appropriate investigative technique, and the NSLs were appropriately authorized. FBI-OGC also concluded that the case agents acted in good faith.
- In two related matters the FBI issued national security letters for telephone toll billing records during authorized national security investigations but the NSL recipient provided the results 35 days after expiration of the authority to conduct the investigation. The FBI-OGC decision stated that the FBI's receipt of the information did not constitute a violation of the Attorney General's NSI Guidelines because no investigative activity was conducted after the investigative authority had expired, and the case agent took appropriate steps to obtain approval to extend the investigation before conducting further investigative activity.

With regard to the FBI's decisions whether to report the possible violations to the JOB, we concurred in FBI-OGC's analysis and conclusions to report 19 of the 26 possible violations to the JOB. With one exception, we also concurred in its analysis and conclusions not to report the 7 remaining possible violations.

The one case in which we disagreed with the FBI-OGC decision not to report the possible violation to the IOB related to the FBI's acquisition of telephone toll billing records and subscriber information relating to a "nonU,S. person" from a telephone company employee on nine occasions without issuing national security letters. FBI-OGC reasoned that because the investigative subject was a "non-U.S. person" agent of a foreign power, the only determination it had to reach was whether the FBI's failure to conform to its internal administrative requirements was reportable "as a matter of policy" to the IOB. FBI-OGC's decision concluded that if the subject of the NSL had been a "U.S. person," this failure would "likely" constitute an IOB violation. Yet, we believe that FBI-OGC's rationale for not reporting the matter is inconsistent with at least four other possible IOB violations that were triggered by national security letters where the investigative subject or the target of the national security letter was a "non-U.S. person" but the matters were reported to the IOB.[151] We therefore disagree with FBI-OGC's determination that this matter should not be reported to the IOB.[152]

2. OIG Analysis Regarding Possible IOB Violations Identified by the FBI

Our examination of the 26 possible IOB violations reported to FBI-OGC relating to the use of national security letters did not reveal deliberate or intentional violations of national security letter statutes, the Attorney General Guidelines, or internal FBI policy. Although the majority of the possible violations - 22 of 26 - arose from FBI errors, most of them occurred because of typographical errors or the case agent's good faith but erroneous belief that the information requested related to an investigative subject. While the errors resulted in the acquisition of information not relevant to an authorized investigation, they did not manifest deliberate attempts to circumvent statutory limitations or Departmental policies, and appropriate remedial action was taken.

However, we believe that three of the possible IOB violations arising from FBI errors were of a more serious nature because they demonstrated FBI agents' unfamiliarity with the constraints on national security letter authorities and inadequate supervision in the field. For example, in one instance, an FBI analyst was unaware of the statutory and internal FBI policy requirements that national security letters can only be issued during a national security investigation and must be signed by the Special Agent in Charge of the field division. In the two other matters probationary agents erroneously believed that they were authorized to obtain records about investigative subjects - without issuing national security letters - from information derived from FISA electronic surveillance orders. In these instances, it is clear that the agents and, in one instance, the squad supervisor, did not understand the legal constraints on the two types of national security letters or the interrelationship between PISA authorities and national security letter authorities.

II. Additional Possible IOB Violations Identified by the OIG During Our Field Visits

In addition to the 26 possible IOB violations identified by the FBI in this 3-year review period, we found 22 additional possible IOB violations in our review of a sample of investigative files in the 4 field offices we visited. In those 77 investigative files, we reviewed 293 national security letters issued from 2003 through 2005. In those files, we identified 22 NSL-related possible IOB violations that arose in the course of 17 separate investigations, none of which was reported to FBI-OGC or the IOB. Thus, we found that 22 percent of the investigative files we reviewed (17 of 77) contained one or more possible IOB violations that were not reported to FBI-OGC or the 'OB.

A. Possible IOB Violations Identified by the OIG

Of the 22 possible IOB violations, 8 arose in eight investigations in Chicago, two arose in two investigations in New York, 8 arose in 4 investigations in Philadelphia, and 4 arose in three investigations in San Francisco. Seventeen occurred in counterterrorism investigations and 5 occurred in counterintelligence investigations. Thirteen possible IOB violations occurred during preliminary investigations, while 9 occurred during full investigations. The 22 possible IOB violations are summarized in Table 6.2.

We describe below the facts relating to these 22 matters, followed by our analysis of these possible violations.

Table 6.2. Summary of 22 Possible IOB Violations Triggered by Use of National Security Letters Identified by the OIG in Four Field Offices

Category of Possible IOB Violations	Number of Possible IOB Violations	
	FBI Error	Third Party Error
Improper Authorization		
Issuing national security letter without obtaining required approval to extend investigation	1	0
Improper Requests Under Pertinent National Security Letter Statute		
Issuing national security letter for material that arguably constituted prohibited content under ECPA	1	0
Issuing national security letter citing ECPA statute that requests RFPA financial records associated with e-mail accounts	1	0
Issuing national security letter for FCRAv consumer full credit report that included certification language either for RFPA financial records or FCRAu consumer or financial institution identifying information	3	0
Issuing national security letter requesting FCRAv consumer full credit report in a counterintelligence case	2	0
Issuing national security letter requesting FCRAv consumer full credit report when SAC approved national security letter for consumer identifying information or identity of financial institutions under FCRAu	4	0
Unauthorized Collection		
Obtaining information not relevant to an authorized national security investigation (subscriber information and telephone toll billing records)	0	4
Obtaining information beyond the time period requested in the national security letter (from 30 to 81 days in excess of request); obtaining consumer full credit report when SAC had approved NSL for limited credit information: obtaining toll billing records when NSL requested subscriber records	0	6
Total FBI or Third Party Errors	**12**	**10**
Total Possible IOB Violations		**22**

Nature of Possible IOB Violation and *NSL Statute at Issue:* The 22 possible IOB violations we identified fell into three categories: improper authorization for the NSL (1), improper requests under the pertinent national security letter statutes (11), and unauthorized collections (10). The possible violations included:

- One NSL for telephone toll billing records was issued 22 days after the investigative authority had lapsed. As a result, under FBI policy and ECPA the NSL was sent in the absence of an authorized national security investigation.
- Nine NSLs involved improper requests under FCRAv, the newest NSL authority, which was established in the Patriot Act. Two of the 9 NSLs issued during one investigation requested consumer full credit reports during a counterintelligence investigation notwithstanding the fact that the statute authorizes consumer full credit

report NSLs only in international terrorism investigations. Three of the 9 NSLs listed FCRAv as the authority for the request but the NSLs included the certification of relevance language either for the RFPA or the FCRAu NSL authority. In addition, 4 of these 9 NSLs were FCRA requests where the types of records approved by field supervisors differed from the records requested in the national security letters.

- Two NSLs referenced the ECPA as authority for the request but sought content information not permitted by the statute. In one instance, the NSL requested content arguably not permitted by the NSL statute.[153] The second NSL requested financial records associated with two e-mail addresses but requested the information under the ECPA rather than the RFPA, which authorizes access to financial records.
- Ten NSLs involved the FBI's receipt of unauthorized information. In 4 instances, the FBI received telephone toll billing records or subscriber information for telephone numbers that were not listed in the national security letters. In these instances the provider either erroneously furnished additional records for another telephone number associated with the requested number or made transcription errors when querying its systems for the records. In 4 instances, the FBI received telephone toll billing records and electronic communication transactional records for longer periods than that specified in the NSL - periods ranging from 30 days to 81 days.[154] One NSL sought subscriber records pursuant to the ECPA, but the recipient provided the FBI with toll billing records. One NSL sought financial institution and consumer identifying information about an individual pursuant to FCRAu. However, the recipient erroneously gave the FBI the individual's consumer full credit report, which is available pursuant to another statute, FCRAv.

The following text box shows an example of agents' confusion regarding the two NSL authorities in the Fair Credit Reporting Act.

POSSIBLE IOB VIOLATION NO. 3

In October 2003, during a counterterrorism investigation, a field division counterterrorism squad obtained approval to issue a national security letter to a credit reporting agency seeking the names and addresses of all financial institutions at which the investigative subject, a "U.S. person," maintained accounts. The national security letter was issued pursuant to the Fair Credit Reporting Act, 15 U.S.C. § 1681u(a), to determine the extent of the subject's financial holdings and to evaluate whether the subject provided material support to terrorist organizations.

In November 2003, a credit reporting agency provided a consumer full credit report on the investigative subject, instead of the more limited information the FBI had requested in the national security letter. Although the FBI was entitled to request a full consumer report if it established the necessary predicate under 15 U.S.C. § 1681v, this authority had not been approved by the Special Agent in Charge. Accordingly, even though the error was made by the credit reporting agency, the FBI's receipt of the additional information would be considered an unauthorized collection subject to reporting to FBI-OGC as a possible IOB violation. According to FBI records, the incident was not reported to FBI-OGC.

We found there was substantial confusion during the period covered by our review about how to address this and other matters related to the unauthorized acquisition of consumer full credit reports, including questions concerning (1) whether the FBI could use the full credit reports produced to the FBI even if they had not been requested; (2) whether agents should destroy the information, seal it, redact it, or ignore it; and (3) whether the matter should be reported to FBI-OGC as a possible IOB violation. The confusion was compounded by the decisions of two of the three major consumer credit bureaus to provide full consumer credit reports in response to all FBI FCRA national security letters, regardless of whether they requested only the limited information available under the original FCRA NSL statute. Ultimately, FBI-OGC decided that when the field agents receive full consumer credit reports in response to national security letters seeking more limited information, the agents should take the information the FBI is entitled to, seal the remainder, and file an IOB report. Following FBI-OGC meetings with credit bureau representatives in 2006, the two credit bureaus have agreed to redact information that is not requested in FBI NSLs.

Status of Investigative Subject and Target of NSL: Twelve subjects of the 17 investigations involving possible IOB violations identified by the OIG were "U.S. persons," 3 were "non-U.S persons," and two appeared to be "U.S. persons." In 18 of the matters, the NSLs sought information about the subjects of the underlying investigations. In the remaining 4 matters, the NSL targets could not be determined.

Source of Error. Twelve of the 22 possible IOB violations identified by the OIG were due to FBI errors, and 10 were due to errors on the part of third-party recipients of the NSLs.

Uploading of information obtained beyond time period specified in NSL request: We identified one instance in which the FBI uploaded into Telephone Applications from an NSL that exceeded the time period requested in the NSL. The NSL was issued during a full counterterrorism investigation of a U.S. person requesting toll billing records on the investigative subject's telephone number for the period September 1, 2002, to July 16, 2003. However, the FBI received and uploaded into its specialized application for telephone data telephone toll billing records information for two months in excess of the requested time period.

B. National Security Letter Issued in a Charlotte, N.C. Terrorism Investigation

In this section, we describe another possible IOB violation arising from the use of national security letter authorities that was not identified by the FBI. We learned of this possible violation through press accounts. For this reason we did not include it in the description of the results of our review of investigative files in the four field offices we visited. However, we believe this violation is noteworthy, and we therefore describe it in this section.

According to press accounts, the FBI's Charlotte Division was looking for information about a former student at North Carolina State University in connection with in the London subway and bus bombings in July 2005, who was later cleared of sus icion.[155] The national security letter requested.

> Applications for admission, applications or statements concerning financial aid and/or financial situation, housing information, emergency contacts, association with any campus organizations, campus health records, and the names, without being redacted, of other students included in the records associated with the following information:.....

According to press accounts, university officials said that the FBI "tried to use a national securi letter to demand much more information than the law allows." The university produced the records in response to a grand jury subpoena.

As discussed in Chapter Two, the ECPA NSL statute authorizes the FBI to obtain telephone toll billing records and subscriber info' illation and electronic communication transactional records. It does not authorize the FBI to obtain educational records.[156] According to FBI records, the matter was not reported to FBI-OGC as a possible IOB violation. It also was not reported as a possible misconduct matter to the FBI's Office of Professional Responsibility.

C. OIG Analysis Regarding Possible IOB Violations Identified or Reviewed by the OIG

At the outset, it is significant to note that in the limited file review we conducted of 77 investigative files in 4 FBI field offices we identified nearly as many NSL-related possible IOB violations (22) as the number of NSL-related possible IOB violations that the FBI identified in reports from all FBI Headquarters and field divisions for the same 3-year period (26). We found that 22 percent of the investigative files that we reviewed contained at least one possible IOB violation that was not reported to FBI-OGC or the IOB.

We have no reason to believe that the number of possible IOB violations we identified in the four field offices we visited was skewed or disproportionate to the number of possible IOB violations that exist in other offices. This suggests that a significant number of NSL-related possible IOB violations throughout the FBI have not been identified or reported by FBI personnel.

However, it is also significant to note that our review did not reveal intentional violations of the national security letter authorities, the Attorney General Guidelines, or internal FBI policy. Rather, we found confusion about the authorities available under the various NSL statutes. For example, our interviews of field personnel and review of e-mail exchanges between NSLB attorneys and Division Counsel indicated that field personnel sometimes confused the two different authorities under the FCRA: the original FCRA provision that authorized access to financial institution and consumer identifying information in both counterterrorism and counterintelligence cases (15 U.S.C. §§ 1681u(a) and (b)), and the Patriot Act provision that amended the FCRA to authorize access to consumer full credit reports in international terrorism investigations where "such information is necessary for the agency's conduct of such investigation, activity or analysis" (15 U.S.C. § 1681v). Although NSLB sent periodic guidance and "all CDC" e-mails to clarify the distinctions between the two NSLs, we found that the problems and confusion persisted.

As was the case with the NSL-related possible IOBs identified by the FBI, the possible violations identified or reviewed by the OIG varied in seriousness. Among the most serious matters resulting from FBI errors were the two NSLs requesting consumer full credit reports in a counterintelligence case and the NSL requesting educational records from a university, ostensibly pursuant to the ECPA. In these three instances, the FBI misused NSL authorities. Less serious infractions resulting from FBI errors were the seven matters in which three levels of supervisory review failed to detect and correct NSLs which contained incorrect certifications or which sought records not referenced in the approval ECs. While the FBI was entitled to obtain the records sought and obtained in these seven NSLs, the lapses in oversight indicate that the FBI should reinforce the need for careful preparation and review of all documentation supporting the use of NSL authorities.

The reasons why the FBI did not identify the 23 possible IOB violations (counting the improper ECPA NSL involving the Charlotte Division) is unclear. Nine of the 23 matters were the types of possible violations that were self-reported by field divisions in the past, as noted in Section I above.[157] Thirteen of the remaining 14 matters involved discrepancies between the NSL approval ECs and the corresponding NSLs, the acquisition of records beyond the time period requested in the NSL, and the acquisition of a consumer full credit report and telephone toll billing records that were not requested by the NSLs. We believe that many of these infractions occurred because case agents and analysts do not carefully review the text of national security letters, do not consistently cross check the approval ECs with the text of proposed national security letters, and do not verify upon receipt that the information supplied by the NSL recipients matches the requests. We also question whether case agents or analysts reviewed the records provided by the NSL recipients to determine if records were received beyond the time period requested or, if they did so, determined that the amount of excess information received was negligible and did not need to be reported.

Our review also found that the FBI did not issue comprehensive guidance describing the types of national security letter-related infractions that need to be reported to FBI-OGC as possible IOBs until November 2006. During our review, we noted frequent exchanges between Division Counsel and NSLB attorneys about what should and should not be reported as possible IOB violations involving NSLs which we believe showed significant confusion about the reporting requirements. However, the FBI did not issue comprehensive guidance about national security letter-related infractions until more than 5 years after the Patriot Act was enacted.[158] We believe the lack of guidance contributed to the high rate of unreported possible IOB violations involving national security letters that we found.

III. Improper Use of National Security Letter Authorities by Units in FBI Headquarters' Counterterrorism Division Identified by the OIG

We identified two ways in which FBI Headquarters units in the Counterterrorism Division circumvented the requirements of national security letter authorities or issued NSLs contrary to the Attorney General's NSI Guidelines and internal FBI policy. First, we learned that on over 700 occasions the FBI obtained telephone toll billing records or subscriber information from 3 telephone companies without first issuing NSLs or grand jury subpoenas. Instead, the FBI issued so-called "exigent letters" signed by FBI Headquarters Counterterrorism Division personnel who were not authorized to sign NSLs. In many instances there was no pending investigation associated with the request at the time the exigent letters were sent. In addition, while some witnesses told us that many exigent letters were issued in connection with fast-paced investigations, many were not issued in exigent circumstances, and the FBI was unable to determine which letters were sent in emergency circumstances due to inadequate recordkeeping. Further, in many instances after obtaining such records from the telephone companies, the FBI issued national security letters after the fact to "cover" the information obtained, but these after-the-fact NSLs sometimes were issued many months later.

Second, we determined that FBI Headquarters personnel regularly issued national security letters seeking electronic communication transactional records exclusively from "control files" rather than from "investigative files," a practice not permitted by FBI policy. If NSLs are issued exclusively from control files, the NSL approval documentation does not indicate whether the NSLs are issued in the course of authorized investigations or Whether the information sought in the NSLs is relevant to those investigations. Documentation of this information is necessary to establish compliance with NSL statutes, the Attorney General's NSI Guidelines, and internal FBI policy.

We describe below these practices, how they were discovered, and what actions the FBI took to address the issues.

A. Using "Exigent Letters" Rather Than ECPA National Security Letters

The Communications Exploitations Section (CXS) in the Counterterrorism Division at FBI Headquarters analyzes terrorist communications in support of the FBI's investigative and intelligence mission. One of the units in the CXS is the Communications Analysis Unit (CAU), established in approximately July 2002. The CAU's mission is to exploit terrorist communications and provide actionable intelligence to the Counterterrorism Division.

The CAU is designated an "operational support unit" rather than an operational unit. The consequence of this status is that under FBI internal policy the CAU cannot initiate counterterrorism investigations under the NSI Guidelines and cannot issue national security letters. NSLB attorneys told us that to the extent the CAU wants to obtain telephone toll billing records or other records under the ECPA NSL statute, the CAU has two options. One, it can ask the Headquarters Counterterrorism Division or an appropriate field division counterterrorism squad to issue a national security letter from an existing investigation to which the request was relevant. In those instances, as described in Chapter Three, in order to meet the NSI Guidelines' and ECPA standards, the CAU needs to generate approval memoranda articulating the relevance of the information sought to the pending investigation. Alternatively, if there is no pending investigation, the CAU can ask Headquarters operating units in the Counterterrorism Division or field office squads to: a) open a new counterterrorism investigation based on predication the CAU supplies that is sufficient to meet the NSI Guidelines and the ECPA, and b) issue a national security letter seeking information relevant to the new investigation.

As discussed in Chapter Three, only Special Agents in Charge of the FBI's field offices and specially delegated senior Headquarters officials are authorized to issue national security letters.

1. FBI Contracts with Three Telephone Companies

Following the September 11 attacks, the FBI's New York Division formed a group to assist in the analysis of telephone toll billing records that were needed for the criminal investigations of the 19 hijackers. A small group of agents and analysts assigned to examine the communication networks of the terrorists evolved into a domestic terrorism squad in the New York Division known as DT-6. During this time, the FBI's New York Division developed close working relationships with private sector companies, including telephone companies that furnished points of contact to facilitate the FBI's access to records held by these companies, including telephone records. The Supervisory Special Agent (SSA) who supervised DT-6 told us that he obtained Headquarters approval of and Headquarters financing for an arrangement whereby a telephone company representative would work with the New York Division to expedite the FBI's access to the telephone company's databases.

The SSA said that case agents on DT-6 generally provided grand jury subpoenas to the telephone company prior to obtaining telephone records. The grand jury subpoenas issued to the telephone company were signed by Assistant United States Attorneys who worked with FBI agents in the criminal investigations growing out of the September 11 attacks.[159] However, in the period following the September 11 attacks, instead of initially sending a grand jury subpoena the case agents frequently furnished a "placeholder" to the telephone company in the form of a letter stating, in essence, that exigent circumstances supported the request. These "placeholder" letters - also referred to as "exigent letters" - were signed by SSAs or subordinate squad personnel.[160]

Between late 2001 and the spring of 2002, the value of the FBI's access to the telephone company prompted the FBI to enter into contracts with three telephone companies between May 2003 and March 2004. The requests for approval to obligate funds for each of these contracts referred to the Counterterrorism Division's need to obtain telephone toll billing data from the communications industry as quickly as possible. The three memoranda stated that:

> Previous methods of issuing subpoenas or National Security Letters (NSL) and having to wait weeks for their service, often via hard copy reports that had to be retyped into FBI databases, is insufficient to meet the FBI's terrorism prevention mission.

The three memoranda also stated that the telephone companies would provide "near real-time servicing" of legal process, and that once legal process was served telephone records would be provided.

The CAU worked directly with telephone company representatives in connection with these contracts. Moreover, on the FBI's Intranet web site, CAU referenced its capacity to facilitate the acquisition of telephone records pursuant to the contracts. CAU presentations to counterterrorism squads in several field divisions also described the unit's capabilities, including its access to telephone company records. The slides used in CAU presentations referred to the CAU's ability to "provide dedicated personnel to service subpoenas/NSLs 24 x 7." In describing how the CAU should receive requests from the field, the slides noted that

> *Field office prepares NSL or FGJS* for CAU to serve on appropriate telecom provider.
> -- Once paper received, CAU will obtain tolls/call details.

Thus, from this presentation, it appears that the CAU contemplated that the FBI would serve national security letters or grand jury subpoenas prior to obtaining telephone toll billing records and subscriber information pursuant to the three contracts, in conformity with the ECPA NSL statute.[161]

The Assistant Director of the Counterterrorism Division told us that based on numerous FBI briefings he received during his tenure, he directed his subordinates to contact the CXS Section Chief to ensure that the capabilities of the three companies were used. However, he also told us that he was unaware that any of the three companies were providing telephone toll billing records without first receiving duly authorized national security letters.

2. The Exigent Letters to Three Telephone Companies

The SSA who supervised DT-6 following the September 11 attacks told us that by late 2001 he and other DT-6 personnel were assigned to assist in the establishment of CAU at FBI Headquarters, and that they would have brought with them to Headquarters a copy of the exigent letter that had been used in the criminal investigations of the September 11 attacks to obtain information from the telephone company in New York. This letter was used by CAU personnel as a model to generate requests to the three telephone companies under contract with the FBI to provide telephone toll billing records or subscriber information. These exigent letters typically stated:

> Due to exigent circumstances, it is requested that records for the attached list of telephone numbers be provided. Subpoenas requesting this information have been submitted to the U.S. Attorney's Office who will process and serve them formally to [information redacted] as expeditiously as possible.

In response to our request, the FBI provided the OIG copies of 739 exigent letters addressed to the three telephone companies dated between March 11, 2003, and December 16, 2005, all but 4 of which were signed. The signed exigent letters included 3 signed by CXS Assistant Section Chiefs, 12 signed by CAU Unit Chiefs, 711 signed by CAU Supervisory Special Agents, 3 signed by CAU special agents, 2 signed by intelligence analysts, 1 signed by an intelligence operations specialist, and 3 that contained signature blocks with no titles. Together, the 739 exigent letters requested information on approximately 3,000 different telephone numbers. The three highest volume exigent letters sought telephone toll billing or subscriber information on 117, 125, and 171 different telephone numbers.

We determined that contrary to the provisions of the contracts and the assertions in CAU's briefings that the FBI would obtain telephone records only after it served NSLs or grand jury subpoenas, the FBI obtained telephone toll billing records and subscriber information prior to serving NSLs or grand jury subpoenas. Moreover, CAU officials told us that contrary to the assertion in the exigent letters, subpoenas requesting the information had not been provided to the U.S. Attorney's Office before the letters were sent to the telephone companies. Two CAU Unit Chiefs said they were confident that national security letters or grand jury subpoenas were ultimately issued to cover the FBI's receipt of information acquired in response to the exigent letters. The Unit Chiefs said that they relied on the telephone company representatives to maintain a log of the requests and to let CAU personnel know if any NSLs or grand jury subpoenas were needed. However, the Unit Chiefs acknowledged that because the CAU did not maintain a log to track whether national security letters or grand jury subpoenas were issued to cover the exigent letter requests and did not maintain signed copies of the exigent letters, they could not provide documentation to verify that national security letters or grand jury subpoenas were in fact issued to cover every exigent letter request.

Pursuant to administrative subpoenas, the OIG obtained from the three telephone companies copies of national security letters and grand jury subpoenas that the FBI served on the telephone companies in connection with FBI requests for telephone toll billing records or subscriber information from 2003 through 2005. The three telephone companies provided 474 national security letters and 458 grand jury subpoenas. However, CAU personnel told us that some of these NSLs and grand jury subpoenas were not related to the exigent letters and that CAU could not isolate which NSLs or grand jury subpoenas given to the OIG by the telephone companies were associated with the exigent letters. CAU officials told us that the only way the CAU could attempt to associate an exigent letter with a national security letter or grand jury subpoena was to query the ACS database system with the telephone numbers referenced in the exigent letters. Because the CAU officials stated that this would be a labor intensive exercise, we asked them to query ACS for the NSLs, grand jury subpoenas, or related documentation associated with 88 exigent letters that we randomly selected from the 739 exigent letters provided to us by the FBI.

The FBI provided the results of ACS queries for the first 25 of the 88 letters. To try to demonstrate that it issued either national security letters or grand jury subpoenas to cover the FBI's acquisition of the records obtained in response to the exigent letters, the FBI pointed to various documents ranging from unsigned national security letters to e-mails referencing the telephone number listed in the exigent letters. Yet, the documents did not demonstrate that national security letters or grand jury subpoenas were issued to cover the records requested in the exigent letters. These documents included:

- Unsigned copies of 14 national security letters. The FBI provided approval ECs associated with only 8 of these 14 NSLs. Two of the NSLs were dated before the date of the corresponding exigent letters, three bore the same date as the corresponding exigent letters, and nine were dated after the date of the corresponding exigent letters. One of the unsigned NSLs was dated 481 days after the date of the corresponding exigent letter, and the rest were dated between 6 and 152 days after the corresponding exigent letters. Two unsigned NSLs were dated 10 and 13 days prior to the date of the corresponding exigent letters.
- Two ECs seeking approval to issue a national security letters, but no copies of the national security letters themselves.
- An e-mail dated 16 days prior to the date of the exigent letter asking CAU to "check" 7 telephone numbers, one of which was referenced in the exigent letter, and a note to the file indicating that the FBI had received records 10 days after the date of an exigent letter in response to a grand jury subpoena to 1 of the 3 telephone companies.[162]
- For the remaining eight exigent letters, documentation that did not reference directly or indirectly that national security letters had been issued relating to the records requested in the exigent letters.[163]

In sum, of the 88 exigent letters we randomly selected from the 739 exigent letters, the FBI produced unsigned national security letters for only 14 of the first 25 exigent letters. The documents provided for the first 25 exigent letters showed that the FBI would be unable to provide reliable documentation to substantiate that national security letters or other legal process was issued to cover the records obtained in response to many of the exigent letters. Therefore, because of this clear finding in the first 25 letters and the labor intensive nature of the exercise, we did not ask the FBI to complete the sample of 88 letters.

3. Absence of Investigative Authority for the Exigent Letters

As discussed in Chapter Three, the national security letter statutes, the Attorney General's NSI Guidelines, and internal FBI policy require that Special Agents in Charge of field divisions or specially delegated Headquarters officials certify that the information sought in the national security letter is relevant to an authorized investigation. Since passage of the Patriot Act, the information requested in certain national security letters does not need to relate to the subject of the FBI's investigation, but can relate to other individuals as long as the information requested is relevant to an authorized national security investigation.

A former CAU Unit Chief told us that many of the exigent letters were generated in connection with significant Headquarters-based investigations as well as investigations in which the FBI provided assistance to foreign counterparts, such as investigations of the July 2005 London bombings. In some instances, CAU personnel said that the requests directed to CAU were communicated by senior Headquarters officials who characterized the requests as urgent. However, when CAU personnel gave the exigent letters to the three telephone companies, they did not provide to their supervisors any documentation demonstrating that the requests were related to pending FBI investigations, and many exigent letters were not sent in exigent circumstances. As described in Chapter Three, these are required elements for NSL approval documentation necessary to establish compliance with the ECPA NSL statute, the NSI Guidelines, and internal FBI policy. Moreover, we learned from interviews of CAU personnel and FBI documents that when CAU requested telephone records from the three telephone companies pursuant to exigent letters, there sometimes were no open or pending national security investigations tied to the request.

We found that in the absence of a pending investigation CAU sent leads either to the Headquarters Counterterrorism Division (ITOS-1 or ITOS-2) or to field offices asking them to initiate new investigations from which the after-the-fact NSLs could be issued. However, CAU personnel told us that the Counterterrorism Division units and field personnel often resisted generating the documentation for these new investigations or declined to act on the leads, primarily for three reasons. First, CAU often did not provide the operating units with sufficient information to justify the initiation of an investigation. Second, on some occasions, the documentation CAU supplied to the field divisions did not disclose that the FBI had already obtained the information from the telephone companies.[164] When the field offices learned that the records had already been received, they complained to NSLB attorneys that this did not seem appropriate. Third, since Headquarters and field divisions were unfamiliar with the reasons underlying the requests, they believed that the CAU leads should receive lower priority than their ongoing investigations.

We concluded that, as a consequence of the CAU's use of the exigent letters to acquire telephone toll billing records and subscriber information from the three telephone companies without first issuing NSLs, CAU personnel circumvented the ECPA NSL statute and violated the NSI Guidelines and internal FBI policies. These matters were compounded by the fact that CAU used exigent letters in non-emergency circumstances, failed to ensure that there were duly authorized investigations to which the request could be tied, and failed to ensure that NSLs were issued promptly after the fact pursuant to existing or new counterterrorism investigations.

4. Efforts by the FBI's National Security Law Branch to Conform CAU's Practices to the Electronic Communications Privacy Act

NSLB attorneys responsible for providing guidance on the FBI's use of national security letter authorities told us that they were not aware of the CAU's practice of using exigent letters until late 2004. When an NSLB Assistant General Counsel learned of the practice at that time, she believed that the practice did not comply with the ECPA national security letter statute. Our review of contemporaneous e-mail communications and our interviews of CAU and NSLB personnel found that for nearly 2 years, beginning in late 2004, NSLB attorneys counseled CAU officials to take a variety of actions, including: discontinue use of exigent letters except in true emergencies; obtain more details to be able to justify associating the information with an existing national security investigation or to request the initiation of a new investigation; issue duly authorized national security letters promptly after the records were provided in response to the exigent letters; modify the letters to reference national security letters rather than grand jury subpoenas; and consider opening "umbrella" investigations out of which national security letters could be issued in the absence of another pending investigation.[165] In addition, NSLB offered to dedicate personnel to expedite issuance of CAU NSL requests (as it had done for other high priority matters requiring expedited NSLs). However, CAU never pursued this latter option.

In June 2006, NSLB provided revised models for exigent letters to the Counterterrorism Division that stated that NSLs (rather than grand jury subpoenas) would be processed and served upon the telephone companies as expeditiously as possible. Pursuant to NSLB advice, the FBI continued to issue exigent letters since June 2006, using the new model letters.

As of March 2007, the FBI is unable to determine whether NSLs or grand jury subpoenas were issued to cover the exigent letters. However, at FBI-OGC's direction, CAU is attempting to determine if NSLs were issued to cover the information obtained in response to each of the exigent letters. If CAU is unable to document appropriate predication for the FBI's retention of information obtained in response to the exigent letters, the Deputy General Counsel of NSLB stated that the FBI will take steps to ensure that appropriate remedial action is taken. Remedial action may include purging of information from FBI databases and reports of possible IOB violations.

The Assistant General Counsel also told us that a different provision of ECPA could be considered in weighing the legality of the FBI's use of the exigent letters: the provision authorizing voluntary emergency disclosures of certain non-content customer communications or records (18 U.S.C. § 2702(c)(4)).[166] The Assistant General Counsel stated that while the FBI did not rely upon this authority in issuing the exigent letters from 2003 through 2005, the FBI's practice may in part be justified by the ECPA's recognition that emergency disclosures may be warranted in high-risk situations. The Assistant General Counsel argued that in serving the exigent letters on the telephone companies the FBI did its best to reconcile its mission to prevent terrorist attacks with the strict requirements of the ECPA NSL statute.

The FBI General Counsel told us that the better practice in exigent circumstances is to provide the telephone companies letters seeking voluntary production pursuant to the emergency voluntary disclosure provision of 18 U.S.C. § 2702 (c)(4) and to follow up promptly with NSLs to document the basis for the request and capture statistics for reporting purposes. But the General Counsel said that, if challenged, the FBI could defend its past use of the exigent letters by relying on the ECPA voluntary emergency disclosure authority. The

General Counsel also noted that the manner in which FBI personnel are required to generate documentation to issue NSLs can make it appear to an outsider that the records were requested without a pending investigation when in fact there is a pending investigation that is not referenced in the approval documentation due to the FBI's recordkeeping and administrative procedures.[167]

5. OIG Analysis of Exigent Letters

The FBI entered into contracts with three telephone companies in CY 2003 and CY 2004 for the purpose of obtaining quick responses to requests for telephone toll billing records and subscriber information. The documentation associated with the contracts indicated that the telephone companies expected to receive, and the FBI agreed to provide, national security letters or other legal process prior to obtaining the responsive records. Moreover, when the CAU described its mission to field personnel, it told them that the CAU expected to receive national security letters or other legal process before it obtained the records from the telephone companies. Neither the former Executive Assistant Director of the Counterterrorism and Counterintelligence Divisions nor any other Headquarters official told us that they approved the FBI's acquisition of records from the three telephone companies other than in response to duly authorized national security letters. Yet, the CAU issued over 700 exigent letters, rather than national security letters, to obtain telephone toll billing records information relating to over 3,000 different telephone numbers.

We found three additional problems with the CAU's exigent letters. First, each of the 739 exigent letters seeking telephone toll billing and subscriber records was signed by CAU Unit Chiefs and subordinate CAU personnel who were not authorized to issue national security letters under the ECPA and internal FBI policy. Second, when the CAU asked Headquarters or field divisions to issue national security letters after the fact in connection with existing investigations or to initiate new investigations from which the national security letters could be issued, the CAU generally did not inform other FBI employees that the records had already been obtained from the three telephone companies. Third, when the CAU asked Headquarters and field divisions to open new investigations out of which they could generate NSLs after the fact, CAU did not consistently provide information establishing predication for the request that was necessary to satisfy the ECPA NSL statute, the Attorney General's NSI Guidelines, and internal FBI policy.

We are not convinced by the legal justifications offered by FBI attorneys during this review for the FBI's acquisition of telephone toll billing records and subscriber information in response to the exigent letters without first issuing NSLs. The first justification offered was the need to reconcile the strict requirements of the ECPA NSL statute with the FBI's mission to prevent terrorist attacks. While the FBI's priority counterterrorism mission may require streamlined procedures to ensure the timely receipt of information in emergencies, the FBI needs to address the problem by expediting the issuance of national security letters or seeking legislative modification to the ECPA voluntary emergency disclosure provision for non-content records. Moreover, the FBI's justification for the exigent letters was undercut because they were (1) used, according to information conveyed to an NSLB Assistant General Counsel, mostly in non-emergency circumstances, (2) not followed in many instances within a reasonable time by the issuance of national security letters, and (3) not catalogued in a fashion that would enable FBI managers or anyone else to validate the justification for the practice or the predication required by the ECPA NSL statute.

We also disagree with the FBI's second justification: that use of the exigent letters could be defended as a use of ECPA's voluntary emergency disclosure authority for acquiring non-content information pursuant to 18 U.S.C. § 2702(c)(4). First, we found that the exigent letters did not request voluntary disclosure. The letters stated, "Due to exigent circumstances, it is requested that records . . . be provided" but added, "a subpoena requesting this information has been submitted to the United States Attorney's Office and "will be processed and served foi wally... as expeditiously as possible." In addition, we found that the emergency voluntary disclosure provision was not relied upon by the CAU at the time, the letters were not signed by FBI officials who had authority to sign ECPA voluntary emergency disclosure letters, and the letters did not recite the factual predication necessary to invoke that authority.[168]

We also are troubled that the FBI issued exigent letters that contained factual misstatements. The exigent letters represented that Islubpoenas requesting this information have been submitted to the U.S. Attorney's Office who will process and serve them folinally to [information redacted] as expeditiously as possible." In fact, in examining the documents CAU provided in support of the first 25 of the 88 randomly selected exigent letters, we could not confirm one instance in which a subpoena had been submitted to any United States Attorney's Office before the exigent letter was sent to the telephone companies. Even if there were understandings with the three telephone companies that some form of legal process would later be provided to cover the records obtained in response to the exigent letters, the FBI made factual misstatements in its official letters to the telephone companies either as to the existence of an emergency justifying shortcuts around lawful procedures or with respect to steps the FBI supposedly had taken to secure lawful process.

In evaluating these matters, it is also important to recognize the significant challenges the FBI was facing during the period covered by our review. After the September 11 terrorist attacks, the FBI implemented major organizational changes to seek to prevent additional terrorist attacks in the United States, such as overhauling its counterterrorism operations, expanding its intelligence capabilities, beginning to upgrade its info'illation technology systems, and seeking to improve coordination with state and local law enforcement agencies. These changes occurred while the FBI and its Counterterrorism Division has had to respond to continuing terrorist threats and conduct many counterterrorism investigations, both internationally and domestically. In addition, the FBI developed specialized operational support units that were under significant pressure to respond quickly to potential terrorist threats. It was in this context that the FBI used exigent letters to acquire telephone toll billing records and subscriber information on approximately 3,000 different telephone numbers without first issuing ECPA national security letters. We also recognize that the FBI's use of so-called "exigent letters" to obtain the records without first issuing NSLs was undertaken without the benefit of advance legal consultation with FBI-OGC.

However, we believe none of these circumstances excuses the FBI's circumvention of the requirements of the ECPA NSL statute and its violations of the Attorney General's NSI Guidelines and internal FBI policy governing the use of national security letters.

B. National Security Letters Issued from Headquarters Control Files Rather Than From Investigative Files

As discussed in Chapter Three, the national security letter statutes and the Attorney General's NSI Guidelines authorize the issuance of national security letters only if the information sought is relevant to an "authorized investigation." Within the FBI, the only types of investigations in which national security letters may be used are national security investigations.

FBI internal policy also distinguishes between "investigative files" and "administrative files." Numerical codes are used to designate the FBI's various investigative programs, and other unique designations are used to establish non-investigative files, sometimes referred to as "control files" or "repository" files. The FBI's National Foreign Intelligence Program (NFIP) Manual states that investigative activity may not be conducted from control files, and that NSLs may only be issued in the course of national security investigations.[169]

However, we found that the FBI on occasion relied exclusively on "control files" rather than "investigative files" to initiate approval for the issuance of national security letters, in violation of internal FBI policy. Moreover, this practice made it difficult for FBI supervisors and others reviewing the proposed national security letters to determine if the required statutory predicate had been satisfied and whether the information sought was relevant to an authorized investigation in accordance with the NSI Guidelines.

1. National Security Letters Issued from a Headquarters Special Project Control File

During the first quarter of 2003, the FBI began to issue national security letters in connection with a classified special project. From 2003 through 2005, the CAU initiated NSL approval memoranda for approximately 300 national security letters in connection with this project, which were generated from a Headquarters control file. All of the resulting NSLs sought telephone toll billing records, subscriber information, or electronic communication transactional records pursuant to the ECPA NSL statute. From the information available during the OIG review, it appears that all of the national security letters were served on the communications provider before any records were given to the FBI, and none of the information sought arose in emergency circumstances. The approval ECs for these NSLs do not refer to the case number of any specific pending FBI investigation.[170]

As noted above, CAU officials are not authorized to sign national security letters. A former CAU Unit Chief told us that, as a result, during the early phase of the project the CAU sent leads to field offices to initiate the process to issue these national security letters, but the CAU often met resistance. The Unit Chief said that some field offices responded diligently and pursued investigative activity to establish predication for opening a new counterterrorism investigation, while others did nothing.

To address the problem of issuing national security letters in the absence of timely field support, the CAU provided additional training to field personnel. In addition, the Unit Chief said that the Counterterrorism Division opened a special project control file from which the CAU sought approval from NSLB to issue national security letters for subscriber infmination. The CAU had used information in the control file to check indices to determine whether there was a nexus to terrorism that justified further investigative activity.

The classified nature of the project was such that few FBI Headquarters officials or OGC attorneys were authorized to know the predication for the NSL requests. This led to frustration and delays when field divisions were asked to respond to the CAU leads for the project. Because the CAU provided limited information about the predication for the leads to field offices, field-based counterterrorism squads sometimes opened threat assessments because they were not able to establish the required predication to open a national security investigation. In these instances, national security letters could not be issued in response to the CAU leads to field offices.

In December 2006, after considering a number of options that would comply with the ECPA NSL statute, the Attorney General's NSI Guidelines, and internal FBI policy, the FBI initiated an "umbrella" investigative file from which national security letters related to this classified project could be issued.

2. National Security Letters Issued by the Electronic Surveillance Operations and Sharing Unit

The second circumstance we identified in the review in which national security letters were issued solely from control files related to leads sent by the Counterterrorism Division's Electronic Surveillance Operations and Sharing; Unit (EOPS) in the CXS. EOPS' mission is to. In 2003, EOPS opened a Headquarters control file to track its activities as well as the results of its analyses.[171]

An EOPS Unit Chief told us that EOPS initiated requests for national security letters in two circumstances. The first and most frequent circumstance was when field offices or Headquarters operational units requested EOPS' assistance in vetting subscriber information about some form of Internet usage. In these circumstances, the EC seeking approval for the national security letter would reference a "dual caption": the field or Headquarters division's investigative file number and the EOPS control file number. EOPS personnel told us that the FBI issued approximately 214 national security letters from 2003 through 2005 under "dual captions" that included an EOPS control file number.

The second and rarer circumstance occurred when, in the absence of a pending Headquarters or field-based national security investigation, EOPS sought approval for issuance of national security letters to verify subscriber or other information when EOPS alone developed the predication to support the request. These EOPS requests were prepared and forwarded for approval and issuance by the NSLB Deputy General Counsel. In these circumstances, EOPS assumed the role of "office of origin" for purposes of the request to NSLB. Documentation provided to us by the FBI indicated that the FBI sent six national security letters from 2003 through 2005 solely on the authority of control files.[172] The six NSLs sought information from Internet service providers. The requests for information initiated by EOPS were in the form of duly authorized national security letters prepared for the signature of the NSLB Deputy General Counsel. The national security letters sought electronic communication transactional records, including the name, address, length of service, and billing records associated with specified e-mail addresses.

As discussed in Chapter Three, the approval EC accompanying an NSL request must document the predication for the national security letter by stating why the information is relevant to an authorized investigation. Yet, none of the six approval ECs accompanying the requests for these NSLs referred to the case number of any specific pending FBI investigation.[173]

A new EOPS Unit Chief recognized in August 2005 that the nature and quality of the work EOPS was generating out of the control file went beyond the conventional use of a control file. The EOPS Unit Chief began consulting with NSLB attorneys to make EOPS' "internal policies and procedures" conform to the FBI's national security letter practices. In December 2005, the Unit Chief sent an e-mail to an NSLB attorney acknowledging that EOPS was using a control file to seek Headquarters approval for the issuance of national security letters in response to numerous "hot projects," and that the Attorney General's NSI Guidelines require that a national security investigation be opened in order to issue national security letters. The Unit Chief noted that NSLB had approved using an EOPS repository or control file for certain unrelated purposes and asked if that control file could also be used for generating requests to issue national security letters.

The EOPS Unit Chief told us, however, that in his opinion EOPS was in compliance with FBI policy and the "spirit" of the Attorney General's Guidelines when it sought national security letters using EOPS as the "office of origin" because (1) the control file contained adequate information to support predication for a national security investigation; and (2) issuance of a national security letter did not constitute a "investigation" within the meaning of the Attorney General Guidelines. The Unit Chief noted that the NSLB Deputy General Counsel had been signing the national security letters, the predication was there, and it was "common sense" that issuing a national security letter was not a "full blown investigation." In the Unit Chiefs view, so long as EOPS developed the requisite predication, the EOPS control file would serve as the investigation that would justify issuance of a national security letter because of the "uniqueness of the situation."

According to the Unit Chief, this would comply with the "spirit of the law," but not the letter of the law.

The NSLB Deputy General Counsel told us that in reviewing the documentation associated with national security letters generated by EOPS that she was asked to sign, she did not focus on the caption of the approval EC but rather on the factual recitation and whether the letter sought information on a "U.S. person" that impinged on First Amendment activity.[174] However, following questions raised by the OIG in this review, the NSLB Deputy General Counsel told us that she has advised the EOPS Unit Chief to discontinue requesting approval of national security letters issued exclusively out of control files and that, as of December 2006, she believes her advice has been followed.

3. OIG Analysis

According to the Attorney General's NSI Guidelines and the FBI's NFIP Manual, the issuance of a national security letter is an investigative technique that can be used only in connection with a national security investigation. Moreover, the national security letter statutes and the NSI Guidelines provide that national security letters may be issued only during authorized investigations. We believe that adherence to these three authorities requires that national security letters be issued from investigative files so that the requesting agent documents the existence of an authorized investigation and the relevance of the information sought to that investigation.

Although the distinction between a "control file" and an "investigative file" may seem obscure and technical, it is important for purposes of documenting compliance with the

ECPA, the NSI Guidelines, and FBI policy. Unless national security letters are issued from investigative files, case agents and their supervisors - and internal and external reviewers - cannot determine whether the requests are tied to substantive investigations that have established the required evidentiary predicate for issuing the national security letters. As the FBI General Counsel told us, the only way to determine if the information requested in a national security letter is relevant to an authorized investigation is to have an investigative file to which the national security letter request can be tied or to have the connection described in the NSL approval EC. Control files are generally created for storing information that does not yet - and may never - satisfy the predicate for initiating a national security investigation. In our review, we found that approval ECs for the special project and EOPS NSLs did not provide documentation tying the requests to specific pending investigations or establishing the relevance of the information sought to pending investigations.

We believe that the CAU officials and the EOPS Unit Chief concluded in good faith that the FBI had sufficient predication either to connect these national security letters with existing investigations or to open new investigations in compliance with the Attorney General's NSI Guidelines. We also believe that the EOPS Unit Chief understood that national security letters should not be issued out of control files. We concluded, however, that issuing national security letters constitutes investigative activity, especially when the Attorney General's NSI Guidelines and the NFIP Manual plainly provide that national security letters are an "investigative technique" and that control files are not considered to be national security investigations.

In sum, we concluded that the Counterterrorism Division's use of control files rather than investigative files in connection with NSLs related to a classified special project and related to certain EOPS' activities, was contrary to internal FBI policy.

IV. Failure to Adhere to FBI Internal Control Policies on the Use of National Security Letter Authorities

Our review also examined FBI investigative files to determine whether the field offices' use of national security letters violated FBI internal control policies. As discussed in Chapter Three, the FBI established procedures for the approval of national security letters to ensure that the requests contained sufficient information to allow field supervisors to confirm that the NSLs complied with applicable legal requirements and FBI policy. Periodic updates to the NFIP Manual and to the NSLB's Intranet web site also informed agents of the legal and internal policy requirements for each type of NSL. In addition, models, or "ponies," of approval electronic communications (ECs) and NSLs, which were available on the NSLB's Intranet web site, assisted case agents in completing the necessary paperwork to secure approval of national security letters.

The two key documents related to national security letters were the EC seeking approval to issue the NSL and the national security letter itself. According to FBI policy, each of these documents was required to reference information required either by the authorizing statutes or by FBI-OGC guidance.

In the sections below, we assess whether the national security letter documents we reviewed complied with these FBI policies. In addition, we discuss the violations of these policies that we found in our field office reviews of FBI investigative files.

1. Lapses in Internal Controls

In our review of the 77 investigative files and 293 national security letters in 4 FBI field offices, we identified repeated failures to adhere to FBI-OGC guidance regarding the documentation necessary for approval of national security letters.[175]

We organized these infractions into three categories:

1) NSL approval memoranda that were not reviewed and initialed by one or more of the required field supervisors or Division Counsel;
2) NSL approval memoranda that did not contain all of the required information; and
3) national security letters that did not contain the recitals or other information required by the authorizing statutes.

A large percentage of the investigative files we reviewed - 46 of 77, or 60 percent - contained one or more of these infractions. Nevertheless, in each of these cases, the national security letters were approved.

a. Failure to Document Review of NSL Approval Memoranda

The NFIP Manual and FBI-OGC guidance require that before a Special Agent in Charge signs a national security letter, the approval documents must be reviewed and initialed by the Supervisory Special Agent or Squad Leader, the Office of Chief Division Counsel, the Assistant Special Agent in Charge (ASAC), and the Special Agent in Charge.

Twenty-two of the 293 approval ECs (7 percent) we reviewed in eight different investigations did not reflect review or approval by these field supervisors or Division Counsel.[176] Seventeen of the 22 approval ECs with these infractions arose during counterterrorism investigations, while 5 arose during counterintelligence investigations. In five of the investigations, the subject of the investigation was a "U.S. person." In three cases, the subject of the investigation was a "non-U.S. person."

The elements missing from the 22 approval ECs were:

- 3 approval ECs did not reflect review and approval by the Special Agents in Charge;
- 18 approval ECs did not reflect review by the Assistant Special Agents in Charge (of which 15 were in a field division that suspended the requirement to route NSLs through the ASACs);
- 8 approval ECs did not reflect review by the Supervisory Special Agent; and
- 3 approval ECs did not reflect review by the Chief Division Counsel or Assistant Division Counsel.

b. Failure to Include Required Information in NSL Approval Memoranda

The NFIP Manual and FBI-OGC guidance require the approval EC to reference the statute authorizing the information requested; the status of the investigative subject as a "U.S. person" or "non-U.S. person"; the type and number of records requested; the predication for the request; leads showing transmittal of the approval EC to NSLB, the pertinent Headquarters operational division, and the squad or field division that was to deliver the national security letter; and the initialed approval of the request by the field supervisors and Chief Division Counsel.

We identified 99 of the 293 approval ECs (34 percent) we examined, in 40 different investigations, in which at least one of the four required elements was missing.[177] Thirty of the 40 files with these infractions were counterterrorism investigations, while 10 were counterintelligence investigations. In 31 instances, the investigative subject was a "U.S. person," in 8 instances, the investigative subject was a "non-U.S. person," and in one instance, the status of the investigative subject could not be determined.

The information missing from the 99 approval ECs was:

- 16 approval ECs did not reference the statute authorizing the FBI to obtain the information or cited the wrong statute;
- 66 approval ECs did not reference the "U.S. person" or "non-U.S. person" status of the investigative subject;
- 34 approval ECs did not specify the type and number of records requested; and
- 7 approval ECs did not recite the required predication for the request.

c. Failure to Include Required Information in National Security Letters

The NFIP Manual and FBI-OGC guidance require national security letters to reference the pertinent statutory authority, the type and number of records requested, the mandatory certification required by the referenced NSL statute, the non-disclosure provision, and the request that the provider deliver the records personally.[178]

We identified 5 of 293 national security letters (2 percent) we examined, in 3 different investigations that did not include at least one of these required elements. One of the infractions arose in a counterterrorism investigation, and four arose in counterintelligence investigations. In all three investigations, the investigative subject was a "U.S. person."

The five national security letters either did not include a reference to an NSL statute or referenced the wrong statute.

Finally, we note that we were unable to comprehensively audit the field divisions' compliance with the requirement that Special Agents in Charge sign national security letters because three of the four divisions we visited did not maintain signed copies of the national security letters. The Special Agent in Charge of the fourth division maintained a control file with copies of all NSLs he signs, but this practice was instituted only during the last year of our review period.

2. OIG Analysis of Failures to Adhere to FBI Internal Control Policies

Complete and accurate documentation of the elements required for approval ECs and national security letters is essential to ensure compliance with the national security letter authorities, the Attorney General Guidelines, and internal FBI policy. If elements of the approval EC or the national security letter are missing, the FBI official signing the national security letter cannot be assured that the required predication, specifications of items sought, and statutory authority are correct.

We found significant numbers of NSL approval documents did not contain the required elements. The most notable elements missing (34 percent) occurred when field personnel failed to include the required information in NSL approval ECs. The absence of accurate information in these approval memoranda increases the risk of incorrect entries in the OGC database for tracking national security letters and may have produced incorrect reports to Congress with respect to the numbers of NSL requests and the status of investigative subjects.

The instances in which field supervisors or Division Counsel failed to document their review of the NSL approval package, while few in number, were also serious. Review of the NSL package is designed to ensure that errors or inadequate predication are identified and corrected before a national security letter is issued.

Overall, we believe that the FBI has now provided needed guidance and support to field personnel to facilitate production of approval documentation compliant with statutory requirements, Attorney General Guidelines, and internal FBI policies. Nonetheless, we believe the FBI should improve its compliance with the internal controls governing the exercise of national security letter authorities by ensuring that its employees consistently and accurately satisfy all elements of the NSL approval documentation.

7. Other Noteworthy Facts and Circumstances Related to the FBI's Use of National Security Letters

As directed by the Patriot Reauthorization Act, in this chapter our report includes other "noteworthy facts and circumstances" related to the FBI's use of national security letters that we found during our review. These matters include the interpretation of the Attorney General Guidelines' requirement to use the "least intrusive collection techniques feasible" with regard to the use of national security letters; uncertainty about the types of telephone toll billing records the FBI may obtain pursuant to an Electronic Communications Privacy Act (ECPA) national security letter; the review by Division Counsel of NSL requests; the issuance of NSLs from control files rather than investigative files, in violation of FBI policy; the FBI's use of "certificate letters" rather than Right to Financial Privacy Act (RFPA) national security letters to obtain records from Federal Reserve Banks; and the FBI's failure to include in its NSL tracking database the use of NSLs to obtain information about individuals who are not subjects of FBI investigations.

I. Using the "Least Intrusive Collection Techniques Feasible"

When FBI agents evaluate the investigative techniques available to them at different stages of FBI investigations - including the use of national security letters - one of the factors they must consider is the intrusiveness of the technique. According to the Attorney General's Guidelines for FBI National Security Investigations and Foreign Intelligence Collection (NSI Guidelines), the intrusiveness of the investigative technique must be compared to the seriousness of the threat to national security that is being investigated and the strength of the information indicating such a threat. The NSI Guidelines, which were in effect for <u>all</u> but the first ten months of this review and remain in effect today, state:

> Choice of Methods. The conduct of investigations and other activities authorized by these Guidelines may present choices between the use of information collection methods that are more or less intrusive, considering such factors as the effect on the privacy of individuals and potential damage to reputation. As Executive Order 12333 § 2.4 provides, "the least intrusive collection techniques feasible" are to be used in such situations. The FBI shall not hesitate to use any lawful techniques consistent with these Guidelines, even if intrusive, where the degree of intrusiveness is warranted in light of the seriousness of a threat to the national security or the strength of the information indicating its existence. This point is to be particularly observed in investigations relating to terrorism.[179]

However, during our review, we found that no clear guidance was given to FBI agents on how to reconcile the limitations expressed in the Attorney General Guidelines, which reflect concerns about the impact on privacy of FBI collection techniques, with the expansive authorities in the NSL statutes.[180]

For example, during our review, several senior FBI attorneys told us that legal precedents suggest that NSLs seeking telephone toll billing records and subscriber information do not implicate privacy interests under the Fourth Amendment. Several also said that they consider NSLs seeking financial records and consumer full credit reports to be more intrusive than NSLs seeking telephone toll billing records or subscriber information. However, the national security letter statutes and internal FBI policies do not address which of the national security letter authorities are more intrusive than others or the relative intrusiveness of NSLs compared to other investigative techniques.

These issues raise difficult questions that regularly arise regarding the FBI's use of national security letters. For example, under the NSI Guidelines, should case agents access NSL information about parties two or three steps removed from their subjects without determining if these contacts reveal suspicious connections? In light of the "least intrusive collection techniques feasible" proviso in the Attorney General Guidelines, is there an evidentiary threshold beyond "relevance to an authorized investigation" that should be considered before financial records or full credit histories are obtained on persons who are not investigative subjects? Are NSLs more or less intrusive than other investigative techniques authorized for use during national security investigations, such as physical surveillance? Yet, if agents are hindered from using all types of NSLs at early stages of investigations, this may compromise the FBI's ability to pursue critical investigations of terrorism or espionage threats or to reach resolution expeditiously that certain subjects do not pose threats.

The FBI Headquarters and field personnel we interviewed said that there is no uniform answer to the difficult question of how to use and sequence NSLs. Instead, they said that individualized decisions are made based on the evidence developed as the investigation proceeds. The FBI General Counsel also expressed this view, stating that she believes that the use and sequencing of national security letters is best left to the experienced judgment of field supervisors. However, several Division Counsel told us that they believe it would be helpful if FBI-OGC's National Security Law Branch (NSLB) provided guidance on the interrelationship between the Attorney General's NSI Guidelines and the NSL statutes.

The impact of the FBI's investigative choices when using national security letters is magnified by three factors. First, as discussed in Chapter Four, the FBI generates tens of thousands of NSLs per year on the authority of Special Agents in Charge, and the predication standard - relevance to an authorized investigation - can easily be satisfied. Second, we found that FBI Division Counsel in field offices have asked NSLB attorneys in FBI Headquarters for ad hoc guidance on application of the "least intrusive collection techniques feasible" proviso, suggesting a need for more clarity or at least a frame of reference.[181] Third, neither the Attorney General's NSI Guidelines nor internal FBI policies require the purging of information derived from NSLs in FBI databases, regardless of the outcome of the investigation. Thus, once information is obtained in response to a national security letter, it is indefinitely retained and retrievable by the many authorized personnel who have access to various FBI databases.

We recognize that there cannot be one model regarding the use of NSLs in all types of national security investigations, and that the FBI cannot issue definitive guidance addressing when and what types of NSLs should issue at each stage of investigations. The judgment of FBI agents and their supervisors, coupled with review by Chief Division Counsel and Special Agents in Charge or senior Headquarters officials, are critical to ensuring the appropriate use of these NSLs and preventing overreaching. However, we believe that the meaning and application of the Attorney General Guidelines' proviso calling for use of the "least intrusive collection techniques feasible" to the FBI's use of national security letter authorities should be addressed in general FBI guidance as well as in the training of special agents, Chief Division Counsel, and all FBI officials authorized to sign NSLs.[182] With the FBI's increasing reliance on national security letters as an investigative technique, such guidance and training would be helpful in assisting FBI personnel in reconciling the important privacy considerations that underlie the Attorney General Guidelines' proviso with the FBI's mission to detect and deter terrorist attacks and espionage threats.

II. Telephone "Toll Billing Records Information"

We found that FBI agents and attorneys frequently have questions regarding the types of records they can obtain when requesting "toll billing records information" pursuant to the ECPA NSL statute.

ECPA does not define the term "toll billing records information" and there is no case law interpreting the provision. Technological developments in the last twenty years also complicate what is meant by "toll billing records information." When the original ECPA NSL statute was enacted in 1986, most individuals had one landline telephone and were billed for each local and long distance telephone call. Now, many individuals have multiple cell phones or disposable cell phones, pre-paid phone cards, fixed rate phone plans, and text messaging capabilities.

In the absence of a statutory definition for "toll billing records information" or case law interpreting this phrase, different electronic communication service providers produce different types of information in response to the FBI's ECPA national security letter requests for these records.[183] For example, some telephone companies have told the FBI that while they maintain records of outgoing calls from a particular telephone number for business purposes, these records are not used for billing purposes and, thus, are not "toll billing records information." Other telephone companies provide long distance records but not records for local calls

To assist case agents in ensuring that the FBI obtains the data permitted by the statute, FBI-OGC's National Security Law Branch has developed sample attachments to NSLs for "toll billing records information" that list the types of records that the NSL recipient "may consider to be 'toll billing records information'." In June 2005, for example, NSLB posted sample attachments on its web site that referenced 12 categories of records, such as "local, regional, long distance, international, wholesale, cellular, paging, toll free, and prepaid calls." The attachment also contained the caveat that the FBI was not requesting, and the recipient should not provide, contents of any electronic communications.

However, we found that ongoing uncertainty about the meaning of the phrase "toll billing records information" has generated multiple inquiries by Division Counsel to NSLB attorneys and confusion on the part of various communication providers. In light of this recurring issue, we recommend that the Department consider seeking a legislative amendment to the ECPA to define the phrase "toll billing records information."

III. The Role of FBI Division Counsel in Reviewing National Security Letters

FBI Division Counsel play a critical role in reviewing and approving national security letters. As discussed in Chapter Three, Division Counsel are responsible for identifying and correcting erroneous information in NSLs and NSL approval memoranda, resolving questions about the scope of the NSL statutes, ensuring adequate predication for NSL requests, and providing advice on issues concerning the collection of any unauthorized information through any national security letters.

However, we believe that the timing of Division Counsel's review of NSLs and the supervisory structure for Division Counsel may affect the independence and aggressiveness of their review.

Division Counsel report to the Special Agents in Charge of the field offices in which they work, not to the Office of General Counsel at FBI Headquarters. As a result, personnel decisions such as performance reviews, compensation, and promotion determinations concerning Division Counsel are made by the Special Agents in Charge (SACs). We also found in our review that because Division Counsel report to SACs rather than to FBI-OGC, some Division Counsel are reluctant to question NSL requests or to challenge requests generated in the course of investigations that were previously approved by the SAC without CDC input.[184]

The tensions arising from the CDCs' reporting relationship with field managers were underscored by the results of an informal survey involving the use of NSL authorities. During our review, the CDC of a large field office reviewed an approval EC for an ECPA NSL that contained only one sentence addressing predication for the request.[185] The CDC believed the NSL should not be approved, but was interested to know if his views were shared by CDCs in other field offices. To elicit their views, the CDC circulated the text of the request to 22 other CDCs, asking if they would have approved the NSL request. Responses to this informal survey revealed a split: 9 CDCs said they would approve the NSL request, while 13 said they would have rejected it.

The responses to the inquiry also generated much discussion as to whether there was sufficient predication for the request. For example, several CDCs said they would prefer to see more than a perfunctory statement that the investigation was authorized in accordance with the Attorney General Guidelines. Others disagreed, stating that so long as the approval EC recites the applicable legal standard, it is sufficient.

Apart from these legal disagreements as to whether the request satisfied the requirements of the ECPA statute, several CDCs said that they would have approved the request for reasons other than the merits of the approval documentation. After the inquiry, an Assistant General Counsel in NSLB (who would not have approved the NSL) spoke to some of the Division Counsel who said they would have approved the request. The Assistant General Counsel told the OIG that she learned that there were certain offices in which the CDC's relationship with the SAC was not "great," and where lawyers are viewed as trying to "stop things." The Assistant General Counsel said that she believed, after speaking to these attorneys, that some of the attorneys who said they would have approved the request would have preferred to reject it, but felt in a bind in challenging the SAC, particularly when the squad supervisor and Assistant Special Agent in Charge had already approved the underlying investigation. The Assistant General Counsel also said she thought several CDCs who would have approved the request did so "only to avoid the political fallout from questioning the initiation of a [national security investigation]."

As a result of the inquiry, FBI-OGC concluded that Division Counsel would benefit from more information in NSL approval documentation. Accordingly, in February 2006 OGC revised its guidance and standard formats for NSLs. Instead of requiring a "brief explanation" of the predication underlying the request, the ECs requesting approval to issue NSLs now are required to provide a "full explanation of the justification for opening and maintaining the investigation on the subject" and to "fully state the relevance of the requested records to the investigation."

Another issue we found regarding the Division Counsel's review of national security letters was that, with exceptions in several of the FBI's largest field offices, Division Counsel do not learn about the underlying national security investigation until they are asked to review the NSL request. Therefore, the first time Division Counsel are likely to learn about the predication for national security investigations is when they see the first NSL in the investigations. As discussed above, until recently the documentation that case agents were required to prepare during the period covered by our review called for a "brief explanation" of the predication for the request. At times, agents merely recited the statutory language in the NSL approval memoranda.[186] Yet, some Division Counsel told us they are reluctant to second guess the predication for national security letters because they are unfamiliar with the underlying investigations - and, as noted above, are reluctant to second guess the operational judgments of senior field office officials. In fact, many CDCs said that the questions they raise with field personnel about the adequacy of predication for NSLs often results in contentious discussions with the requesting case agents and their supervisors.[187]

Finally, in considering the responses to the CDC's informal survey, the Assistant General Counsel and two NSLB Deputy General Counsel said they were very concerned that some CDCs believe they cannot exercise their independent professional judgment on the use of NSL authorities due to these concerns. We believe that, while the reporting structure for the Office of Chief Division Counsel raises questions that are beyond the scope of this review, they likely affect the CDC's role in approving the use of many other investigative authorities. We therefore recommend that the FBI consider measures to ensure that Chief Division

Counsel and Assistant Division Counsel provide a hard review, and independent oversight, of NSL requests.

IV. Issuing NSLs from "Control Files" Rather Than from "Investigative Files"

The Attorney General's NSI Guidelines and internal FBI policy authorize agents to initiate national security investigations when the required predication exists for a national security investigation. When these investigations are approved, the investigation is assigned a unique identifier that is referred to as the investigative file number. In contrast to these "investigative files," case agents may also seek approval to open "control files," sometimes referred to as "administrative files" or "repository files," which are created to store other types of FBI information. However, FBI policy does not permit investigative activity - such as issuing national security letters - to be conducted from a control file. Moreover, if a national security letter is issued from a control file, the NSL approval memorandum may not be accompanied by documentation explaining how the NSL request is tied to an existing national security investigation or the relevance of the information requested to that investigation.

As part of the FBI's post-September 11 reorganization, the Counterterrorism Division established several "operational support sections" that provide analytical support to counterterrorism investigations. As discussed in Chapter Six, we identified two circumstances in which over 300 national security letters were generated by Headquarters Counterterrorism Division personnel exclusively from "control files" rather than from investigative files.

FBI Headquarters officials, including Counterterrorism Division officials and NSLB attorneys, told us that the nature and quality of the work generated by these operational support units in coordination with other Headquarters and field divisions made these officials confident that there was sufficient predication for the NSLs issued exclusively from control files. However, these officials acknowledged that issuing NSLs exclusively from control files does not conform to internal FBI policy and makes it difficult to determine if the statutory and Attorney General's NSI Guidelines' requirements for issuing NSLs have been satisfied. We understand that the Counterterrorism Division, in consultation with FBI-OGC, has taken steps in response to the OIG's identification of this issue to ensure that future NSL requests are issued from investigative files rather than from control files so that these requests conform to NSL statutes, the Attorney General's NSI Guidelines, and internal FBI policy.

V. Obtaining Records from Federal Reserve Banks in Response to "Certificate Letters" Rather Than by Issuing RFPA NSLs

We identified instances in which the FBI sent at least 19 "certificate letters" to a Federal Reserve Bank seeking "financial records" concerning 244 named individuals instead of issuing NSLs pursuant to the Right to Financial Privacy Act (RFPA).[188] Most of the individuals whose records were sought were subjects of FBI investigations, but some were other individuals. The certificate letters were issued between May 2003 and August 2004 and were signed by a Unit Chief in the Headquarters Counterterrorism Division's Terrorist

Financing Operations Section (TFOS), a TFOS Acting Unit Chief, or Supervisory Special Agents assigned to TFOS. While the letters did not consistently specify what type of "financial records" were sought, TFOS officials told us that the FBI obtained "Fedwire records" in response to the letters.[189] Although the letters were issued at least 18 months after passage of the Patriot Act, they recited the pre-Patriot Act legal standard for acquiring the records.[190] The FBI General Counsel and other FBI-OGC attorneys told us that they were not aware that the FBI had obtained records from a Federal Reserve Bank without first issuing RFPA NSLs.

NSLB attorneys first learned of the certificate letters in July 2004, when a TFOS Acting Assistant Section Chief told an NSLB Assistant General Counsel that the certificate letters merely asked the Federal Reserve Bank whether it had information on the referenced bank account and that TFOS obtained the records themselves only after they served RFPA NSLs. TFOS personnel also told the Assistant General Counsel that the letters were used with few exceptions only in emergency situations, and that NSLs or grand jury subpoenas were issued relatively soon after the records were provided to the FBI to cover the records obtained in response to the certificate letters. While some TFOS personnel told the Assistant General Counsel that Federal Reserve Bank employees who dealt with TFOS did not believe NSLs were required in order for the FBI to obtain the records because the Federal Reserve Banks were "quasi-governmental bodies," the Assistant General Counsel believed at the time that NSLs were required before the FBI could obtain the records. The Assistant General Counsel instructed TFOS in August 2004 that any requests for information from Federal Reserve Banks be reviewed to ensure that they do not seek financial records in the initial requests and that such requests should omit the reference to the RFPA NSL statute.

Contrary to the statements made to the Assistant General Counsel by TFOS personnel noted above, the Assistant General Counsel discovered by accident in the fall of 2004 that the certificate letters requested the records themselves, not just that a search be conducted. The Assistant General Counsel also learned that the certificate letters were often used in non-emergency situations; and there were delays as long as six months in issuing NSLs after obtaining the information. Following these discoveries, in December 2004 the Assistant General Counsel again counseled TFOS to revise the certificate letters to ask that only a search be conducted and that the FBI should only obtain the records after issuing duly authorized NSLs except in genuine emergencies.

The Assistant General Counsel also met with attorneys in the Federal Reserve's Office of the General Counsel (OGC) who said that the Federal Reserve's position on whether to require NSLs depended on who the FBI's point of contact was at the Federal Reserve. The Assistant General Counsel told us that the issue was resolved when Federal Reserve OGC attorneys told the Assistant General Counsel that the Federal Reserve considered itself to be a "financial institution" and therefore would require NSLs before releasing financial records under the RFPA.

Prior to the conclusion of this review, the OIG contacted Federal Reserve Bank attorneys who stated that they believe Federal Reserve Banks are not "financial institutions" for purposes of the RFPA NSL statute and that Fedwire records are not "financial records" under the statute. Nonetheless, the Federal Reserve OGC attorneys said that Federal Reserve Banks as a matter of policy require that the FBI issue RFPA NSLs before the FBI may obtain Fedwire records and "financial records." After reviewing the certificate letters, these attorneys also stated that the Federal Reserve Banks should not have provided Fedwire records in response to the certificate letters because the certificate letters are not duly authorized RFPA NSLs.

The OIG also asked FBI-OGC and the OIG General Counsel for their legal opinion as to whether Feder al Reserve Banks are "financial institutions" for purposes of the RFPA NSL statute and whether Fedwire records are "financial records" under the statute. Although we do not reach a definitive conclusion in this review, we cannot conclude that the FBI's practice of issuing certificate letters signed by subordinate TFOS personnel violated the RFPA.

We also note our concern about (1) the ability of NSLB attorneys in FBI-OGC to obtain accurate and complete information about the FBI's use of NSL authorities; and (2) the delay in TFOS' compliance with NSLB's advice. 'I'F'OS personnel provided inaccurate information to the Assistant General Counsel who inquired about TFOS' practice of issuing certificate letters rather than NSLs and failed to ensure that the initial advice given to TFOS was promptly communicated and implemented. As a consequence of the inaccurate information conveyed to NSLB and the delay in implementing NSLB's advice, the FBI issued at least three additional certificate letters to a Federal Reserve Bank in contravention of NSLB's legal advice.

VI. The OGC Database Does Not Identify the Targets of National Security Letters When They are Different from the Subjects of the Underlying Investigations

As discussed in Chapter Three, since passage of the Patriot Act the standard for issuing national security letters has changed and the FBI no longer needs to identify individualized suspicions about the targets of the NSLs. Instead, the FBI is authorized to collect information on any individuals so long as the information is relevant to an authorized investigation and, with respect to investigations of "U.S. persons," the investigations are not conducted solely on the basis of activities protected by the First Amendment. Thus, the target of an NSL is frequently not the same person as the subject of the underlying investigation. For example, if the response to an NSL for toll billing records on the subject's telephone number identifies a telephone number that the subject contacted frequently during a time period relevant to the investigation, the FBI may issue another NSL requesting subscriber information for that telephone number.

As described in Chapter Four, for purposes of preparing the congressional reports on NSL usage, the FBI-OGC NSL tracking database (OGC database) captures the numbers of investigations of different U.S. Persons and non-U.S. persons that generated NSL requests. However, the OGC database does not capture data on whether the target of the NSL is the subject of the underlying investigation or another individual. As a result, because the target of an NSL is frequently not the same person as the subject of the underlying investigation, the FBI does not know, and cannot estimate, the number of NSL requests relating to persons who are not investigative subjects.

Our review assessed this issue in the sample of investigative files we examined in four field offices. Of the 293 national security letters we examined, we identified 13 instances (4 percent) in which the NSLs requested information on individuals other than the investigative subjects.

We also found that during the period of our review, FBI-OGC did not consistently require case agents to include in the memoranda seeking approval to issue NSLs whether the NSL target was the subject of the underlying investigation. In 2006, the FBI modified its guidance to require, with the exception of NSLs seeking subscriber information, that agents indicate in the approval EC whether the request is for a person other than the subject of the investigation, or in addition to that subject, and to state the U.S. person or non-U.S. person status of those individuals.

We believe the FBI should also modify the FBI database to include data, which is contained in the approval ECs, reflecting the number of NSL requests for information on U.S. persons and non-U.S. persons who are not the investigative subjects but are the targets of NSLs. In light of the Patriot Act's expansion of the FBI's authority to collect information about individuals who are not subjects of its investigations, we believe the OGC database should contain this information so that the issue is subject to internal and external oversight.

8. Conclusions and Recommendations

As required by the Patriot Reauthorization Act, this OIG review examined the FBI's use of national security letters from calendar years 2003 through 2005. The Act required the OIG to examine how many requests were issued by the FBI; any noteworthy facts or circumstances relating to such use, including any improper or illegal use of such authority; the importance of the information acquired to the intelligence activities of the Department of Justice or to others; the manner in which such information is collected, retained, analyzed, and disseminated by the Department; whether and how often the Department utilized such information to produce an analytical intelligence product for distribution within the Department of Justice, to the intelligence community, or to others; and whether and how often the Department provided such information to law enforcement authorities for use in criminal proceedings.

Our review found that the FBI's use of national security letter requests has grown dramatically since enactment of the Patriot Act in October 2001. The FBI issued approximately 8,500 NSL requests in CY 2000, the last full year prior to passage of the Patriot Act. After the Patriot Act, the number of NSL requests increased to approximately 39,000 in 2003, approximately 56,000 in 2004, and approximately 47,000 in 2005. During the period covered by our review, the FBI issued a total of 143,074 NSL requests pursuant to national security letter authorities.

When considering these statistics, it is important to note that one national security letter may contain more than one request for information. For example, the 39,000 NSL requests in 2003 were contained in approximately 12,000 letters, and the 47,000 requests in 2005 were contained in approximately 19,000 letters.

Most NSL usage (about 74 percent of all NSL requests) occurred during counterterrorism investigations. About 26 percent of all NSL requests were issued during counterintelligence investigations, and less than 1 percent of the requests were generated during foreign computer intrusion cyber investigations.

In addition, the use of national security letters in FBI counterterrorism investigations increased from approximately 15 percent of investigations opened during 2003 to approximately 29 percent of the counterterrorism investigations opened during 2005.

We found that the use of NSL requests related to "U.S. persons" and "non-U.S. persons" shifted during our 3-year review period. The percentage of requests generated from investigations of U.S. persons increased from about 39 percent of all NSL requests issued in 2003 to about 53 percent of all NSL requests during 2005.

National security letters seeking telephone toll billing records or subscriber information or electronic communication (e-mail) transactional records or subscriber information accounted for the overwhelming majority of NSL re uests durin the reviiiriod percent), percent) and percent).

It is important to note that these statistics, which were obtained from the FBI electronic database that tracks NSL usage, understate the total number of national security letter requests. We found that the OGC database is inaccurate and does not include all national security letter requests issued by the FBI.

Because of inaccuracies in the OGC database, we compared data in this database to a sample of investigative files in four FBI field offices that we visited. Overall, we found approximately 17 percent more national security *letters* and 22 percent more national security letter *requests* in the case files we examined in four field offices than were recorded in the OGC database. As a result, we believe that the total numbers of NSLs and NSL requests issued by the FBI are significantly higher than the FBI reported.

Further, we found the OGC database did not accurately reflect the status of investigative subjects or other targets of NSLs and that the Department's semiannual classified reports to Congress on NSL usage were also inaccurate. Specifically, the data provided in the Department's semiannual classified reports regarding the number of requests for records, the number of different persons or organizations that were the subjects of investigations in which records were requested, and the classification of those individuals' status as "U.S. persons or organizations" and "non-U.S. persons or organizations" were all inaccurate. We found that 12 percent of the case files we examined did not accurately report the status of the target of the NSL as being a U.S. person or a non-U.S. person. In each of these instances, the FBI database indicated that the subject was a non-U.S. person while the approval memoranda in the investigative file indicated the subject was a U.S. person or a presumed U.S. person.

With respect to the effectiveness of national security letters, FBI Headquarters and field personnel told us that they believe national security letters are indispensable investigative tools that serve as building blocks in many counterterrorism and counterintelligence investigations. National security letters have various uses, including obtaining evidence to support FISA applications for electronic surveillance, pen register/trap and trace devices, or physical searches; developing communication or financial links between subjects of FBI investigations and between those subjects and others; providing evidence to initiate new investigations, expand investigations, or enable agents to close investigations; providing investigative leads; and corroborating information obtained by other investigative techniques.

FBI agents and analysts also use information obtained from national security letters, in combination with other information, to prepare analytical intelligence products for distribution within the FBI and to other Department components, and for dissemination to other federal agencies, Joint Terrorism Task Forccs, and other members of the intelligence community. We found that information derived from national security letters is routinely shared with United States Attorneys' Offices pursuant to various Departmental directives requiring terrorism prosecutors and intelligence research specialists to be familiar with FBI counterterrorism investigations. When prosecutors review FBI investigative files, they also may see information obtained through national security letters. However, because information derived from national security letters is not marked or tagged as such, it is impossible to determine when and how often the FBI provided information derived from national security letters to law enforcement authorities for use in criminal proceedings.

We also determined that information obtained from national security letters is routinely stored in the FBI's Automated Case Support (ACS) system; Telephone Applications, a specialized FBI application for storing telephone data; the FBI's Investigative Data Warehouse database; and other databases. FBI personnel and Joint Terrorism Task Force members who have the appropriate clearances to use these databases would therefore have access to information obtained from national security letters.

As required by the Patriot Reauthorization Act, our review also examined instances of improper or illegal use of national security letters. First, our review examined national security letter violations that the FBI was required to report to the President's Intelligence Oversight Board (IOB). Executive Order 12863 directs the IOB to inform the President of any activities that the IOB believes "may be unlawful or contrary to Executive order or presidential directive." The FBI identified 26 possible violations involving the use of national security letter authorities from 2003 through 2005, of which 19 were reported to the IOB. These 19 involved the issuance of NSLs without proper authorization, improper requests under the statutes cited in the national security letters, and unauthorized collection of telephone or Internet e-mail transactional records, including records containing data beyond the time period requested in the national security letters. Of these 26 possible violations, 22 were the result of FBI errors, while 4 were caused by mistakes made by recipients of the national security letters.

Second, in addition to the violations reported by the FBI, we reviewed documents relating to national security letters in a sample of FBI investigative files in four FBI field offices. In our review of 77 FBI investigative files, we found that 17 of these files - 22 percent - contained one or more possible violations relating to national security letters that were not identified by the FBI. These possible violations included infractions that were similar to those identified by the FBI and considered as possible IOB violations, but also included instances in which the FBI issued national security letters for different information than what had been approved by the field supervisor. Based on our review and the significant percentage of files that contained unreported possible violations (22 percent), we believe that a significant number of NSL-related possible violations are not being identified or reported by the FBI.

Third, we identified many instances in which the FBI obtained telephone toll billing records and subscriber information from 3 telephone companies pursuant to more than 700 "exigent letters" signed by personnel in the Counterterrorism Division without first issuing national security letters. We concluded that the FBI's acquisition of this information circumvented the ECPA NSL statute and violated the Attorney General's Guidelines for FBI National Security Investigations and Foreign Intelligence Collection (NSI Guidelines) and internal FBI policy. These matters were compounded by the fact that the FBI used the exigent letters in non- emergency circumstances, failed to ensure that there were duly authorized investigations to which the requests could be tied, and failed to ensure that NSLs were issued promptly after the fact, pursuant to existing or new counterterrorism investigations. In addition, the exigent letters inaccurately represented that the FBI had already requested subpoenas for the information when, in fact, it had not.

Fourth, we determined that in two circumstances during 2003 though 2005 FBI Headquarters Counterterrorism Division generated over 300 national security letters exclusively from "control files" rather than from "investigative files" in violation of FBI policy. In these instances, FBI agents did not generate and supervisors did not approve documentation demonstrating that the factual predicate required by the Electronic Communications Privacy Act, the Attorney General's Guidelines for FBI National Security Investigations and Foreign Intelligence Collection, and internal FBI policy had been established. When NSLs are issued from control files rather than from investigative files, internal and external reviewers cannot determine whether the requests are tied to investigations that establish the required evidentiary predicate for issuing the national security letters.

Fifth, we examined FBI investigative files in four field offices to determine whether FBI case agents and supervisors adhered to FBI policies designed to ensure appropriate supervisory review of the use of national security letter authorities. We found that 60 percent of the investigative files we examined contained one or more violations of FBI internal control policies relating to national security letters. These included failures to document supervisory review of national security letter approval memoranda and failures to include required information such as the authorizing statute, the status of the investigative subject, or the number or types of records requested in NSL approval memoranda. Moreover, because the FBI does not retain copies of signed national security letters, we were unable to conduct a comprehensive audit of the FBI's compliance with its internal control policies and the statutory certifications required for national security letters.

Our review describes several other "noteworthy facts or circumstances" we identified. For example, we found that the FBI has not provided clear guidance describing how case agents and supervisors should apply the Attorney General Guidelines' requirement to use the "least intrusive collection techniques feasible" in their use and sequencing of national security letters. In addition, we found confusion among FBI attorneys and communication providers over the meaning of the phrase "telephone toll billing records information" in the ECPA NSL statute. We also saw indications that some Chief Division Counsel and Assistant Division Counsel are reluctant to provide an independent review of national security letter requests because these attorneys report to the Special Agents in Charge who have already approved the underlying investigation.

Finally, in evaluating the FBI's use of national security letters it is important to note the significant challenges the FBI was facing during the period covered by our review and the major organizational changes it was undergoing. Moreover, it is also important to recognize that in most cases the FBI was seeking to obtain information that it could have obtained properly if it had it followed applicable statutes, guidelines, and internal policies. We also did not find any indication that the FBI's misuse of NSL authorities constituted criminal misconduct.

However, as described above, we found that that the FBI used NSLs in violation of applicable NSL statutes, Attorney General Guidelines, and internal FBI policies. In addition, we found that the FBI circumvented the requirements of the ECPA NSL statute when it issued at least 739 "exigent letters" to obtain telephone toll billing records and subscriber information from three telephone companies without first issuing NSLs. Moreover, in a few other instances, the FBI sought or obtained information to which it was not entitled under the NSL authorities when it sought educational records through issuance of an ECPA NSL, when it sought and obtained telephone toll billing records in the absence of a national security investigation, when it sought and obtained consumer full credit reports in a counterintelligence investigation, and when it sought and obtained financial records and telephone toll billing records without first issuing NSLs.

Based on our review, we believe that the FBI should consider the following recommendations relating to the use of national security letters. We recommend that the FBI:

1. Require all Headquarters and field personnel who are authorized to issue national security letter to create a control file for the purpose of retaining signed copies of all national security letters they issue.
2. Improve the FBI-OGC NSL tracking database to ensure that it captures timely, complete, and accurate data on NSLs and NSL requests.
3. Improve the FBI-OGC NSL database to include data reflecting NSL requests for information about individuals who are not the investigative subjects but are the targets of NSL requests.
4. Consider issuing additional guidance to field offices that will assist in identifying possible IOB violations arising from use of national security letter authorities, such as (a) measures to reduce or eliminate typographical and other errors in national security letters so that the FBI does not collect unauthorized information; (b) best practices for identifying the receipt of unauthorized information in the response to national security letters due to third-party errors; (c) clarifying the distinctions between the two NSL authorities in the Fair Credit Reporting Act (15 U.S.C. §§ 1681u and 1681v); and (d) reinforcing internal FBI policy requiring that NSLs must be issued from investigative files, not from control files.
5. Consider seeking legislative amendment to the Electronic Communications Privacy Act to define the phrase "telephone toll billing records information."
6. Consider measures that would enable FBI agents and analysts to (a) label or tag their use of information derived from national security letters in analytical intelligence products and (b) identify when and how often information derived from NSLs is provided to law enforcement authorities for use in criminal proceedings.
7. Take steps to ensure that the FBI does not improperly issue exigent letters.
8. Take steps to ensure that, where appropriate, the FBI makes requests for information in accordance with the requirements of national security letter authorities.
9. Implement measures to ensure that FBI-OGC is consulted about activities undertaken by FBI Headquarters National Security Branch, including its operational support activities, that could generate requests for records from third parties that the FBI is authorized to obtain exclusively though the use of its national security letter authorities.
10. Ensure that Chief Division Counsel and Assistant Division Counsel provide close and independent review of requests to issue national security letters.

We believe that these recommendations, if fully implemented, can improve the accuracy of the reporting of the FBI's use of national security letters and ensure the FBI's compliance with the requirements governing their use. As directed by the Patriot Reauthorization Act, the

OIG will examine the FBI's use of national security letter authorities and report on their use in calendar year 2006.

UNCLASSIFIED APPENDIX

The Attorney General
Washington, D.C.

March 1, 2007

The Honorable Glenn A. Fine
Inspector General
Office of the Inspector General
United States Department of Justice
950 Pennsylvania Avenue, N.W.
Washington, D.C. 20530

Dear Mr. Fine:

I appreciate your work and the opportunity to comment on your Review of the Federal Bureau of Investigation's Use of National Security Letters.

The problems identified in your review are serious and must be addressed immediately. I have spoken with FBI Director Bob Mueller about your findings and recommendations. He already has taken specific steps to correct past mistakes and to ensure that the Bureau will use National Security Letters (NSLs) in an appropriate manner in compliance with all applicable laws and internal policy requirements.

I have asked the Department's National Security Division and the Privacy and Civil Liberties Office to work with the Bureau in implementing these corrective actions and to consider any further review and reforms that are needed. They will report to me regularly on their progress. In addition, I ask that you report to me in four months on the FBI's implementation of your recommendations.

Your review also evaluated the effectiveness of NSLs and rightly found them to have "contributed significantly to many counterterrorism and counterintelligence investigations." NSLs are vital investigative tools and are critical to our efforts to fight and win the war on terror. They can and must be used appropriately and in a manner that protects the civil liberties of all Americans. I have confidence in the Director's ability to implement the changes necessary to ensure the proper use of these authorities.

Sincerely,

Alberto R. Gonzales

UNCLASSIFIED

DIRECTOR OF NATIONAL INTELLIGENCE
WASHINGTON, DC 20511

E/S 00145

MEMORANDUM FOR: Glenn A. Fine
Inspector General
Department of Justice

SUBJECT: (U) Department of Justice Office of the Inspector General's Draft Report: "A Review of the Federal Bureau of Investigation's Use of National Security Letters"

(U) Thank you for requesting my comments, pursuant to Section 119(d) of the USA PATRIOT Improvement and Reauthorization Act of 2005, on the Department of Justice (DOJ) Office of the Inspector General's Draft Report entitled "A Review of the Federal Bureau of Investigation's Use of National Security Letters" (Report).

(U) I appreciate your efforts, and the efforts of your staff, in producing an in-depth Report on this important issue. I have significant concerns about the issues raised in the Report. I anticipate that many of the recommendations contained in the Report will be implemented in order to ensure that the Federal Bureau of Investigation (FBI) has improved processes and procedures to ensure full compliance with all laws and regulations in its use of National Security Letters (NSLs). To ensure that the FBI's changes are successful, and that the FBI's use of NSLs is consistent with the U.S. Constitution, statutes, Executive Orders, and regulations, I directed the General Counsel and the Civil Liberties Protection Officer of the Office of the Director of National Intelligence to work with DOJ and the FBI to remedy deficiencies identified in your final report, as appropriate.

(U) My highest priority is protecting America while ensuring that all activities undertaken to protect our citizens by the Intelligence Community fully comply with all laws. While not lessening my concern about the issues identified in the Report, I think it is important to note that NSLs are critical tools in counterterrorism and other investigations. As your Report notes, information obtained from NSLs "contributed significantly to many counterterrorism and counterintelligence investigations." Many of these details on sensitive investigative matters must remain classified, but your Report contains important examples where NSLs have provided critical information to protect America. Indeed, as your Report notes, FBI personnel believe NSLs are "indispensable investigative tools." Of course, as with all investigative tools, it is vital that NSLs are used in a manner that complies with all applicable laws and regulations.

(U) Thank you again for your efforts.

JMMcConnell
J. M. McConnell

28 FEB 07
Date

U.S. Department of Justice

Federal Bureau of Investigation

Office of the Director

Washington, D.C. 20535-0001

March 6, 2007

Honorable Glenn A. Fine
Inspector General
United States Department of Justice
Suite 4706
950 Pennsylvania Avenue, N.W.
Washington, DC 20530

SUBJECT: U.S. Department of Justice, Office of the Inspector General - **"A Review of the Federal Bureau of Investigation's Use of National Security Letters (NSL)."**

Dear Mr. Fine:

The FBI appreciates this opportunity to respond to findings and recommendations made in your report entitled "A Review of the Federal Bureau of Investigation's Use of National Security Letters" (hereinafter "Report"). This letter conveys the FBI's responses to the recommendations, and I request that it be appended to the Report. The Office of the Inspector General (OIG) has identified areas of serious concern related to the FBI's use of National Security Letters (NSLs). The FBI has already taken several steps to correct the deficiencies identified in the Report. These steps are described in more detail below and include strengthening internal controls, changing policies and procedures to improve oversight of the NSL approval process, barring certain practices identified in the Report, and ordering an expedited inspection. We will continue to work with the OIG to gauge our progress in these reforms.

Before addressing the specific findings and recommendations in the Report, the FBI offers two general comments applicable to the FBI's use of this critical national security investigative tool. First, I appreciate the OIG's discussion in the Report of the importance of National Security Letters to our counterterrorism and intelligence missions. When Congress expanded the FBI's ability to use this vital tool, some expressed concern about a potential for abuse. It is important to note that the OIG found no intentional or deliberate misuse of these authorities but highlighted several areas where we must increase our internal audit and oversight of these tools. We are doing so, and we will work in concert with the Department's National Security Division and Privacy and Civil Liberties Office to implement these reforms.

As the Report notes, NSLs are indispensable investigative tools that permit the FBI to gather the basic building blocks in national security investigations, enabling the FBI both to advance such investigations and, when warranted, to close such inquiries with a higher degree of confidence that the subject does not pose a terrorism threat. On page 46 of the Report and in the ensuing pages, the Report catalogues 8 vital functions NSLs play in the FBI's mission to protect the American people. For instance, the Report cites examples where NSLs helped enable investigators to establish potential contacts of an investigative subject and to determine whether a terror cell may be operating in a particular location. As the Report notes, these are the types of "bread and butter" capabilities FBI Agents rely on to advance national security investigations.

With these functions in mind, I deeply appreciate the OIG's observation that any discussion of the FBI's use of National Security Letters must take into consideration the environment in which the FBI -- particularly the Counterterrorism Division (CTD) -- has functioned for the last five years. Since September 11, 2001, the FBI has transformed its operations while working at a breakneck pace to keep the country safe. As the OIG noted, the FBI has "overhaul[ed] its counterterrorism operations, expand[ed] its intelligence capabilities, [begun] to upgrade its information technology systems, and [sought] to improve coordination with state and local law enforcement agencies." It is important to note that during the period reviewed, CTD was investigating and responding to a constant stream of terror threats. For instance, the investigation into the Al Qaeda plot that culminated in the attacks of September 11 was still ongoing in 2003 when CTD began investigating potential plots to destroy U.S.-bound aircraft and individuals surveilling economic targets in the United States. The 2005 bombings in London prompted intensive investigations of any known U.S. connections. These high-profile investigations occurred at the same time as CTD was conducting literally hundreds of lower profile investigations.

I believe those first two points -- the extraordinary workload of CTD since September 11 and the importance of National Security Letters to our national security efforts -are critical to remember when considering the OIG's congressionally mandated assessment of "improper or illegal" use of national security letter authorities. I am pleased that the OIG found no criminal use of these authorities nor any deliberate or intentional violations of the national security letter statutes or the Attorney General Guidelines. Nevertheless, I conclude from the OIG's fmdings that we must redouble our efforts to ensure that there is no repetition of mistakes of the past in the use of these authorities, however lacking in willfulness was the intent. To that end, it is worth noting that the FBI considers all reports of possible violations of its legal authorities seriously and requires regular reporting, legal review, and referrals to the appropriate entities. If unauthorized information is obtained, whether due to FBI or third-party error, that information is sealed, sequestered, and where appropriate, destroyed. In addition, employee conduct is reviewed and disciplined appropriately.

As the Report makes clear, in the majority of cases, the desire of Agents to expedite the conduct of national security investigations for the protection of the American public resulted in the FBI obtaining information to which it was entitled. While well-intentioned, the shortcuts identified by the OIG were unacceptable. Because they may have been facilitated in part by unclear internal guidance, we have already published improved internal guidance and have prohibited certain practices that the OIG criticized. We are also developing a comprehensive training module to address any uncertainty that exists within our employee ranks about the legal strictures that govern the use of National Security Letters. That training will be mandatory for Special Agents in Charge (SAC), Chief Division Counsels (CDC), and counterterrorism and counterintelligence Agents. Finally, because the vast majority of the uses of NSLs that the OIG flagged as improper originated with the CTD, I ordered an expedited, special inspection of that area of responsibility within CTD and the practices identified by the OIG.

Second, prior to commencement of the IG review, the FBI had identified deficiencies in our system for generating the data necessary for required congressional reporting of NSL usage. Those deficiencies, which were first flagged for Congress in March 28, 2006, resulted in errors in the numbers reported to Congress. We appreciate the OIG identifying additional deficiencies that we had not noted in the way we track and report usage of NSLs. Independent of this report, we have made substantial progress in developing an automated system to prepare NSLs and their associated documentation, which will automatically gather data for congressional reporting. This system, which will be described in more detail below, should alleviate many of the concerns identified by the FBI and the OIG. Other deficiencies identified by the OIG have already been corrected for future reporting purposes.

Recommendations:

OIG's recommendations below outline important and necessary controls when issuing National Security Letters and maintaining corresponding (statistical) records.

Recommendation #1: Require all Headquarters and field personnel who are authorized to issue National Security Letters to create a control file for the purpose of retaining signed copies of all National Security Letters they issue.

The FBI agrees with the OIG recommendation that the FBI should retain a signed copy of the National Security Letter and is implementing a policy that would require the originating office to maintain a copy of the signed NSL in the investigative sub-folder of the authorized investigation to which the NSL is relevant. The FBI believes that maintaining the NSL copy with the corresponding investigative file is more appropriate than creating a control file for this purpose.

Recommendation #2: Improve the FBI-Office of General Counsel (OGC) NSL tracking database to ensure that it captures timely, complete, and accurate information on NSLs and NSL requests.

Recommendation #3: Improve the FBI-OGC NSL database to include data reflecting NSL requests for information about individuals who are not the investigative subjects but are the targets of NSL requests.

The FBI agrees with these OIG recommendations. In fact, the FBI began addressing this issue in February 2006, when contractors produced an initial proposal for an automated system to prepare and track National Security Letters. This system is intended to be built as part of the existing, highly succeessful FISA Management System (FISAMs). For the last year, the FBI, with the assistance of its contractors, has been in the process of designing a database that is referred to as the NSL sub-system of FISAMs. The NSL sub-system is scheduled for testing in the Washington Field Office in July 2007, with the expansion of the system to other field offices pending successful testing.

The NSL sub-system is designed to require the user to enter certain data before the workflow can proceed and requires specific reviews and approvals before the request for the NSL can proceed. Through this process, the FBI can automatically ensure that certain legal and administrative requirements are met and that required reporting data is accurately collected. For example, by requiring the user to identify the investigative file from which the NSL is to be issued, the system will be able to verify the status of that file to ensure that it is still open and current (e.g., request date is within six months of the opening or an extension has been filed for the investigation) and ensure that NSLs are not being requested out of control or administrative files. The system will require the user to separately identify the target of the investigative file and the person whose records are being obtained through the requested NSL, if different. This will allow the FBI to accurately count the number of different persons about whom we gather data through NSLs. The system will also require that specific data elements be entered before the process can continue, such as requiring that the target's status as a U.S. person (USPER) or nonU.S. person (NON-USPER) be entered.

The NSL sub-system is being designed so that the FBI employee requesting an NSL will enter data only once. The system will then generate both the NSL and the authorizing Electronic Communication (EC) for signature, thereby ensuring that the two documents match exactly and minimizing the opportunity for transcription errors that give rise to unauthorized collections that must be reported to the Intelligence Oversight Board (JOB). As with the FISA Management System, this subsystem will have a comprehensive reporting capability.

With regard to other deficiencies indicated in your report that affect the accuracy of our congressional reporting, the default settings in our existing "database" have been changed: the default position for the U.S. person status of the "target" of the NSL has been changed to U.S. person and "0" can no longer be entered for the number of facilities on which data is requested by an NSL.

Recommendation #4: Consider issuing additional guidance to field offices that will assist in identifying possible IOB violations arising from use of national security letter authorities, such as (a) measures to reduce or eliminate typographical and other errors in National Security Letters so that the FBI does not collect unauthorized information; (b) best practices for identifying the receipt of unauthorized information in the response to National Security Letters due to third-party errors; (c) clarifying the distinctions between the two NSL authorities in the Fair Credit Reporting Act (15 U.S.C. §§ 1681u and 1681v); and (d) reinforcing internal FBI policy requiring that NSLs must be issued from investigative files, not from control files.

The FBI agrees with the OIG recommendation. As indicated above, the NSL subsystem is anticipated to reduce if not eliminate typographical errors that result in unauthorized collection of information. OGC issued comprehensive advice on November 11, 2006, with respect to reporting unauthorized collection of all types and provided guidance with respect to the sequestration of such materials. OGC will issue additional comprehensive NSL guidance that will, among other things, highlight the legal differences between the two NSL authorities that appear in the Fair Credit Reporting Act. Given the finding of the IG of at least two instances in which an NSL was issued under 15 U.S.C. § 1681v in counterintelligence investigations, we are directing each field office to inspect its counterintelligence files to determine whether it has made the same mistake. If any additional instances of that error are found, appropriate remedial action, including reports to the Intelligence Oversight Board, will be taken. The FBI does not believe that the issuance of

National Security Letters from control files is legally improper if, as was the case, the NSLs sought information that was relevant to authorized national security investigations that were open at the time the NSLs were issued. The FBI recognizes, however, that referring solely to a control file in the EC that seeks issuance of the NSL does not adequately document the existence of a national security investigation to which the material sought is relevant. Therefore, we are reiterating existing FBI policy that National Security Letters should be issued exclusively from investigative files and that such investigative files should be referenced on the supporting EC. Finally, although many of the possible IOB violations identified by the IG do not rise to the level of violations that are required to be reported to the JOB, the field has been instructed to report all to OGC for further evaluation.

Recommendation #5: Consider seeking legislative amendment to the Electronic Communications Privacy Act to define the phrase "telephone toll billing records information."

The FBI agrees with the OIG recommendation. The FBI agrees with the OIG's recommendation to seek a clarification of statutory definition of "telephone toll billing records information."

Recommendation #6: Consider measures that would enable FBI Agents and analysts to (a) label or tag their use of information derived from National Security Letters and (b) identify when and how often information derived from NSLs is provided to law enforcement authorities for use in criminal proceedings.

FBI agrees with the OIG recommendation, I have asked OGC to work with the FBI's National Security Branch and the Office of the Director of National Intelligence to ensure we carefully consider this recommendation balancing our operational needs, information sharing policy, and privacy concerns.

Recommendation #7: Take steps to ensure that the FBI does not improperly use exigent letters.

Recommendation #8: Take steps to ensure that where appropriate the FBI makes requests for information in accordance with the requirements of National Security Letter authorities.

The FBI agrees with the OIG recommendations. It is important to note that an "exigent" letter as that term is used in the Report is not an emergency disclosure under 18 U.S.C. 2702 (c) but rather a letter asking for records from a service provider upon the promise of a forthcoming NSL or grand jury subpoena. The "exigent letter" discussed in the Report never sought the content of any communications. While the FBI does not believe that the use of exigent letters is improper in itself, it recognizes that they have been used improperly as noted in the Report. Therefore, as a matter of policy, the FBI has barred their use.

Recommendation #9: Implement measures to ensure that FBI-OGC is consulted about activities undertaken by FBI Headquarters National Security Branch, including its operational support activities, that could generate requests for records from third parties that the FBI is authorized to obtain exclusively through the use of National Security Letter authorities.

The FBI agrees with the OIG recommendation. As part of the OGC's issuance of comprehensive guidance on National Security Letters, it will implement a more rigorous approval process to include the following: (1) for National Security Letters issued by Field Offices, the EC supporting the National Security Letter must be reviewed and approved by the Chief Division Counsel or Assistant Division Counsel (ADC); and (2) for National Security Letters issued by Headquarters, the EC must be reviewed and approved by the National Security Law Branch of the Office of General Counsel.

Recommendation #10: Ensure that Chief Division Counsel and Assistant Division Counsel provide close and independent review of requests to issue National Security Letters.

The FBI agrees with the OIG recommendation. The FBI has taken steps to address this issue already. In February 2006, the Office of the General Counsel, National Security Law Branch, reminded all Chief Division Counsels of the importance of their role in the National Security Letter approval process. In March 2006, the National Security Law Branch included on its website a narrative description of the role of the CDCs and the ADCs in approving National Security Letters. Additionally, the FBI General Counsel has reminded all Special Agents in Charge that their office's CDCs have an obligation to provide accurate, independent legal advice and that the SACs should strive to encourage such independent advice from the CDCs. Finally, the General Counsel will stress to the CDCs during the next regularly scheduled teleconference the importance of their exercising independent legal judgment in all FBI matters, including those surrounding the NSL process.

The FBI is committed to protecting the people of the United States in a manner consistent with its statutory authority, guidelines, and policy. I appreciate this opportunity to respond to your recommendations and will update you and the appropriate congressional committees with regard to our implementation progress.

Sincerely yours,

Robert S. Mueller, III
Director

NATIONAL SECURITY LETTER STATUTES IN EFFECT PRIOR TO USA PATRIOT IMPROVEMENT AND REAUTHORIZATION ACT OF 2005

Right to Financial Privacy Act
12 U.S.C. § 3414

(a) (1) Nothing in this chapter (except sections 3415, 3417, 3418, and 3421 of this title) shall apply to the production and disclosure of financial records pursuant to requests from--

(A) a Government authority authorized to conduct foreign counter- or foreign positive- intelligence activities for purposes of conducting such activities;

(B) the Secret Service for the purpose of conducting its protective functions (18 U.S.C. 3056; 3 U.S.C. 202, Public Law 90-331, as amended); or

(C) a Government authority authorized to conduct investigations of, or intelligence or counterintelligence analyses related to, international terrorism for the purpose of conducting such investigations or analyses.

(2) In the instances specified in paragraph (1), the Government authority shall submit to the financial institution the certificate required in section 3403(b) of this title signed by a supervisory official of a rank designated by the head of the Government authority.

(3) No financial institution, or officer, employee, or agent of such institution, shall disclose to any person that a Government authority described in paragraph (1) has sought or obtained access to a customer's financial records.

(4) The Government authority specified in paragraph (1) shall compile an annual tabulation of the occasions in which this section was used.

(5)

(A) Financial institutions, and officers, employees, and agents thereof, shall comply with a request for a customer's or entity's fmancial records made pursuant to this subsection by the Federal Bureau of Investigation when the Director of the Federal Bureau of Investigation (or the Director's designee in a position not lower than Deputy Assistant Director at Bureau headquarters or a Special Agent in Charge in a Bureau field office designated by the Director) certifies in writing to the financial institution that such records are sought for foreign counter intelligence purposes to protect against international terrorism or clandestine intelligence activities, provided that such an investigation of a United States person is not conducted solely upon the basis of activities protected by the first amendment to the Constitution of the United States.

(B) The Federal Bureau of Investigation may disseminate information obtained pursuant to this paragraph only as provided in guidelines approved by the Attorney General for foreign intelligence collection and foreign counterintelligence investigations conducted by the Federal Bureau of Investigation, and, with respect to dissemination to an agency of the United

States, only if such information is clearly relevant to the authorized responsibilities of such agency.

(C) On the dates provided in section 415b of Title 50, the Attorney General shall fully inform the congressional intelligence committees (as defined in section 401a of Title 50) concerning all requests made pursuant to this paragraph.

(D) No financial institution, or officer, employee, or agent of such institution, shall disclose to any person that the Federal Bureau of Investigation has sought or obtained access to a customer's or entity's financial records under this paragraph.

(b) (1) Nothing in this chapter shall prohibit a Government authority from obtaining financial records from a financial institution if the Government authority determines that delay in obtaining access to such records would create imminent danger of--

(A) physical injury to any person;

(B) serious property damage; or

(C) flight to avoid prosecution.

(2) In the instances specified in paragraph (1), the Government shall submit to the financial institution the certificate required in section 3403(b) of this title signed by a supervisory official of a rank designated by the head of the Government authority.

(3) Within five days of obtaining access to financial records under this subsection, the Government authority shall file with the appropriate court a signed, sworn statement of a supervisory official of a rank designated by the head of the Government authority setting forth the grounds for the emergency access. The Government authority shall thereafter comply with the notice provisions of section 3409(c) of this title.

(4) The Government authority specified in paragraph (1) shall compile an annual tabulation of the occasions in which this section was used.

(d) For purposes of this section, and sections 3415 and 3417 of this title insofar as they relate to the operation of this section, the term "financial institution" has the same meaning as in subsections (a)(2) and (c)(1) of section 5312 of Title 31, except that, for purposes of this section, such term shall include only such a financial institution any part of which is located inside any State or territory of the United States, the District of Columbia, Puerto Rico, Guam, American Samoa, the Commonwealth of the Northern Mariana Islands, or the United States Virgin Islands.

Fair Credit Reporting Act
Financial Institution and Consumer Identifying Information

15 U.S.C. § 1681u

(a) Identity of financial institutions

Notwithstanding section 1681 b of this title or any other provision of this subchapter, a consumer reporting agency shall furnish to the Federal Bureau of Investigation the names and addresses of all financial institutions (as that term is defined in section 3401 of Title 12) at which a consumer maintains or has maintained an account, to the extent that information is in the files of the agency, when presented with a written request for that information, signed by the Director of the Federal Bureau of Investigation, or the Director's designee in a position not lower than Deputy Assistant Director at Bureau headquarters or a Special Agent in Charge of a Bureau field office designated by the Director, which certifies compliance with this section. The Director or the Director's designee may make such a certification only if the Director or the Director's designee has determined in writing, that such information is sought for the conduct of an authorized investigation to protect against international terrorism or clandestine intelligence activities, provided that such an investigation of a United States person is not conducted solely upon the basis of activities protected by the first amendment to the Constitution of the United States.

(b) Identifying information

Notwithstanding the provisions of section 1681 b of this title or any other provision of this subchapter, a consumer reporting agency shall furnish identifying information respecting a consumer, limited to name, address, former addresses, places of employment, or former places of employment, to the Federal Bureau of Investigation when presented with a written request, signed by the Director or the Director's designee in a position not lower than Deputy Assistant Director at Bureau headquarters or a Special Agent in Charge of a Bureau field office designated by the Director, which certifies compliance with this subsection. The Director or the Director's designee may make such a certification only if the Director or the Director's designee has determined in writing that such information is sought for the conduct of an authorized investigation to protect against international terrorism or clandestine intelligence activities, provided that such an investigation of a United States person is not conducted solely upon the basis of activities protected by the first amendment to the Constitution of the United States.

(c) Court order for disclosure of consumer reports

Notwithstanding section 168lb of this title or any other provision of this subchapter, if requested in writing by the Director of the Federal Bureau of Investigation, or a designee of the Director in a position not lower than Deputy Assistant Director at Bureau headquarters or a Special Agent in Charge in a Bureau field office designated by the Director, a court may issue an order ex parte directing a consumer reporting agency to furnish a consumer report to the Federal Bureau of Investigation, upon a showing in camera that the consumer report is sought for the conduct of an authorized investigation to protect against international terrorism or clandestine intelligence activities, provided that such an investigation of a United States person is not conducted solely upon the basis of activities protected by the first amendment to the Constitution of the United States.

The terms of an order issued under this subsection shall not disclose that the order is issued for purposes of a counterintelligence investigation.

(d) Confidentiality

No consumer reporting agency or officer, employee, or agent of a consumer reporting agency shall disclose to any person, other than those officers, employees, or agents of a consumer reporting agency necessary to fulfill the requirement to disclose information to the Federal Bureau of Investigation under this section, that the Federal Bureau of Investigation has sought or obtained the identity of financial institutions or a consumer report respecting any consumer under subsection (a), (b), or (c) of this section, and no consumer reporting agency or officer, employee, or agent of a consumer reporting agency shall include in any consumer report any information that would indicate that the Federal Bureau of Investigation has sought or obtained such information or a consumer report.

(e) Payment of fees

The Federal Bureau of Investigation shall, subject to the availability of appropriations, pay to the consumer reporting agency assembling or providing report or information in accordance with procedures established under this section a fee for reimbursement for such costs as are reasonably necessary and which have been directly incurred in searching, reproducing, or transporting books, papers, records, or other data required or requested to be produced under this section.

(f) Limit on dissemination

The Federal Bureau of Investigation may not disseminate information obtained pursuant to this section outside of the Federal Bureau of Investigation, except to other Federal agencies as may be necessary for the approval or conduct of a foreign counterintelligence investigation, or, where the information concerns a person subject to the Uniform Code of Military Justice, to appropriate investigative authorities within the military department concerned as may be necessary for the conduct of a joint foreign counterintelligence investigation.

(g) Rules of construction

Nothing in this section shall be construed to prohibit information from being furnished by the Federal Bureau of Investigation pursuant to a subpoena or court order, in connection with a judicial or administrative proceeding to enforce the provisions of this subchapter. Nothing in this section shall be construed to authorize or permit the withholding of information from the Congress.

(h) Reports to Congress

(1) On a semiannual basis, the Attorney General shall fully inform the Permanent Select Committee on Intelligence and the Committee on Banking, Finance and Urban Affairs of the House of Representatives, and the Select Committee on Intelligence and the Committee on Banking, Housing, and Urban Affairs of the Senate concerning all requests made pursuant to subsections (a), (b), and (c) of this section.

(2) In the case of the semiannual reports required to be submitted under paragraph (1) to the Permanent Select Committee on Intelligence of the House of Representatives and the Select Committee on Intelligence of the Senate, the submittal dates for such reports shall be as provided in section 415b of Title 50.

(i) Damages

Any agency or department of the United States obtaining or disclosing any consumer reports, records, or information contained therein in violation of this section is liable to the consumer to whom such consumer reports, records, or information relate in an amount equal to the sum of-

(1) $100, without regard to the volume of consumer reports, records, or information involved;

(2) any actual damages sustained by the consumer as a result of the disclosure;

(3) if the violation is found to have been willful or intentional, such punitive damages as a court may allow; and

(4) in the case of any successful action to enforce liability under this subsection, the costs of the action, together with reasonable attorney fees, as determined by the court.

(j) Disciplinary actions for violations

If a court determines that any agency or department of the United States has violated any provision of this section and the court finds that the circumstances surrounding the violation raise questions of whether or not an officer or employee of the agency or department acted willfully or intentionally with respect to the violation, the agency or department shall promptly initiate a proceeding to determine whether or not disciplinary action is warranted against the officer or employee who was responsible for the violation.

(k) Good-faith exception

Notwithstanding any other provision of this subchapter, any consumer reporting agency or agent or employee thereof making disclosure of consumer reports or identifying information pursuant to this subsection in good-faith reliance upon a certification of the Federal Bureau of Investigation pursuant to provisions of this section shall not be liable to any person for such disclosure under this subchapter, the constitution of any State, or any law or regulation of any State or any political subdivision of any State.

(1) Limitation of remedies

Notwithstanding any other provision of this subchapter, the remedies and sanctions set forth in this section shall be the only judicial remedies and sanctions for violation of this section.

(m) Injunctive relief

In addition to any other remedy contained in this section, injunctive relief shall be available to require compliance with the procedures of this section. In the event of any successful action under this subsection, costs together with reasonable attorney fees, as determined by the court, may be recovered.

Fair Credit Reporting Act
Consumer Full Credit Report

15 U.S.C. § 1681v

(a) Disclosure

Notwithstanding section 168lb of this title or any other provision of this subchapter, a consumer reporting agency shall furnish a consumer report of a consumer and all other information in a consumer's file to a government agency authorized to conduct investigations of, or intelligence or counterintelligence activities or analysis related to, international terrorism when presented with a written certification by such government agency that such information is necessary for the agency's conduct or such investigation, activity or analysis.

(b) Form of certification

The certification described in subsection (a) of this section shall be signed by a supervisory official designated by the head of a Federal agency or an officer of a Federal agency whose appointment to office is required to be made by the President, by and with the advice and consent of the Senate.

(c) Confidentiality

No consumer reporting agency, or officer, employee, or agent of such consumer reporting agency, shall disclose to any person, or specify in any consumer report, that a government agency has sought or obtained access to information under subsection (a) of this section.

(d) Rule of construction

Nothing in section 1681u of this title shall be construed to limit the authority of the Director of the Federal Bureau of Investigation under this section.

(e) Safe harbor

Notwithstanding any other provision of this subchapter, any consumer reporting agency or agent or employee thereof making disclosure of consumer reports or other information pursuant to this section in good-faith reliance upon a certification of a government agency pursuant to the provisions of this section shall not be liable to any person for such disclosure under this subchapter, the constitution of any State, or any law or regulation of any State or any political subdivision of any State.

Electronic Communications Privacy Act 18 U.S.C. § 2709

(a) **Duty to provide.**--A wire or electronic communication service provider shall comply with a request for subscriber information and toll billing records information, or electronic communication transactional records in its custody or possession made by the Director of the Federal Bureau of Investigation under subsection (b) of this section.

(b) **Required certification.**--The Director of the Federal Bureau of Investigation, or his designee in a position not lower than Deputy Assistant Director at Bureau headquarters or a Special Agent in Charge in a Bureau field office designated by the Director, may--

(1) request the name, address, length of service, and local and long distance toll billing records of a person or entity if the Director (or his designee) certifies in writing to the wire or electronic communication service provider to which the request is made that the name, address, length of service, and toll billing records sought are relevant to an authorized investigation to protect against international terrorism or clandestine intelligence activities, provided that such an investigation of a United States person is not conducted solely on the basis of activities protected by the first amendment to the Constitution of the United States; and

(2) request the name, address, and length of service of a person or entity if the Director (or his designee) certifies in writing to the wire or electronic

communication service provider to which the request is made that the information sought is relevant to an authorized investigation to protect against international terrorism or clandestine intelligence activities, provided that such an investigation of a United States person is not conducted solely upon the basis of activities protected by the first amendment to the Constitution of the United States.

(c) **Prohibition of certain disclosure.**--No wire or electronic communication service provider, or officer, employee, or agent thereof, shall disclose to any person that the Federal Bureau of Investigation has sought or obtained access to information or records under this section.

(d) **Dissemination by bureau.**—The Federal Bureau of Investigation may disseminate information and records obtained under this section only as provided in guidelines approved by the Attorney General for foreign intelligence collection and foreign counterintelligence investigations conducted by the Federal Bureau of Investigation, and, with respect to dissemination to an agency of the United States, only if such information is clearly relevant to the authorized responsibilities of such agency.

(e) **Requirement that certain congressional bodies be informed.**--On a semiannual basis the Director of the Federal Bureau of Investigation shall fully inform the Permanent Select Committee on Intelligence of the House of Representatives and the Select Committee on Intelligence of the Senate, and the Committee on the Judiciary of the House of Representatives and the Committee on the Judiciary of the Senate, concerning all requests made under subsection (b) of this section.

National Security Act
50 U.S.C. § 436

(a) Generally

(1) Any authorized investigative agency may request from any financial agency, financial institution, or holding company, or from any consumer reporting agency, such financial records, other financial information, and consumer reports as may be necessary in order to conduct any authorized law enforcement investigation, counterintelligence inquiry, or security determination. Any authorized investigative agency may also request records maintained by any commercial entity within the United States pertaining to travel by an employee in the executive branch of Government outside the United States.

(2) Requests may be made under this section where--

(A) the records sought pertain to a person who is or was an employee in the executive branch of Government required by the President in an Executive order or regulation, as a condition of access to classified information, to provide consent, during a background investigation and for such time as access to the information is maintained, and for a period of not more than three years thereafter, permitting access to financial records, other financial information, consumer reports, and travel records; and

(B)(i) there are reasonable grounds to believe, based on credible information, that the person is, or may be, disclosing classified information in an unauthorized manner to a foreign power or agent of a foreign power;

(ii) information the employing agency deems credible indicates the person has incurred excessive indebtedness or has acquired a level of affluence which cannot be explained by other information known to the agency; or

(iii) circumstances indicate the person had the capability and opportunity to disclose classified information which is known to have been lost or compromised to a foreign power or an agent of a foreign power.

(3) Each such request--

(A) shall be accompanied by a written certification signed by the department or agency head or deputy department or agency head concerned, or by a senior official designated for this purpose by the department or agency head concerned (whose rank shall be no lower than Assistant Secretary or Assistant Director), and shall certify that--

(i) the person concerned is or was an employee within the meaning of paragraph (2)(A);

(ii) the request is being made pursuant to an authorized inquiry or investigation and is authorized under this section; and

(iii) the records or information to be reviewed are records or information which the employee has previously agreed to make available to the authorized investigative agency for review;

(B) shall contain a copy of the agreement referred to in subparagraph (A)(iii);

(C) shall identify specifically or by category the records or information to be reviewed; and

(D) shall inform the recipient of the request of the prohibition described in subsection (b) of this section.

(b) Disclosure of requests

Notwithstanding any other provision of law, no governmental or private entity, or officer, employee, or agent of such entity, may disclose to any person, other than those officers, employees, or agents of such entity necessary to satisfy a request made under this section, that such entity has received or satisfied a request made by an authorized investigative agency under this section.

(c) Records or information; inspection or copying

(1) Notwithstanding any other provision of law (other than section 6103 of Title 26), an entity receiving a request for records or information under subsection (a) of this section shall, if the request satisfies the requirements of this section, make available such records or information within 30 days for inspection or copying, as may be appropriate, by the agency requesting such records or information.

(2) Any entity (including any officer, employee, or agent thereof) that discloses records or information for inspection or copying pursuant to this section in good faith reliance upon the certifications made by an agency pursuant to this section shall not be liable for any such disclosure to any person under this subchapter, the constitution of any State, or any law or regulation of any State or any political subdivision of any State.

(d) Reimbursement of costs

Any agency requesting records or information under this section may, subject to the availability of appropriations, reimburse a private entity for any cost reasonably incurred by such entity in responding to such request, including the cost of identifying, reproducing, or transporting records or other data.

(e) Dissemination of records or information received

An agency receiving records or information pursuant to a request under this section may disseminate the records or information obtained pursuant to such request outside the agency only--

(1) to the agency employing the employee who is the subject of the records or information;

(2) to the Department of Justice for law enforcement or counterintelligence purposes; or

(3) with respect to dissemination to an agency of the United States, if such information is clearly relevant to the authorized responsibilities of such agency.

(f) Construction of section

Nothing in this section may be construed to affect the authority of an investigative agency to obtain information pursuant to the Right to Financial Privacy Act (12 U.S.C. 3401 et seq.) or the Fair Credit Reporting Act (15 U.S.C. 1681 et seq.).

End Notes

* This report includes information that the Department of Justice considered to be classified and therefore could not be publicly released. To create this public version of the report, the OIG redacted (deleted) the portions of the report that the Department considered to be classified, and we indicate where those redactions were made. However, the Executive Summary of the report is completely unclassified. In addition, the OIG has provided copies of the full classified report to the Department, the Director of National Intelligence, and Congress.

[1] The Patriot Reauthorization Act also directed the OIG to conduct reviews for the same two time periods on the use and effectiveness of Section 215 of the Patriot Act, a new authority under the Patriot Act that authorizes the FBI to obtain business record orders from the Foreign Intelligence Surveillance Court. The OIG's first report on the use and effectiveness of Section 215 orders is contained in a separate report issued in conjunction with this review of NSLs.

[2] Patriot Reauthorization Act § 119(b).

[3] The term "USA PATRIOT Act" is an acronym for the Uniting and Strengthening America by Providing Appropriate Tools Required to Intercept and Obstruct Terrorism Act of 2001, Pub. L. No. 107-56, 115 Stat. 272 (2001). It is commonly referred to as "the Patriot Act."

[4] 15 U.S.C. § 1681v (Supp. IV 2005).

[5] During the time period covered by this review, calendar years 2003 through 2005, the Attorney General Guidelines for national security investigations were revised. From January 1, 2003, through October 31, 2003, investigations of international terrorism or espionage were governed by the Attorney General Guidelines for FBI Foreign Intelligence Collection and Foreign Counterintelligence Investigations (FCI Guidelines)(March 1999). Effective October 31, 2003, these investigations were conducted pursuant to the Attorney General's Guidelines for FBI National Security Investigations and Foreign Intelligence Collection (NSI Guidelines).

[6] H.R. Rep. No. 95-1383, at 33 (1978).

[7] 12 U.S.C. §§ 3401-3422 (2000).

[8] 12 U.S.C. § 3414(a)(5)(A) (2000 & Supp. IV 2005).

[9] 18 U.S.C. § 2709 (1988).

[10] 18 U.S.C. § 2709(b)(2) (2000 & Supp. IV 2005).

[11] The ECPA permits access only to "subscriber and toll billing records information" or "electronic communication transactional records," as distinguished from the content of telephone conversations or e-mail communications.

[12] 15 U.S.C. § 1681 et seq.

[13] Intelligence Authorization Act for Fiscal Year 1996, Pub. L. No. 104-93, § 601(a), 109 Stat. 961, codified at 15 U.S.C. § 1681u (Supp. V. 1999).

[14] 15 U.S.C. § 1681u(a)-(b) (2000 & Supp. IV 2005).

[15] Patriot Act, § 358(g) (2001).

[16] Patriot Act, § 358(g) (2001).

[17] See H.R. Rep. No. 103-541 (1994) and H.R. Conf. Rep. No. 103-753 (1994), reprinted in 1994 U.S.C.C.A.N. 2703.

[18] 50 U.S.C. § 436(a)(1) (2000).

[19] The Department was required to include in its semiannual classified reports only the number of NSL requests issued pursuant to the RFPA (financial records), the ECPA (telephone toll billing records, electronic communication transactional records and subscriber information (telephone or e-mail)), and the original FCRA NSL statute (consumer and financial institution identifying information), FCRAu. The Department was not required to report the number of NSL requests issued pursuant to the Patriot Act amendment to the FCRA (consumer full credit reports) or the National Security Act NSL statute (financial records, other financial information, and consumer reports). The requirement for public reports on certain NSL usage did not take effect until March 2006, which is after the period covered by this review.

[20] FBI-OGC utilizes a manual workflow process to enter required information into ACS. The information is transcribed into a Microsoft Access database which, during the period covered by our review, had limited analytical capabilities.

[21] See Memorandum for the Attorney General, *Semiannual Report for Requests for Financial Records Made Pursuant to Title 12, United States Code (U.S.C.) Section 3414, Paragraph (0)(5), National Security Investigations/Foreign Collection* (March 23, 2006), at 2.

[22] As shown in Chart 4.1, the number of ECPA NSL requests increased in CY 2004, and then decreased in CY 2005. We determined that the spike in ECPA NSL requests in CY 2004 occurred because of the issuance of 9 ECPA NSLs in one investigation that contained requests for subscriber information on a total of 11,100 separate telephone numbers. If those nine NSLs are excluded from CY 2004, the number of NSL requests would show a moderate, but steady increase over the three years.

[23] The total number of requests in Chart 1.1 is not the same as in chart 4.1 because Chart 1.1 excludes NSL requests in cyber investigations and NSL requests that are not required to be reported to Congress.

[24] Chart 4.2 does not contain the same totals as Chart 4.1 because not all NSL requests reported to Congress identified whether they related to an investigation of a U.S. person or a non-U.S. person. Of the total number of NSL requests reported in the Department's semiannual classified reports to Congress for CY 2003 through CY 2005 (which included the ECPA, RFPA and FCRAu requests), 52,199 NSL requests identified whether the request for information related to a U.S. person or a non-U.S. person. The remaining NSL requests were for the ECPA NSLs seeking subscriber information for telephone numbers and Internet e-mail accounts and did not identify the subject's status as a U.S. person or non-U.S. person.

[25] See 12 U.S.C. § 3414(a)(5)(B)(Right to Financial Privacy Act); 18 U.S.C. § 2709(d)(Electronic Communications Privacy Act); 15 U.S.C.A. §1681u(f)(Fair Credit Reporting Act); and 50 U.S.C.A. § 436 (National Security Act). While the NSL statute permitting access to consumer full credit reports, 15 U.S.C. §1681v, does not explicitly authorize dissemination, it does not limit such dissemination.

[26] In this report, we use the terms "improper or illegal use," as contained in the Patriot Reauthorization Act. As noted below, the improper or illegal uses of the national security letter authorities we found in our review did not involve criminal misconduct. However, as also noted below, the improper or illegal uses we found included serious misuses of national security letter authority.

[27] The FBI has developed an internal process for the self-reporting of possible IOB violations to FBI-OGC. During the period covered by our review, FBI-OGC issued 2 guidance memoranda describing the process by which FBI personnel were required to report such violations to FBI-OGC within 14 days of discovery. The reports were to include a description of the status of the subjects of the investigative activity, the legal authority for the investigation, the potential violation, and the date of the incident. FBI-OGC then reviewed the report, prepared a written opinion as to whether the matter should be sent to the IOB, and prepared the written communication to the IOB for those matters it decided to report.

[28] When we examined the records provided to the FBI in response to this NSL, however, we determined that the requested information was not furnished to the FBI.

[29] Our report also discusses another noteworthy possible IOB violation involving the issuance of an NSL seeking educational records from a North Carolina university. In that matter, which we learned of through press accounts, the FBI's Charlotte Division was in the process of seeking a grand jury subpoena for educational records about an investigative subject to determine whether the subject was involved in the July 2005 London subway and bus bombings. The NSL sought several categories of records, including applications for admission, housing information, emergency contacts, and campus health records. According to press accounts, university officials said that the FBI had tried to use an NSL to demand more information than the law permitted and declined to honor the national security letter. A grand jury subpoena was thereafter served on the university, and the university produced the records. In this instance, the FBI sought records it was not authorized to obtain pursuant to an ECPA national security letter.

[30] Following the September 11 attacks, the FBI's New York Division established a relationship with one of the major telephone companies to obtain quick responses to requests for telephone toll billing records or

subscriber information in connection with its criminal investigations of the 19 hijackers. Although the New York Division generally obtained grand jury subpoenas to obtain this information, it frequently provided a "placeholder letter," sometimes referred to as an "exigent letter," to the telephone company if the grand jury subpoena was not yet available.

[31] Similarly, when CAU on occasion asked the NSLB Deputy General Counsel to issue national security letters to cover information already obtained from the telephone companies in response to the exigent letters, CAU sometimes did not disclose in the approval documentation that the records already had been provided in response to the exigent letters. An NSLB Assistant General Counsel complained to CAU personnel about these omissions in December 2004.

[32] The FBI's reference to grand jury subpoenas in the exigent letters rather than to national security letters appears to be the result of CAU's use of the New York Division's model letter for exigent letters sent to a telephone company in connection with the New York Division's criminal investigations of the September 11 hijackers.

[33] The classified nature of the project was such that few FBI Headquarters officials or FBI-OGC attorneys were authorized to know the predication for the requests.

[34] Problems with the FBI's NSL database make it impossible to determine the precise number of national security letters the FBI issued in this second category.

[35] NSI Guidelines, § I(B)(2).

[36] USA PATRIOT Improvement and Reauthorization Act of 2005, Pub. L. No. 109177, § 119(a), 120 Stat. 192 (2006) (Patriot Reauthorization Act).

[37] Although the Act only required the OIG to include calendar years 2003 through 2004 in the first report, we elected to also include 2005 in this first report. The second report, which is due to Congress on December 31, 2007, will cover calendar year 2006.

[38] The Patriot Reauthorization Act also directed the OIG to conduct reviews on the use and effectiveness of Section 215 orders for business records, another investigative authority that was expanded by the Patriot Act. The OIG's first report on the use and effectiveness of Section 215 orders is contained in a separate report issued in conjunction with this review of NSLs.

[39] The term "USA PATRIOT Act" is an acronym for the law entitled the Uniting and Strengthening America by Providing Appropriate Tools Required to Intercept and Obstruct Terrorism Act of 2001, Pub. L. No. 107-56, 115 Stat. 272 (2001). This law is commonly referred to as "the Patriot Act."

[40] The statutes do not authorize the FBI to collect the content of telephone calls and e-mail. For that information, the FBI must obtain court approval or voluntary production of the records pursuant to 18 U.S.C. § 2702(b)(8) (2000).

[41] Patriot Reauthorization Act, § 119(b).

[42] FBI investigations of terrorism and espionage are called "national security investigations," which are conducted pursuant to the Attorney General's Guidelines for FBI National Security Investigations and Foreign Intelligence Collection (Oct. 31, 2003) (NSI Guidelines). NSLs are not authorized in connection with FBI conduct of ordinary criminal investigations or domestic terrorism investigations.

[43] The five statutes are:

1)18 U.S.C. § 2709 (covering subscriber information and telephone toll billing records infoiination and electronic communication transactional records);

2)12 U.S.C. § 3414 (covering financial records);

3)15 U.S.C. § 1681u (covering the names and addresses of all financial institutions at which a consumer maintains or has maintained an account; and the consumer's name, address, former addresses, places of employment or formet places of employment);

4)15 U.S.C. § 1681v (covering consumer reports and all other information in a consumer's file in international terrorism investigations); and

5)50 U.S.C. § 436 (covering financial records, other financial information, and consumer reports in law enforcement investigations, counterintelligence inquiries, or security determinations). See Appendix A of this report for the text of the five statutes prior to the effective date of the Patriot Reauthorization Act.

The phrase "national security letter" was not used in any of the authorizing statutes, but was commonly used to refer to these authorities. The term was first used in legislation in the Patriot Reauthorization Act.

[44] See, e.g., 18 U.S.C. § 2709 (2000) ; 50 U.S.C. §§ 1801-1811 (2000).

[45] S. 1448, The Intelligence to Prevent Terrorism Act of 2001 and Other Legislative Proposals in the Wake of the September 11, 2001 Attacks: Hearing Before the Senate Select Comm On Intelligence, 107th Cong. (2002); Dismantling the Financial Infrastructure of Global Terrorism: Hearing Before the House Comm. on Fin. Servs., 107th Cong. (2002); The Role of Technology in Preventing the Entry of Terrorists into the United States: Hearing Before the Senate Subcomm. on Tech., Terrorism, Gov't Info. of the Comm. on the Judiciary, 107th Cong. (2002).

[46] Hearing Before the House Comm. on the Judiciary, 107th Cong. 57-58 (2001) (Administration's Draft Anti-Terrorism Act of 2001). This view also was reflected in post-Patriot Act testimony at hearings considering whether to reauthorize the NSL authorities in the Patriot Act. See Tools Against Terror: How the Administration is Implementing New Laws in the Fight to Protect Our Homeland: Hearing Before the

Subcomm. on Technology, Terrorism, and Gov't Info. of the Senate Comm. on the Judiciary, 107th Cong. 139 (2002) (statement of Dennis Lormel, Chief, Terrorist Financing Operations Section, Counterterrorism Division, FBI) ("Delays in obtaining NSLs has long been identified as a significant problem relative to the conduct of counterintelligence and counterterrorism investigations.")

[47] Prior to the Patriot Act, approximately 10 FBI Headquarters officials were authorized to sign national security letters, including the Director, Deputy Director, and the Assistant Directors and Deputy Assistant Directors of the Counterterrorism and Counterintelligence Divisions. Under the Patriot Act, the heads of the FBI's 56 field offices (Assistant Directors in Charge or Special Agents in Charge) may also issue NSLs. Since enactment of the Patriot Act, approval to sign NSLs has also been delegated to the Deputy Director, Executive Assistant Director (EAD), and Assistant EAD for the National Security Branch; Assistant Directors and all Deputy Assistant Directors for the Counterterrorism, Counterintelligence, and Cyber Divisions; all Special Agents in Charge of the New York, Washington, D.C., and Los Angeles field offices, which are headed by Assistant Directors in Charge; the General Counsel; and the Deputy General Counsel for the National Security Law Branch in the Office of the General Counsel.

[48] 15 U.S.C. § 1681v (Supp. IV 2005).

[49] 15 U.S.C. § 1681u (2000).

[50] The national security letter authority in the National Security Act, which allows collection of financial records and infoi 'nation, consumer reports, and travel records, did not require reports to Congress. See 50 U.S.C. § 436 (2000).

[51] Pub. L. No. 109-177, § 102(a) (2006). The Patriot Reauthorization Act modified the non-disclosure requirements regarding national security letters. An NSL recipient may now disclose the NSL in connection with seeking legal advice or complying with the NSL. In addition, the Patriot Reauthorization Act permits the NSL recipient to challenge compliance with the NSL and the non-disclosure requirement in federal court. In addition, the government may seek judicial enforcement of NSLs in the event of non-compliance.

[52] See Letter from William E Moschella, Assistant Attorney General, to L. Ralph Mecham, Director, Administrative Office of the United States Courts (April 28, 2006), at 3.

[53] Id. In Chapter Four we describe the categories of NSL requests that are included and excluded from the public report.

[54] H.R. Rep. No. 95-1383, at 33 (1978), reprinted in 1978 U.S.C.C.A.N. 9273, 9305. The RFPA was enacted in response to the Supreme Court's decision in United States v. Miller, 425 U.S. 435 (1976), which held that customers of banking services had no expectation of privacy under the Fourth Amendment and therefore could not contest government access to their records.

[55] 12 U.S.C. §§ 3401-3422 (2000).

[56] 12 U.S.C. § 3414(a)(5)(A) (2000).

[57] 12 U.S.C. § 3414(a)(5)(A) (2000 & Supp. IV 2005). Financial records accessible to the FBI under the RFPA were also subject to compulsory process through subpoenas, search warrants, and formal requests, all of which, with limited exceptions, required notice to the customer.

[58] See 12 U.S.C. § 3414(d) (2000 & Supp. IV 2005), as amended by the Intelligence Authorization Act for Fiscal Year 2004, Pub. L. No. 108-77, § 374(a) (2004), which incorporated the definition of "financial institution" set forth in 31 U.S.C. §§ 5312(a)(2) and (c)(1).

[59] 12 U.S.C. § 3414(a)(5)(B) (2000).

[60] 18 U.S.C. § 2709 (1988).

[61] A "pen register" is a device that records the numbers that a target telephone is dialing. A "trap and trace" device captures the telephone numbers that dial a target telephone. See 18 U.S.C. § 3127 (2000).

[62] 18 U.S.C. § 2709(b)(1)(B) (2000).

[63] 18 U.S.C. § 2709(b)(2) (2000 & Supp. IV 2005).

[64] Pub. L. No. 103-142, § 2, 107 Stat. 1491 (1993). The 1993 amendment also provided additional congressional reporting requirements. Id.

[65] Intelligence Authorization Act for Fiscal Year 1997, Pub. L. No. 104-293, § 601(a), 110 Stat. 3461 (1996).

[66] 18 U.S.C. § 2709(c) (2000).

[67] 18 U.S.C. § 2709(d) (2000).

[68] 18 U.S.C. § 2709(a) (2000). ECPA requires a warrant for the interception and surveillance of the content of a telephone call or e-mail communication. See 18 U.S.C. §§ 2511 (Wiretap Act) and 3121 (Pen Register Act). See also 18 U.S.C. § 2702(b)(8) (2000).

[69] 15 U.S.C. § 1681 et seq (2000).

[70] Intelligence Authorization Act for Fiscal Year 1996, Pub. L. No. 104-93, § 601(a), 109 Stat. 961, codified at 15 U.S.C. § 1681u (Supp. V. 1999).

[71] 15 U.S.C. § 1681u (2000).

[72] 15 U.S.C. § 1681u(a)-(b) (2000 & Supp. IV 2005).

[73] Patriot Act, § 358(g) (2001). Unlike other NSL statutes, the full credit report NSL authority is available not only to the FBI but also to other federal government agencies. This provision does not contain an express prohibition on dissemination.

[74] See H.R. Rep. No. 103-541 (1994) and H.R. Conf. Rep. No. 103-753 (1994), reprinted in 1994 U.S.C.C.A.N. 2703.

[75] 50 U.S.C. § 436(a)(1) (2000).

[76] These NSLs were used to obtain bank account, credit card, and loan transaction information to support the predicate for the FBI's espionage investigation of Aldrich Ames. See Commission for Review of FBI Security Programs (March 31, 2002) (Webster Commission), at 66.

[77] Both sets of Guidelines are partially classified.

[78] FCI Guidelines, § II(D).

[79] In January 2003, the Attorney General issued a memorandum modifying the FCI Guidelines by authorizing designated Headquarters officials and Special Agents in Charge designated by the FBI Director to issue ECPA, RFPA, and FCRAu NSLs during preliminary inquiries.

[80] NSI Guidelines, § II(A). The authorized techniques permitted during threat assessments are classified.

[81] The additional techniques permitted during preliminary investigations are classified.

[82] NSI Guidelines, Introduction, A.

[83] The additional techniques permitted during full investigations are classified.

[84] NSI Guidelines, § I(B)(2).

[85] Terrorism investigations often have a potential criminal nexus under statutes proscribing material support of terrorism and conspiracy, and federal statutes criminalizing threats against public facilities, aircraft, and other transportation systems, as well as possession of weapons of mass destruction.

[86] 18 U.S.C. §§ 2709(b)(1) and 2709(b)(2); 12 U.S.C. § 3414 (a)(5)(A); 15 U.S.C. § 1681u(a); 15 U.S.C. § 1681v(a).

[87] We discuss in Chapter Seven the circumstances that led to a February 2006 modification of models for NSL approval ECs, which now require a "full explanation of the justification for opening and maintaining the investigation of the subject" and to "fully state the relevance of the requested records to the investigation."

[88] For purposes of the reporting requirement, a "United States person" is defined as

> a citizen of the United States, an alien lawfully admitted for permanent residence . . an unincorporated association a substantial number of members of which are citizens of the United States or aliens lawfully admitted for permanent residence, or a corporation which is incorporated in the United States . . . ."

50 U.S.C. § 1801(i). The congressional reporting requirements are described in Chapter Four.

[89] Certifying officials are not authorized to further delegate signature authority. Accordingly, Acting Special Agents in Charge are not authorized to sign national security letters.

[90] While NSLB encourages Headquarters operating divisions to utilize the NSLB Deputy General Counsel as the authorizing official, they are not required to do so. However, a legal review through NSLB is required.

[91] See EC from FBI-OGC to All Field Offices, *Legal Advice and Opinions; Service of National Security Letters* (June 29, 2005). The recipient could return responsive documents to the FBI via the same method. However, FBI personnel in the field offices we visited told us that the national security letters and responsive documents were usually personally delivered.

[92] In one field office we visited, the Special Agent in Charge maintains a control file with copies of signed national security letters, but this does not serve as a tracking system for responses.

[93] FBI officials told us that some of the smaller communication providers and Internet service providers furnish NSL data in hard copy form. This placed a significant burden on FBI support personnel who sometimes were required to manually enter the data into a word processing program for uploading and analysis.

[94] Telephone Applications contains raw data derived from NSLs, known as "metadata," including the call duration. It does not store the contents of telephone conversations. During the period covered by our review, approximately 17,000 FBI personnel and approximately 2,000 non-FBI personnel had accounts permitting them to access the FBI's specialized application for telephone record data.

[95] Case agents may restrict FBI and non-FBI personnel from accessing certain electronic files in ACS and other databases in highly sensitive cases.

[96] In Chapter Five, we describe how information derived from national security letters is used in the development of these intelligence products.

[97] Eventually, in November 2006 NSLB sent guidance to the field that outlined the steps to be taken in these circumstances. The guidance memorandum stated that the agent should send the information to the CDC for sequestering, pending resolution of the matter. The memorandum also stated that NSLB would determine whether the sequestered information must be destroyed, returned to the provider, or may be used by the FBI, and whether the matter is reportable to the IOB.

[98] We identified one instance in which the FBI uploaded into the Telephone Applications database data the FBI had improperly acquired in response to an ECPA NSL. We describe this matter in Chapter Six.

[99] According to the FBI, the Investigative Data Warehouse contains data from approximately 50 different FBI and other government agency databases and holds over 560 million records. The FBI estimated in December 2006 that approximately 12,000 FBI and non-FBI personnel have user accounts to access IDW, approximately 30 percent of which were issued to non-FBI personnel, such as Task Force Officers on the Joint Terrorism Task

Forces (JTTFs). *FBI Oversight:* Hearing Before the Senate Comm. on the Judiciary, 109th Cong. 6 (2006) (statement of Robert S. Mueller, III, Director, Federal Bureau of Investigations.

[100] The Department was required to report the number of NSL requests issued pursuant to the RFPA (financial records), the ECPA (telephone toll billing records, electronic communication transactional records and subscriber information (telephone or e-mail)), and the original FCRA NSL statute (consumer and financial institution identifying information), FCRAu. The Department was not required to report the number of NSL requests issued pursuant to the Patriot Act amendment to the FCRA (consumer full credit reports) or the National Security Act (financial records, other financial information, and consumer reports) NSL statutes. In addition the requirement for public reports on certain NSL usage did not take effect until March 2006, which is after the period covered by this review.

[101] 50 U.S.C. § 1801(i) defines a "United States Person" as:

a citizen of the United States, an alien lawfully admitted for permanent residence . . an unincorporated association a substantial number of members of which are citizens of the United States or aliens lawfully admitted for permanent residence, or a corporation which is incorporated in the United States . . . ."

[102] FBI-OGC utilizes a manual workflow process to enter required information into ACS. The infoimation is transcribed into a Microsoft Access database which, during the period covered by our review, had limited analytical capabilities.

[103] We did not include 55 NSLs that requested information pursuant to FCRAv (full consumer credit reports) because the Department was not required to report that information to Congress during the period covered by our review. We also did not include 12 NSLs for which we could not find a corresponding entry in the OGC database either because the entry (1) was not made; (2) contained typographical errors that prevented us from finding the corresponding entry; or (3) was among those that were lost following a OGC database computer malfunction during the time period of our review.

[104] Most of these (approximately 4,500) were ECPA subscriber information requests. The differences between the NSL requests included in the semiannual classified reports to Congress and the NSL requests included in the OGC database for the other types of NSLs were negligible.

[105] Memorandum for the Attorney General, *Semiannual Report for Requests for Financial Records Made Pursuant to Title 12, United States Code (U.S.C.) Section 3414, Paragraph (a)(5), National Security Investigations/ Foreign Collection* (March 23, 2006), at 2; Memorandum for the Attorney General, *Semiannual Report of Requests for Telephone Subscriber or Toll Billing/ Electronic Communications Transactional Records Made Pursuant to Title 18, United States Code (U.S.C.), Section 2709, Foreign Counterintelligence/ International Terrorism* (March 23, 2006), at 2; and Memorandum for the Attorney General, Semiannual *Report of Requests for Financial Institution and Consumer Identifying Information, and Consumer Credit Reports, Pursuant to Title 15, United States Code (U.S.C.), Section 1681u, for Foreign Counterintelligence/ International Terrorism* (March 23, 2006), at 2.

[106] The computer malfunction made it impossible for the OIG to reconstruct electronically the total number of NSL requests issued during the period covered by our review. As a result, the percentages noted in the Classified Appendix for the NSL requests are based on the total number of requests entered in the database made available to the OIG in May 2006. We estimated that as of that time, the OGC database contained approximately 94 percent of the NSL requests made from 2003 through 2005.

[107] NSLB personnel told us that they are aware of this issue and attempt to eliminate these errors by searching the printed reports manually, identifying subject names that appear the same, although not spelled identically, and eliminating those that they are able to determine are the same person.

[110] Memorandum for the Attorney General, *Annual Report of Total National Security Letter Requests for Information Concerning Different U.S. Persons (Excluding National Security Letters for Subscriber Information) Made Pursuant to the USA PATRIOT Improvement* and *Reauthorization Act of 2005, Public Law 109-177*, at 2.

[108] As noted earlier, we refer to the number of NSL requests rather than letters because one national security letter may include more than one "NSL request." See Chart 1.1 on page 4.

[109] The number of NSL requests we identified significantly exceeds the number reported in the first public annual report issued by the Department because the Department was not required to include all NSL requests in that report. The Department's public report stated that in CY 2005 the FBI issued 9,254 NSL requests for information relating to U.S. persons instead of the NSL requests we identified because the public report did not include NSL requests under the ECPA for telephone and e-mail subscriber information, NSL requests under FCRAv for consumer full credit reports, or NSL requests related to "non-U.S. Persons."

[110] A detailed discussion of the FBI's use of each of the four types of NSLs in counterterrorism and counterintelligence investigations is included in the Classified Appendix.

[111] Chart 4.2 does not contain the same totals as Chart 4.1 because not all NSL requests reported to Congress identified whether they related to an investigation of a U.S. person or a non-U.S. person. Of the NSL requests reported in the Department's semiannual classified reports to Congress for CY 2003 through CY 2005 (which included the ECPA, RFPA and FCRAu requests), 52,199 NSL requests identified whether the request for information related to a U.S. person or a non-U.S. person. The remaining NSL requests were for the ECPA

NSLs seeking subscriber information for telephone numbers and Internet e-mail accounts and did not identify the subject's status as a U.S. person or non-U.S. person.

113 Although FBI data identified whether individual NSLs were related to counterterrorism or counterintelligence investigations, the data provided by the FBI regarding counterintelligence investigations open during CY 2003 through CY 2005 was not sufficiently reliable for us to identify the total number of open counterintelligence investigations and the number of those investigations that involved NSLs. Therefore, we are unable to identify any trends in NSL usage in counterintelligence investigations during the period covered by our review.

114 The total number of investigations open during the three years is less than the sum of the investigations open in each of the years because many investigations remained active during more than one of the years and are counted in each of the years they were open.

115 In Chapter Three, we described the FBI's collection and retention of information derived from national security letters.

116 The final report of the National Commission on Terrorist Attacks Upon the United States (9/11 Commission) contained a monograph on terrorist financing that discussed the limited utility of national security letters in the pre-Patriot Act period. The report noted that Minneapolis FBI agents investigating links between a network of money remitters and a terrorist group chose to use tools available in criminal investigations rather than national security letters for two reasons. First, "the FBI could obtain subpoenas almost instantly, whereas NSLs took 6 to 12 months to obtain." Second, national security letters could only be approved by officials at FBI Headquarters. See *Report of the National Commission on Terrorist Attacks Upon the United States,* Terrorist Financing Staff Monograph, Al-Barakaat Case Study (August 21, 2004).

117 See, e.g., 18 U.S.C. § 2709(b) (2000).

118 These factors were also noted by a Department official in congressional testimony. The official stated that the predication requirement "put the cart before the horse" because agents could not issue national security letters to establish "specific and articulable facts indicating that the individuals in question were agents of a foreign power." *Material Witness Provisions of the Criminal Code, and the Implementation of the USA PATRIOT Act: Section 505 That Addresses National Security Letter and Section 804 That Addresses Jurisdiction Over Crimes Committed at U.S. Facilities Abroad:* Healing Before the Subcomm. on Crime, Terrorism, and Homeland Security of the House Comm. on the Judiciary, 109th Cong. 9-10 (statement of Matthew Berry, Office of Legal Policy, U.S. Department of Justice).

119 Our review of the Department's semiannual classified reports to Congress on NSL usage showed that the FBI issued approximately 8,500 NSL requests in CY 2000 and approximately 7,800 NSL requests in CY 1999.

120 The former NSLB Deputy General Counsel stated that establishing the statutory predication prior to the Patriot Act was much easier in counterintelligence cases, where the subject was almost always affiliated with a foreign nation.

121 Attorney General's Guidelines for FBI National Security Investigations and Foreign Intelligence Collection (NSI Guidelines)(October 31, 2003).

122 *FBI Oversight:* Hearing Before the Senate Comm. on the Judiciary, 109th Cong. 6 (2006) (statement of Robert S. Mueller, III, Director, Federal Bureau of Investigations.

123 See www.fbi.gov.

124 See, e.g., Memorandum of Understanding Between the Intelligence Community, Federal Law Enforcement Agencies, and the Department of Homeland Security Concerning Information Sharing (March 4, 2003).

125 NSI Guidelines, § VII(B).

126 See 12 U.S.C. § 3414(a)(5)(B)(Right to Financial Privacy Act); 18 U.S.C. § 2709(d)(Electronic Communications Privacy Act); 15 U.S.C.A. §1681u(f)(Fair Credit Reporting Act); and 50 U.S.C.A. § 436 (National Security Act). While the NSL statute permitting access to consumer full credit reports, 15 U.S.C. §1681v, does not explicitly authorize dissemination, it does not limit such dissemination.

127 The supervisor of a FIG squad explained that when FIG analysts receive raw NSL-derived information, such as telephone or bank records, their analyses based on this data are uploaded into ACS and provided to operational squads in the form of electronic communications. These tactical analyses may later become part of finished intelligence products, such as Intelligence Bulletins or Intelligence Assessments, that FBI Headquarters may authorize for dissemination to other members of the intelligence community. Since members of the FIG do not reference what information was derived from NSLs, the source of the information would not be associated with the data because it is assimilated into a finished intelligence product.

128 NSI Guidelines, VII(B)(2).

129 Each of the FBI's 56 domestic field divisions contains at least one ji , and as of March 2005 the FBI operated J'ITfs in 100 U.S. cities.

130 NSI Guidelines, VII(B)(3).

131 For example, members of the JTTF in a major FBI field division include representatives from the United States Attorney's Office, United States Marshals Service, United States Postal Service, United States Secret Service, Department of Homeland Security, Federal Protective Service, United States Coast Guard, Department of Defense, Central Intelligence Agency, as well as representatives from state and local law enforcement, including the state police and the city police department.

[132] NSI Guidelines, VII(B)(3).

[133] NSI Guidelines, VII(B)(6).

[134] Only Designated Intelligence Disclosure Officials are authorized to decide that intelligence information may be released to foreign governments. The FBI Director is a DIDO and has delegated DIDO authority to other senior FBI officials.

[135] Following the September 11 terrorist attacks, the Department implemented an anti-terrorism plan that directed the commitment of all available resources and manpower to address efforts to detect and prevent terrorism. Two important aspects of the plan were the establishment of Anti-Terrorism Advisory Councils (ATACs) within each judicial district and the expansion of Joint Terrorism Task Forces. ATACs were directed to convene federal law enforcement agencies and state and local law enforcement officials who, together, would constitute the ATAC for each district. The ATACs were charged with coordinating "the dissemination of information and the development of prosecutive strategy" about suspected terrorists and "implement the most effective strategy for incapacitating them." See Memorandum from John Ashcroft, Attorney General, U.S. Department of Justice, to All United States Attorneys, *Anti-Terrorism Plan* (Sept. 17, 2001).

[136] Memorandum from James B. Comey, Deputy Attorney General, U.S. Department of Justice, to United States Attorneys and Anti-Terrorism Advisory Council Coordinators (June 25, 2004), at 2.

[137] Intelligence research specialists in USAOs assist the ATACs in coordinating anti-terrorist activities by, among other activities, generating analyses of the relevance and reliability of threat information and investigative leads. See Office of the Inspector General, U.S. Department of Justice, A *Review of United States Attorneys' Offices Use of Intelligence Research Specialists* (December 2005).

In some districts, the ATAC Coordinators and intelligence research specialists are full members of the district's Joint Terrorism Task Force. In those circumstances, these Department personnel have access to FBI databases. As noted above, several FBI databases contain either raw data obtained from NSLs or analytical products derived from them.

[138] In June 2006, the Department's Counsel for the Office of Intelligence Policy and Review (OIPR) asked the Department's Office of Legal Counsel (OLC) to render an opinion on whether the FBI is required under the Foreign Intelligence Surveillance Act (FISA) to obtain Attorney General approval prior to disseminating certain information for law enforcement purposes that is developed from national security letters. The FBI and the Department's Criminal Division Counterterrorism Section submitted legal analyses and their positions to OLC in conjunction with this request. Specifically, the Counsel for OIPR asked whether Attorney General approval is required under the FISA before the FBI seeks to obtain a grand jury subpoena based on the results of NSLs that were issued for telephone toll records on telephone numbers identified through its use of FISA authorities. The FISA requires that information obtained through the use of orders for electronic surveillance, physical searches, and pen registers/trap and trace devices

shall not be disclosed for law enforcement purposes unless such disclosure is accompanied by a statement that such information, or any information derived therefrom, may be used in a criminal proceeding with advance authorization of the Attorney General.

U.S.C. §§ 1806(b)(electronic surveillance), 1825 (c)(physical searches), 1845(b)(pen registers/trap and trace devices). The Counsel also asked whether the term "criminal proceeding" means all federal grand jury proceedings, including the issuance or grand jury subpoenas, as well as search warrants, indictments, and trials. In late 2006, after receiving the views of relevant entities, OLC referred the question to the Department's National Security Division for a determination of the best policy approach that comports with the FISA. In February 2007, NSD contacted the FBI and other members of the intelligence community for the purpose of meeting to determine the best policy approach. If Attorney General approval were needed, the Counsel believes and FBI officials confirmed that there would be significant operational implications for the ability of prosecutors and FBI agents to quickly follow leads generated from FISA collection.

[139] By contrast as noted above, when FBI case agents obtain information from the use of FISA authorities, the information is marked or tagged so that its derivation is clear.

[140] In the absence of a tagged digital record or a centralized repository reflecting instances in which information derived from national security letters is provided to law enforcement authorities for use in criminal proceedings, FBI attorneys suggested that we collect data on how often case agents referred targets of national security investigations to law enforcement authorities for possible prosecution. These referrals would capture the universe of investigations in which national security letters were authorized to be issued, and the results of information derived from national security letters issued in these investigations may have been shared with prosecutors, even if the source of the information was not explicitly noted.

[141] By contrast, case agents and supervisors assigned to counterintelligence squads said that there is rarely a criminal nexus in these investigations, and therefore information derived from national security letters would typically not be provided to law enforcement authorities.

[142] One field division provided an approximation of the number of times it used NSL-derived information in criminal proceedings. That division stated that it used NSL-derived information in approximately 105 criminal proceedings from 2003 through 2005. The division reported that NSLs were used only in terrorism-related criminal proceedings, not in any espionage-related criminal proceedings.

[143] If national security letters were not signed by Special Agents in Charge or specially delegated senior Headquarters officials, this would be a violation of the national security letter statutes, the Attorney General's NSI Guidelines, and internal FBI policy.

[144] See Office of the Inspector General, U.S. Department of Justice, *Report to Congress on Implementation of Section 1001 of the USA PATRIOT Act* (March 8, 2006).

[145] The NSL-related possible IOB violations identified in the report occurred during Fiscal Years 2004 and 2005 and included incidents in which third parties provided e-mail content information that was not requested or authorized; an NSL that was issued after the investigation was extended without authorization; an NSL that was issued for the wrong subject with a similar name; and NSLs that were issued with typographical errors that led to the unauthorized collection information not relevant to an authorized national security investigation.

[146] Of the 48 possible IOB violations in both categories, 28 occurred during preliminary investigations, 19 occurred during full investigations, and 1 occurred in the absence of a national security investigation. Thirty-two of the possible IOB violations occurred during counterterrorism investigations, 15 occurred during counterintelligence investigations, and 1 occurred in the absence of a national security investigation.

[147] Section I(C)(1) of the NSI Guidelines, defines a "United States person" as:
a. an individual who is a United States citizen or alien lawfully admitted for permanent residence;
b. an unincorporated association substantially composed of individuals who are United States persons; or
c. a corporation incorporated in the United States.

[148] In one of the matters, the subject was a presumed "non-U.S. person," in one there was no subject, and in another the status of the subject could not be determined.

[149] According to the CDC in one of the field offices we visited, case agents are advised to return telephone toll billing records it improperly acquires to the communication providers. If the providers do not want them back, the agents are advised to destroy the records and document the destruction with an Electronic Communication (EC). This field office did not usually send toll billing records to FBI-OGC for sequestration or destruction.

[150] According to internal FBI guidance, by longstanding agreement between the FBI and the JOB, E.O. 12334 has been interpreted to
mandate the reporting of any violation of a provision of the foreign counterintelligence guidelines or other guidelines or regulations approved by the Attorney General, in accordance with E.O. 12333, if such provision was designed in full or in part to ensure the protection of the individual rights of a U.S. person.

[151] None of the FBI-OGC decision memoranda describing matters reported to the IOB involving non-U.S. Persons explained why these matters were reported to the IOB notwithstanding the status of the subject of the investigation or the NSL target.

[152] In November 2006, FBI-OGC issued guidance to all divisions for reports of possible IOB violations. The memorandum states that Section 2.4 of Executive Order 12863 has been interpreted to mandate the reporting of Attorney General Guidelines' violations "if such provision was designed to ensure the protection of individual rights." Accordingly, we do not believe that future decisions concerning whether to report possible IOB violations will be made solely on the basis of the non-U.S. person status of the investigative subject or the NSL target.

[153] When we examined the records provided to the FBI in response to this NSL, however, we determined that the requested data was not furnished to the FBI.

[154] We did not include in this category unauthorized collection of telephone toll billing records or subscriber information due to instances in which the communication provider furnished records beyond the time period specified in the NSL because of the communications provider's billing cycle.

[155] Barton Gellman, *The FBI's Secret Scrutiny: In Hunt for Terrorists, Bureau Examines Records of Ordinary Americans,* The Washington Post, Nov. 6, 2005, at Al.

[156] The production of educational records is governed by the Family Education Rights and Privacy Act of 1974 (FERPA), commonly referred to as "the Buckley Amendment." See 20 U.S.C. § 1232g. Generally, the Buckley Amendment prohibits the funding of an educational agency or institution that has a policy or practice of disclosing a student's records without parental or student consent if the student is over the age of 18. The law contains 16 exceptions to this general rule, one of which is known as the "law enforcement exception." In responding to a federal grand jury subpoena, the institution is not required to seek consent but must notify the parents and student in advance of compliance. See 20 U.S.C. § 1232g(b)(2)(B). However, for good cause shown, a court may order the institution not to disclose the existence of the subpoena or the institution's response. 20 U.S.C. § 1232g(b)(1)(J)(i).

[157] These included issuing national security letters when the investigative authority had lapsed, issuing full credit report FCRA national security letters in a counterintelligence investigation, and unauthorized collections resulting from FBI typographical errors or third-party errors.

[158] The Inspection Division guidance dated February 10, 2005, generally described the revised procedures for reporting possible IOB violations. But this guidance did not address possible IOB violations that could arise from the FBI's expanded use of national security letters after the Patriot Act.

[159] The SSA told us that an attorney with the telephone company established a tracking system to ensure that grand jury subpoenas were issued to cover all of the records obtained from the telephone company employees. The

SSA also said that he checked regularly with a point of contact at the telephone company to determine if the FBI had fallen behind in providing legal process for these records. The SSA said he was confident that grand jury subpoenas were issued to cover every request.

160 The SSA said that DT-6 case agents would sometimes provide the placeholder letters to the telephone company to initiate the search for records. The SSA said that in most instances by the time the records were available, a grand jury subpoena was ready to be served for the records.

161 NSLB attorneys told us that NSLB attorneys were not consulted about the three contracts with the telephone companies or the procedures and administrative steps that CAU took following their implementation to obtain telephone toll billing records pursuant to the contracts. The FBI-OGC attorneys and a former CAU Unit Chief told us that to their knowledge the only OGC lawyers involved in reviewing the contracts were procurement lawyers.

162 We cannot ascertain whether the subpoena was issued before or after the date of the "exigent letter."

163 These documents included references to analyses of telephone data (5), an EC approving the closing of a preliminary investigation that was initiated after the date of the corresponding exigent letter (1), an EC documenting service of an NSL on a different telephone company than the one listed in the exigent letter (1); and an incomplete draft of an NSL requesting records listed in the corresponding exigent letter (1). We did not regard these to be reliable evidence that national security letters were issued in these instances for the records sought in the corresponding exigent letters.

164 Similarly, when CAU on occasion asked the NSLB Deputy General Counsel to issue national security letters to cover information already obtained from the telephone companies in response to the exigent letters, CAU sometimes did not disclose in the approval documentation that the records already had been provided in response to the exigent letters. An NSLB Assistant General Counsel complained to CAU personnel about these omissions in December 2004.

165 The Assistant General Counsel at first proposed the establishment of six "generic" or "umbrella" investigations files representing the recurring types of threats investigated by the Counterterrorism Division. The proposal contemplated that the FBI would issue national security letters from these files in exigent circumstances when there were no other pending investigations to which the request could be tied. After obtaining approval from NSLB supervisors to pursue this approach, the CAU Unit Chief told the NSLB Assistant General Counsel in September 2005 that generic national security investigations would not be needed because, contrary to his earlier statements, CAU would be able to connect each exigent letter request with an existing Headquarters or field division-initiated national security investigation. The Assistant General Counsel told us that she also was informed at this time by the CAU Unit Chief that the emergency requests were "few and far between."

166 18 U.S.C. § 2702 (c) provides:

Voluntary disclosure of customer communications or records.

(c) Exceptions for disclosure of customer records. - A provider described in subsection (a) may divulge a record or other information pertaining to a subscriber to or customer of such service (not including the contents of communications covered by subsection (a) (1) or (a) (2)) .. .

(4) to a governmental entity, if the provider, in good faith, believes than an emergency involving danger or death or serious physical injury to any person requires disclosure without delay of information relating to the emergency; . . . .

167 FBI-OGC attorneys told us that the FBI's acquisition of telephone toll billing records and subscriber information in response to the exigent letters has not been reported to the IOB as possible violations of law, Attorney General Guidelines, or internal FBI policy. We believe that under guidance in effect during the period covered by our review these matters should be reported as possible IOB violations.

168 Internal FBI guidance states that the only FBI officials authorized to sign voluntary emergency disclosure requests pursuant to 18 U.S.C. § 2702(c)(4) are Special Agents in Charge, Assistant Special Agents in Charge, Section Chiefs, or more senior officials.

169 Section 19-03(L)(1) of the NFIP Manual states:

[C]ontrol files are separate files established for the purpose of administering specific phases of an investigative matter or program and would not be considered a [preliminary investigation] or [full investigation.]

July 25, 2004.

170 When we examined a sample of the approval ECs for these NSLs, we noted that some referred to telephone numbers or e-mail accounts believed to be associated with terrorist networks, while others stated that CAU had developed information from public and other sources identifying telephone numbers in contact with known terrorists.

171 The Electronic Communication (EC) seeking approval to open this control file stated that its purpose was to "serve as a repository for communications concerning EOPS special projects, technical exploitation operations, and for tracking leads and taskings outside of EOPS operational case files." This type of approval EC would not reference investigative activity or facts supporting investigative activity. The subfile created in June 2005 from which the national security letters discussed in this section were issued also did not reference contemplated investigative activity.

[172] Three of the approval ECs referenced only an EOPS control file, while the three remaining approval ECs referenced an FBI legat office control file.
Problems with the FBI's NSL database make it impossible to determine the precise number of national security letters the FBI issued in this second category. The database's limitations are discussed in Chapter Four and in the Classified Appendix.

[173] Three of the six approval ECs sought issuance of ECPA NSLs regarding e-mail addresses identified as being used by a suspected terrorist. The remaining approval ECs sought records pertaining to an e-mail address identified as being associated with a terrorist group, an e-mail account that was in contact with e-mail accounts identified through FISA authorities, and an e-mail address that generated a threat to an intelligence community complaint center.

[174] The caption would have shown whether EOPS was requesting the national security letter exclusively out of its control file, out of an investigative file from Headquarters or a field division, or pursuant to a "dual caption" denoting more than one file.

[175] Based on our understanding of IOB reporting policies, these infractions did not rise to the level of possible IOB violations.

[176] Field personnel who are required to review NSLs are supposed to initial the approval EC. The approval ECs noted in this section did not contain the reviewer's initials, and we found no other documentation of approval in the investigative files.

[177] We did not include in this category failures to include the required transmittals either to Headquarters operating divisions or field divisions for service. Sixty-six of the 293 approval ECs failed to include one or more of the required leads.

[178] The absence of the Special Agent in Charge's signature on the national security letter would be considered a possible IOB violation and is not included in this category.

[179]NSI Guidelines, § I(B)(2).

[180] OGC sent guidance on November 28, 2001, that referred to the "least intrusive" means proviso contained in the applicable FCI Guidelines. The guidance stated that
supervisors should keep [the proviso] in mind when deciding whether or not a particular use of NSL authority is appropriate. The greater availability of NSLs does not mean that they should be used in every case.

[181] For example, the need for guidance was raised by a CDC in the context of considering whether it is appropriate to issue financial record and consumer full credit report NSLs in every terrorism investigation.

[182] One senior NSLB attorney told us that he does not believe that the training given to Special Agents in Charge adequately focuses on the use of NSL authorities, particularly in light of the volume of NSLs that field divisions are issuing. This attorney and other FBI Headquarters personnel told us that when NSLs are addressed at SAC training conferences, the focus is on the statutory requirements and internal FBI policies, such as the fact that SACs may not delegate authority to sign NSLs to Acting Special Agents in Charge or others.
However, SAC conferences have addressed a more intrusive investigative technique used in national security investigations. The FBI General Counsel told us that Special Agents in Charge were encouraged at a Senior Leadership Conference to terminate "full content" electronic surveillance pursuant to the Foreign Intelligence Surveillance Act if the technique is no longer productive, rather than continue to request authority to renew the surveillance orders over many years. Yet, there has been no comparable discussion of the use of NSL authorities.

[183] An Assistant General Counsel in NSLB told us that some telephone companies maintain records of individual calls made from a telephone number but do not bill for the calls. Instead, they "bundle" their services for a fixed fee. Some of these companies have told the FBI that they do not consider data retained for "unbilled calls" to be "toll billing records information."

[184] CDCs are not required to review the documentation seeking approval to initiate national security investigations.

[185] The request stated:
[An international terrorism] investigation of subject, a US PERSON, was authorized in accordance with the [Attorney General Guidelines] because the subject is in contact with the subjects of other international terrorism investigations. These subscriber and toll billing records are being requested to determine the identity of others with whom the subject communicates.

[186] NSLB posted the following guidance on its Intranet web site in March 2006 following passage of the Patriot Reauthorization Act:
A perfunctory recitation that (1) the subject is the target of the investigation, (2) he has a telephone, and (3) therefore, it follows that an NSL for his telephone records is relevant to the authorized investigation will not suffice. Otherwise, any target with a telephone or a bank account is subject to an NSL. And that is not the standard for issuance of an NSL.

[187] One CDC who said he would not have approved the request stated that questions he has raised to explore the predication of NSLs and the relevance of the information sought to the investigations have caused more dissension in the office than any other issues he has encountered in over 20 years with the FBI.

[188] The FBI did not retain signed copies of the certificate letters and, therefore, Counterterrorism Division personnel could not confirm the total number of the letters.

[189] Fedwire is the Federal Reserve's electronic funds and securities transfer service. Banks and other depository institutions use Fedwire "to move balances to correspondent banks and to send funds to other institutions on behalf of customers." See www.newyorkfed.org.

[190] The letters contained certifications that there were "specific and articulable facts giving reason to believe that the customer or entity whose records are sought is a foreign power or an agent of a foreign power as defined in 50 U.S.C. § 1801."

INDEX